Disappearing Futures

Also Available from Bloomsbury

Assassins of Memory, Henry A. Giroux
The Burden of Conscience, Henry A. Giroux
Teachers as Intellectuals, Henry A. Giroux
Theory and Resistance in Education, Henry A. Giroux
Fascism on Trial, Henry A. Giroux and Anthony R. DiMaggio
Insurrections, Henry A. Giroux
Race, Politics, and Pandemic Pedagogy, Henry A. Giroux
Pedagogy of Resistance, Henry A. Giroux
On Critical Pedagogy, 2nd edition, Henry A. Giroux

Disappearing Futures

Education Against the Politics of Disposability

Henry A. Giroux

BLOOMSBURY ACADEMIC
LONDON • NEW YORK • OXFORD • NEW DELHI • SYDNEY

BLOOMSBURY ACADEMIC
Bloomsbury Publishing Plc, 50 Bedford Square, London, WC1B 3DP, UK
Bloomsbury Publishing Inc, 1359 Broadway, New York, NY 10018, USA
Bloomsbury Publishing Ireland, 29 Earlsfort Terrace, Dublin 2, D02 AY28, Ireland

BLOOMSBURY, BLOOMSBURY ACADEMIC and the Diana logo
are trademarks of Bloomsbury Publishing Plc

First published in Great Britain 2026

A catalogue record for this book is available from the British Library.

A catalog record for this book is available from the Library of Congress.

ISBN: HB: 978-1-350-60303-5
PB: 978-1-350-60302-8
ePDF: 978-1-350-60304-2
eBook: 978-1-350-60305-9

Typeset by Integra Software Services Pvt Ltd.
Printed and bound in Great Britain

For product safety related questions contact productsafety@bloomsbury.com.

To find out more about our authors and books visit www.bloomsbury.com
and sign up for our newsletters.

The sea rises, the light fails, lovers cling to each other and children cling to us. The moment we cease to hold each other, the moment we break faith with one another, the sea engulfs us and the light goes out.

James Baldwin

We, too, are so dazzled by power and money that we forget the fragility of our existence: we forget that we are all in the ghetto, that the ghetto is fenced in, that outside the fence are the lords of death, and a little way off the train is waiting.

Primo Levi

For Rania, always.
For Maria Filippakou, whose compassion widens the horizon of hope.
For the children—your futures stolen by genocide refuse silence and call us to justice.

CONTENTS

ACKNOWLEDGMENTS

I could not have authored this book without the wisdom, patience, and unwavering support of my wife, Rania, whose presence steadies my life and enriches every page. I am equally grateful to Christi Caricato, for her help in preparing the research for project. My student assistants, Alisar Saba and Liam Feldman, offered extraordinary care and insight, reading and refining each draft with a generosity of spirit that sustained the work as it evolved. I am indebted to dear friends who have long accompanied me in thought and struggle, especially my dear brothers Donaldo Macedo, Ken Saltman, and Peter McLaren. To Carol Becker, Antonia Darder, Peter Mayo, Robin Goodman, Isaac Cordal, Lawrence Grossberg, Dean Birkenkamp, Brad Evans, and William Paul, whose encouragement and solidarity continue to make the burdens lighter and the work more meaningful. I am especially grateful to Teresa Savoia, my Italian translator for splendid work she has done with my books. I also want to thank Jackie Edmondson for her steadfast support, generosity of spirit, and quiet courage. As President of the University of Southern Maine, she stands as an inspiring example of what principled leadership can be, rooted in a deep commitment to critical inquiry, intellectual freedom, and the pursuit of justice.

I also want to express my gratitude to the close associates who have helped publish my work: Maya Schenwar and Alana Price at Truthout, Sharon Kyle and Dick Price at *LA Progressive*, Jeffrey St. Clair at *CounterPunch*, Jeffrey R. Di Leo at Symploke, David M. Arditi at Fast Capitalism, Stephen McCloskey at the Center for Global Education, Alex Means at *The Review of Education, Pedagogy, and Cultural Studies*, Andrew O'Hehir at *Salon*, and Graeme Farnell in Scotland. Thanks to a number of international publications, which has been instrumental in reprinting much of my work, and for that, I am deeply appreciative.

Many of the ideas in this book appeared in various forms in *Truthout, CounterPunch, Studia Krytczne, Policy and Practice, Fast Capitalism, Symploke, Salon, Review of Education, Pedagogy, and Cultural Studies*, and the *Journal of Holy Land and Palestine Studies.*

The support I have received from colleagues in Poland, Brazil, Greece, Chile, the United Kingdom, Italy, and Spain is well-appreciated.

Finally, I am grateful to Mark Richardson at Bloomsbury, a brilliant and supportive editor and wonderful human being. A writer's dream.

Introduction: The Fire This Time: Confronting America's Authoritarian Turn

As we stand at the crossroads of a crumbling democracy, we face the slow unraveling of a future once imagined as just and humane, a future born of promise yet scarred by contradictions. The United States, long intoxicated by the myth of its own exceptionalism, was founded on the uneasy marriage of so-called freedom and racial terror. For a time, democracy, fragile, imperfect, yet luminous in its aspirations, moved slowly forward, a flicker of hope against the weight of history. That flicker is fading. The dream of a more just society grows faint beneath the tightening grip of white supremacy, authoritarian power, and corporate greed. The horizon of democratic possibility narrows as violence, ignorance, and despair become the dominant registers of political life.

We are witnessing the emergence of a new form of fascism that cancels out the very idea of the future. We are left staring into what Franco "Bifo" Berardi calls "an annihilating nihilism," a death-driven politics that thrives on cruelty, celebrates ignorance, and drains the world of its capacity to imagine otherwise.[1] Under the Trump regime, the scourge of white supremacy and staggering levels of inequality are reproduced in a fascist mode of governance marked by incompetence, extremism, and corruption.

The current historical moment is defined by what Chandra Talpade Mohanty calls "thresholds of disappearance—the proliferation of depoliticized multiplicities"—those institutions and spaces that "domesticate power differences, transforming systemic projects of resistance to commodified, private acts of rebellion."[2] In this landscape, neoliberal culture and pedagogy form one of the most consequential thresholds of disappearance, draining politics of substance and stripping education of its radical possibilities. At stake is the recognition that education has become an urgent site of struggle, a decisive political terrain where agency takes shape, desires are mobilized, oppression is normalized, hope is militarized, and resistance must be rekindled.

This book begins in that darkness, not to yield to despair, but to confront it, to name its sources, to expose its pedagogy of violence, and to rekindle the radical imagination that refuses to die. To resist this annihilating present is to reclaim the language of possibility, to insist that even in times of moral asphyxiation, the future remains a site of struggle, not surrender.

We live in perilous times.[3] The mobilizing passions of fascism are no longer a distant echo of history; they are here, surging through the United States and across the world like a tidal wave, relentlessly crashing against the shores of democracy.[4] Americans are living through orchestrated campaigns of social and racial purification and a repressive crackdown on free speech, and voting rights, amounting to an aggressive state-sponsored ideological cleansing of democracy itself.

First, the idea of government as a democratizing public good and institution of social responsibility, that once held power to account, protected the vulnerable, and nurtured the ideals of justice and collective responsibility, is now held in contempt by the Trump regime. The common good, once the essence of democratic life, has become the enemy of the authoritarian neoliberal state. It is not merely being neglected, it is being assaulted, stripped bare, and left to rot in the shadows of privatization, greed, lawlessness, militarization, and brutality, the major features of a dehumanizing and cruel register of capitalism. This new phase of market domination or what I call gangster capitalism operates through a fusion of market tyranny, unchecked white nationalism, and state violence. Public institutions are gutted, courts are under siege, regulatory bodies are politicized and disempowered, protesters are defined as enemies of the state, politics has become an extension of violence, and the mechanisms of governance now serve only the most ruthless forms of concentrated financial and political power.

Second, we are witnessing a campaign of ideological cleansing, a scorched-earth assault on the very possibility of critical consciousness. Education, both public and higher, once an alleged sanctuary for reflection, dissent, and civic imagination is being defunded, attacked, and stripped of its democratizing mission. The classroom, once a space where truth could be spoken to power, is now reworked as a site of surveillance and obedience. Education as a practice of freedom meant to cultivate informed judgment, moral courage, and collective responsibility is being refashioned into an instrument of control.

The essential pillars of democratic education, academic freedom, critical inquiry, tenure, diversity, and equity, are being dismantled with calculated precision. Language asserts itself as a colonizing force rather than as an act of dialogue and hospitality; memory is colonized as history is erased and refashioned in the spirit of the Confederacy, white supremacy, and a warrior culture. As explored later, this assault on critical thought, language, remembering, agency, and democratic values is no accident; it lies at the very heart of the authoritarian project, which seeks to weaponize pedagogy itself, turning education from a practice of freedom into a machinery of indoctrination. This is no peripheral skirmish; it is a central front in the authoritarian war on democracy.

Faculty who criticize authoritarianism, oppose ICE's lawless brutality, and protest against Israel's genocidal war on Palestinians have been either fired, doxxed, or threatened. For example, Rutgers University historian Mark Bray, author of *Antifa: The Anti-Fascist Handbook*, was doxxed, harassed, and threatened after publicly critiquing the rise of fascism and Trump's authoritarian politics.[5] His home address was circulated online, his classes were disrupted by right-wing activists, and he was briefly prevented from leaving the country when his family's flight was mysteriously cancelled hours before departure. Bray was leaving the US for Spain for fear of violence to him and his family (and was only able to leave once his case drew national attention). Bray's ordeal exposes how dissenting scholars are being turned into targets in a political culture where education itself has become a battlefield. The aim is clear: to silence critique, criminalize thought, and transform the university into a space of fear rather than freedom.

A similar pattern of punitive backlash emerged when Derek Peterson, an African studies and history professor, used a commencement address at Michigan State University to praise pro-Palestinian student protesters for having "opened our hearts to the injustice and inhumanity of Israel's war in Gaza." His remarks were swiftly met with a wave of far-right political condemnation, with Republican officials and some Jewish organizations denouncing the speech as antisemitic and improperly political. In an act that further underscores the climate of institutional capitulation, university president Domenico Grasso publicly apologized, labeling the comments "hurtful and insensitive." What might have been an affirmation of moral witness was instead cravenly named as transgression, revealing how readily the charge of antisemitism can be mobilized, in some cases, to deflect criticism of state violence and to narrow the space for dissent, turning universities into sites of managed silence rather than critical engagement.[6]

As is now a matter of public record, books that illuminate injustice, affirm histories of resistance, and introduce critical ideas are being banned. Entire fields of knowledge, gender studies, critical race theory, decolonial thought—are being outlawed. Professors are fired, blacklisted, harassed or deported for daring to speak the truth, especially those who denounce the genocidal violence being waged by Israel, which has now killed over 70,000 Palestinians, many of them children.[7] Journalists are doxxed, detained, or demonized.[8] Cultural institutions and social platforms that function as powerful educational forces are defunded or coerced into silence. The arts, once sacred, are now suspect; social media platforms and news outlets are intimidated, policed, and purged.

Elite law firms are targeted, silenced, or forced into complicity by the Trump administration. Scott Cummings rightly argues that President Donald Trump's March 14, 2025 speech to the Department of Justice was meant as a declaration of war against lawyers.[9] Some prestigious firms and attorneys, once guardians of justice, now grovel before authoritarianism in acts of staggering complicity.[10] This extends to elite universities, Columbia, Brown, University of Virginia, Berkeley, and others, which have compromised their autonomy and moral authority to appease far-right demands. This posture of appeasement recalls Neville Chamberlain's disastrous concessions to Hitler in 1938, emboldening fascism and weakening democratic resolve.[11] Today the same spirit of appeasement hangs over the United States, not merely as a fog that obscures moral clarity, but as a poisonous mist that seeps into the lungs of democracy itself, suffocating resistance and nourishing the growth of authoritarian power.

Third, and perhaps most alarming is the escalating campaign of racial cleansing, a war against the most vulnerable. Immigrants are caged in detention centers, separated from their families, deported without due process to facilities in Louisiana or to Guantánamo, a prelude to the regime of disappearance explored later in this book.[12] Muslims are vilified and targeted; Black and Brown communities over-policed and under-protected, sacrificed to the machinery of carceral violence.[13]

The human toll of this machinery is already becoming visible in chilling ways. Deaths inside immigration detention centers are accelerating, now occurring at a rate of "roughly one every six days." Since the onset of Donald Trump's mass deportation campaign, more than forty people have died in custody, an unprecedented number in such a short span. These are not isolated tragedies but warning signs, evidence of a system sliding toward zones of abandonment where neglect, abuse, and disposability converge. If left unchecked, such spaces risk evolving into carceral death worlds, hidden in plain sight, where the logic of detention merges with a politics that renders certain lives unworthy of care, protection, or even survival.[14]

As noted in Chapter 2, students and activists, many of whom are people of color, have been suddenly seized, vanished into detention centers, and branded as enemies of the state, not for crimes committed, but for daring to dissent. Targeted through censorship and disciplinary crackdowns, their voices have been silenced by a culture of intimidation that treats critical thought as a crime rather than a civic duty. These are not mistakes of law enforcement; they are calculated acts of silencing, repression, and political abduction. They echo the darkest lessons of the twentieth century; Gestapo round-ups in Nazi Germany, the disappearances of over 30,000 students during Argentina's Dirty War, retooled for an American present.

In addition, Trump's militarization of institutions, cities, and everyday life has stripped citizenship of its meaning. The machinery of state power now extends beyond surveillance and policing to outright erasure. As later chapters show, these tactics dissolve the boundaries between citizen, repression, and exile and render belonging itself precarious. In this new order, deportation becomes the twin of dispossession, working hand in hand with the destruction of citizenship. The state is not merely expelling bodies; effectively rendering people stateless—exiled not only from the nation, but from the very idea of human rights. As bodies are abducted, the law too vanishes, sinking into a bottomless abyss that offers no resistance to the cascade of illegalities unleashed in its name.

The war on bodies and rights is also a war on memory and imagination, the very capacities through which democratic life renews itself. It is an authoritarian onslaught on thought itself, designed to erase connection and the dream of a different future.[15] Policies once deemed unthinkable now parade as common sense.

Consider just one glimpse of the horror now unfolding: immigrants deemed disposable by the United States have vanished into prisons beyond its borders, abducted not for any crime but simply for seeking refuge. Some are shipped into the hemisphere's most brutal detention sites, maximum-security torture chambers run by authoritarian regimes, where they are treated as less than human. This is the architecture of disposability made concrete: people stripped of rights, expelled from visibility, and cast into a global carceral abyss.[16] This administration has kidnapped international students protesting Israel's genocide of the Palestinian peoples. Student visas are revoked in the dead of night. Their dorm rooms raided, their wrists bound in handcuffs, they are forced into unmarked cars by agents of a system that is both cruel and clandestine. These are not arrests, they are abductions. While some of these injustices have been overturned in the lower courts, there is no guarantee that this will not continue.

Visa revocations have become a defining weapon of the Trump regime, a blunt instrument of repression aimed not only at university students protesting for Palestinian rights, but at any non-citizen who dares to dissent. What was once a bureaucratic procedure has been transformed into a political purge, a tool of ideological cleansing. Even figures of immense global stature, such as Nigerian Nobel Laureate Wole Soyinka or Colombian president Gustavo Petro, have not been spared. Under Trump, the revocation of visas is about silencing opposition and sending a horrifying message that in the new fascist order, citizenship itself becomes conditional on obedience.[17]

At work here is not justice, but the slow machinery of fear made flesh. Dissent is now branded as terrorism; those who challenge Trump's authoritarian grip vanish into the void, arrested, erased, rendered disposable. It gets worse. In what appears to be an outright act of state violence, the Trump administration has "conducted more than a dozen strikes on boats and semi-submersible craft from South America that have killed at least 69 people."[18] The administration insists the victims were all involved in drug smuggling, yet it has presented no credible evidence to support such claims, only the familiar pattern of accusation standing in for proof. But even if some had been engaged in illicit trade, these extrajudicial killings remain indefensible. They expose a deeper logic at work: Trump's regime decides who counts as fully human and who can be written off as disposable, using the label of "criminal" as a license for state violence. In this moral universe, the mere hint of wrongdoing becomes enough to sanction execution, revealing a politics that collapses law into calculated cruelty and treats vulnerable populations as expendable.

One of the most visible acts of state terrorism is Trump's unparalleled war on higher education; Trump's authoritarian apparatus has turned colleges and universities into ideological battlegrounds.[19] As Chris Hedges observes, the administration has threatened to strip federal funding from more than sixty elite higher education institutions under the guise of protecting Jewish students, while already pulling $500 million from Columbia University, an action that has nothing to do with combating antisemitism.[20] The charge is a smokescreen, a cynical pretext to silence protest and crush dissent, especially in support of Palestinian freedom. As Edward Said Professor of Modern Arab Studies Emeritus at Columbia University Rashid Khalidi makes clear, "It was never about eliminating antisemitism. It was always about silencing Palestine. That is what the gagging of protesting students, and now the gagging of faculty, was always meant to lead to."[21]

As Ian Buruma observes, there is a cruel irony in the Trump administration's self-styled defense of the Jewish people, given its deep entanglement with antisemitic extremists and its embrace of "blood-and-soil nationalism."[22] The Holocaust scholar Amos Goldberg deepens this insight, warning that the charge of antisemitism is increasingly weaponized to silence critics of Israel. This distortion, he explains, not only serves as a verbal bludgeon and form of intellectual thuggery to erase history but also clears a dangerous path toward authoritarianism. He writes:

> ... the "fight against antisemitism" – as a central lesson supposedly learned from the Holocaust – now serves as a pretext for dismantling effective criticism of genocide, and as a tool for governments to suppress basic democratic institutions – first and foremost, universities – while gradually or rapidly sliding into authoritarianism, or perhaps something worse. The examples from the United States are well known, but similar dynamics are unfolding elsewhere as well, especially in Germany, where authorities violently suppress any protest against the genocide in the name of "fighting antisemitism."[23]

According to Jason Stanley, elite universities once proud of their intellectual autonomy are being transformed into fortified zones of surveillance and submission.[24] Columbia is among the most glaring; the campus at one point resembled a police precinct more than a place of progressive ideas and democratic values. Only now are a few commentators and universities awakening to this siege, one many of us have named for decades. Americans are no longer drifting toward authoritarianism; they are living inside it.

Fourth, Trump is consolidating a police state. He is using the military as a political weapon against Americans who disagree with him, while claiming the occupied cities are cesspools of crime and therefore "should be militarized."[25] The white-supremacist message is clear: race equals criminality. Trump now wages war at home by deploying the military to cities branded as crime-ridden, even going so far as to claim that he can send any branch of the military into American cities, without accountability to either the courts or Congress.[26]

Under Trump's orders, military forces now prowl American streets, not as protectors, but as instruments of terror. They descend upon a number of American cities, largely populated by people of color, to intimidate immigrants, brutalize racialized people, and crush dissent beneath the weight of armored vehicles and riot shields. Trump has declared war on these so-called dangerous cities, but what he truly fears is democracy itself.[27] The United States government has turned its arsenal inward, waging war on its own people. The warrior culture, largely exported abroad in Gaza and Iran, has now come home, infecting the body politic with a fever of militarized violence, turning neighborhoods into battlefields and citizens into enemies. "I'd like to use some of these dangerous cities as training grounds for our military," Trump boasted, a declaration that strips away all pretenses.[28]

Trump's goal is to turn domestic repression into military theater, using the armed forces to further his political agenda and trample the Constitution underfoot. Rights are no longer guaranteed; they are trampled. ICE, transformed into an army of masked enforcers, militarizes politics itself, terrorizing immigrants, Black and Brown citizens, and millions of others branded as either disposable or criminal.[29] Trump's war on cities is matched by his authoritarian war on his dissenters and political enemies.

He has called for the imprisonment of political enemies such as former FBI Director James Comey and Letitia James, as well as Chicago Mayor Brandon Johnson and Illinois Governor J. B. Pritzker.[30] Both Comey and James are already under formal accusation, with Trump vowing that more charges will follow. Fortunately, both cases thus far have been rejected as baseless by the courts. In response, Senate Minority Leader Chuck Schumer warns that Trump has turned the Justice Department into his "personal attack dog."[31] This persecution is part of a wider strategy to turn justice into vengeance. There is no appeal to our better moral and democratic ideals here. This approach to governance thrives on retribution. This is the ideology of fascist barbarism, with its knee-jerk contempt for anything that is thoughtful, critical, and pluralistic.

In this fascist choreography, the Justice Department becomes an instrument of retribution, the weaponized arm of a regime that criminalizes existence itself, punishing all who refuse to conform to its white-Christian-nationalist fantasy of purity, obedience, and subjugation. As Judd Legum observes, "federal agents are terrorizing American citizens."[32] The United States is living within the architecture of authoritarianism.

Under such circumstances, it is crucial for people to pay attention to the political crisis that is unfolding. This means being attentive, learning from history, and analyzing the mobilizing passions of fascism as a system, one directly related to gangster capitalism and white supremacy. Language matters: those who fight the fascist tide must rethink education, resistance, and solidarity. Action is imperative: build alliances, flood the streets, defend critical education, amplify resistance, and refuse to be silent. To ignore history is to surrender to ignorance. History calls for attentiveness and a readiness to learn from both its triumphs and its failures. It teaches us how institutional brutality is repeated when memory fades and how justice advances when knowledge becomes action. Efforts to censor or distort history must be met with vigilance and resistance. Any attempt to freeze or censor it must be challenged. The only question is whether anti-fascist forces will rise to meet it.

In the face of this rising tide of opposition filling the streets of the United States, resistance must no longer be fragmented or polite. As Sherrilyn Ifill notes, "It is not enough to fight, you have to meet the moment."[33] Cultural critics, educators, artists, journalists, social workers, and others must wield their craft like weapons, telling prohibited stories, defying censorship, reigniting imagination. Educators must defend classrooms as sanctuaries of truth, even when the risks are great.

As I argue throughout this book, academics and administrators must form a common front to stop the attack on higher education. Journalists must break the silence, naming injustice with moral clarity. Organizers and everyday people must converge into a broad front of democratic refusal. This is a moment not just for outrage but for audacity, for reclaiming hope as a political act, and courage as a shared ethic.

As the drums of war, both global and domestic, grow louder, we must confront a hard truth: words alone will not halt the terror, the abductions, the violence, or the bombs. The task, then, is to transform the entire cultural sphere, from social media and screen culture to podcasts, classrooms, and interviews, into vital pedagogical spaces where power is exposed, named, and contested. These are not neutral platforms but battlegrounds over meaning, memory, and agency. Resistance, if it is to matter, must move beyond critique and become organized, a collective force, linking the awakening of public consciousness to mass action. It must take root across multiple sites, in the streets through direct action, in workplaces through solidarity, and in universities through critical engagement, forging alliances capable of both understanding power and confronting it. Fascism feeds on fear and isolation. As Robin D. G. Kelley states, it must be met with solidarity, imagination, and relentless struggle rooted in revived class politics.[34] In a culture defined by immediacy, manufactured misery, and staggering inequality, power must be called out for what it does, not for what it promises. Naming its violence is only the beginning. The language of critique, solidarity, compassion, and hope must deepen into forms of mass collective action capable of breaking its grip. The scorched-earth history of capitalism, along with its contemporary rituals of harshness and brutality, must be confronted with a politics willing to imagine a different future and fight for it.

History teaches us that fascism thrives on bigotry, racism, and hatred, poisonous ideologies that offer false promises of fulfilment, especially in times of economic despair. Yet, its most potent weapon is the normalization of silence and complicity among the masses. In such dark times, silence itself becomes a form of complicity, as noted by figures like Albert Einstein, Martin Luther King Jr., and Audre Lorde. The silence born of fear, ignorance, and indifference must be broken. As resistance to Trump intensifies, and it will, the silence must be unmasked for what it truly is: an act of acquiescence. What must be done now is to use dissent, defiance, and civic courage to break the silence and reclaim our collective will to act.

Capitalism exalts values that oppose democracy, it thrives on inequality and teaches punitive violence as virtue. This essence of barbarism is woven into the very logic of capitalism; to ignore this is to misunderstand the nature of our current slide into authoritarianism at home and abroad. How capitalism is legitimized and how it produces subjects, modes of agency, and values that are inherently necropolitical are the searing questions of our age. What many young people recognize is that as neoliberal capitalism tightens its grip on the United States, it cancels out their future, at least a future of equality, justice, and hope.

What is increasingly clear in this war on democracy is that the machinery of domination is not driven by economics alone, it is also fueled by culture. Culture today operates as a powerful educational force, especially in an age saturated with digital technologies, algorithmic control, and the seductive illusions of artificial intelligence. Americans are witnessing not only an unprecedented expansion of surveillance technologies, such as Palantir and Pegasus spyware—but also the rise of a repressive, hate-filled algorithmic culture, one that shapes how we see, how we feel, what we desire, and, most insidiously, what we learn to ignore.[35] When culture becomes an instrument of power rather than a space for imagination and critique, it functions pedagogically to legitimize injustice and numb the collective conscience. It creates a notion of dread that instills a crippling sense of disorientation, trepidation, and loneliness.[36] As explored in Chapter 1, neoliberalism has transformed this cultural machinery into a pedagogy of cruelty, normalizing inequality, rewarding indifference, and creating the social conditions in which fascism takes root.

This darkness is not without precedent, nor is it without models of resistance. During the rise of fascism in Europe, teachers and intellectuals in Nazi-occupied France joined the underground, distributing banned literature and teaching forbidden truths in secret classrooms. In apartheid South

Africa, students in Soweto sparked a nationwide uprising, defying bullets with the cry that *liberation begins with education*. In the American South, Black freedom fighters risked their lives to build freedom schools, challenge police terror, and reimagine democracy in the face of white supremacy. The Zapatistas in Chiapas created autonomous zones rooted in dignity, justice, and Indigenous knowledge. Palestinian writers, youth, freedom fighters, and teachers continue to protests under siege. They insist through every poem and lesson that memory will survive, and resistance will endure.

Today, movements like Black Lives Matter, Abolitionist Futures, Extinction Rebellion, Sunrise Movement, March for Our Lives, No Kings movement, and Indigenous Rights Movements are keeping alive the traditions of collective struggle. Despite the shameful crackdowns by the government and in some cases universities themselves, courageous campus coalitions are resisting militarized policing and corporate capture of higher education. Migrant justice organizations are building sanctuary networks to protect those the state seeks to expel. The "No Kings" protests included millions marching across the US protesting and creating awareness of both the deep-rooted authoritarianism of the Trump administration and the fortitude of people acting together to oppose it. These are not just moments of protest; they are blueprints for democratic rebirth. The task now is to connect these diverse struggles to a broad-based movement for change with the power to wage strikes, engage in direct action, teach-ins, and use any viable nonviolent form of resistance to overcome the fascist nightmare spreading across the globe.[37]

If Trump's theater of suffering is a necropolitical order that thrives on despair and domination, youth resistance along with the growing struggles of the masses opposing fascism is its counter-aesthetic, an assertion of life, movement, and the refusal to submit. Hope here is not naive optimism but radical insistence that history is not over.

Under Trump, the United States has entered a period of dread, ruthlessness, and cultural despair.[38] The future darkens as millions lose their jobs, health care becomes a privilege reserved for the wealthy, and food insecurity looms over millions. Under Trump, the state has been hijacked by a sociopathic billionaire elite, thriving on insatiable greed while undermining and displaying contempt for human needs and the common good. With their opulence on full display, they govern for the accumulation of capital and the concentration of power. Civil rights are eroding, cities have become training grounds for the military, and staggering levels of inequality have concentrated power in the hands of a predatory financial elite. The democratic gains of the last half century are vanishing before our eyes.

The Democratic Party, stripped of moral conviction and political imagination, has collapsed into a hollow centrism, an empty vessel adrift in a sea of political and moral paralysis. As Trump bulldozes the Constitution and transforms the republic into a warfare state, Democrats respond with platitudes instead of power. They refuse to call for mass movements, summon people into the streets, call for strikes, and call to dismantle the machinery of the war economy and the obscene inequality it sustains.[39] They are the soft face of neoliberalism's hard cruelty, servants to the corporate–military–techno complex they claim to restrain. They largely support Netanyahu's genocidal war in Gaza and the West Bank and have done little to stop Trump's march to fascism.

In their cowardice, they have become collaborators, not opponents, of authoritarian rule. Their politics of accommodation mask a failure of moral will. Rather than ignite collective resistance, they drift in the shallow waters of corporate centrism, where compromise replaces courage and the language of reform masks complicity. What remains is a party drained of purpose, incapable of moral outrage, and deaf to history's warning. Drowning in their own vapid centrism, they offer no vision, no movement, no dream, only the cold echo of a political corpse.

As Chris Hedges reminds us, "Donald Trump is a symptom of our diseased society. He is not its cause. He is what is vomited up out of decay."[40] Trump is the political expression of a deeper pathology; the long-standing assault neoliberalism has waged against democracy itself. This is gangster capitalism in its purest form: a politics rooted in greed, racial hatred, and the legacy of colonial domination; its endpoint is an updated version of American fascism.

The struggle before us, then, is not merely to prevent Trump and his enablers from seizing the machinery of government, but to confront and overthrow the conditions that made him possible, the corporate state and the death-dealing logic of neoliberalism. What is required is not only an economic revolution but a moral and political one: a radical reordering of consciousness, values, and social relations.

As Jean-Luc Mélenchon argues, we need a new language for solidarity and civic morality that breaks with gangster capitalism and its elevation of greed over human need. "It is the path we take," he writes, "when we question the consequences of our actions: Are they really good for everyone? To be something real, virtue must necessarily be an action, in the here and now."[41]

As we stand before the terrifying rise of authoritarianism, it becomes clear that the fire we face is not distant or abstract but burning in the present. This is the moment to make education central to politics, to shape history with intention, to summon a collective courage rooted in the demands of freedom, equality, and justice, to act together with a militant hope that does not yield. Fascism will not prevail unless we let it.

To fight fascism today is to fight for education as the art of becoming human: a practice of listening, remembering, and imagining otherwise. Critical pedagogy offers us, as educators, artists, and cultural workers, the opportunity to rehearse freedom. Pedagogy as a practice of liberation prepares the world to begin again. A new future will come into being and endure only as long as we have the courage to make memory, imagination, and action the foundation for militant and collective resistance. In times such as these, resistance is the condition of survival.

This book is more than a chronicle of the rise of authoritarianism; it is a rallying cry, a blueprint for resurrecting democracy in the face of its erasure. Throughout these pages, I weave together the threads of power, culture, and resistance, exposing how the authoritarian project seeks to dismantle not only institutions but the very fabric of society, its memory, its values, its future. At its core, the book affirms that culture and education are pivotal in shaping new forms of agency and identity, essential to holding power accountable, rekindling the fire of moral witnessing, and igniting an organized groundswell of opposition that dares to envision a future beyond the tyranny of the present. From the war on dissent and the militarization of daily life to the erosion of educational spaces and the criminalization of critical thought, it lays bare the many ways democracy is being stripped of substance, shattered, and disfigured. Yet it also illuminates the diverse, powerful forces pushing back, from the defiant actions of youth to the reclaiming of education as a sanctuary of resistance.

Throughout the book, I argue that the resurgence of fascism around the globe must be understood not only as a form of governance, but also as a pedagogical regime and cultural battlefield that narrows the imagination, occupies memory, censors history, and wages war on thought itself. Through the propagation of cultural and educational violence, it spreads hatred, racism, ultranationalism, and a pathological desire for national rebirth rooted in white supremacy and racial cleansing. Central to fascism as a pedagogical regime lies an immense media apparatus, controlled by a handful of billionaires aggressively working to shape public consciousness and consent, turning language, images, and habits into forms of subordination. Fascism expands the reach of culture into every corner of daily life, turning art, media, education, and memory into instruments of domination. To rescue democracy, we must recognize that politics alone cannot save it. What is needed is a cultural and pedagogical revolution that challenges capitalist values of greed, unchecked self-interest, competition, and commodification. Only by building an emancipatory cultural regime, rooted in solidarity, equality, and the common good, can we nurture the consciousness, imagination, and courage necessary to confront fascism and reclaim the meaning of a radical democracy.

This book examines how fascism emerges while challenging us to rethink how we resist it, calling for a new vision of democracy. We must begin to imagine another way of being in the world, a new language of freedom, solidarity, and justice capable of turning despair into collective action and outrage into hope. We must envision a future where the idea and promise of democracy are reimagined in the service of a radical democracy, one that can be constructed and strengthened only through collective struggle and solidarity.

SECTION ONE

The Machinery of Fascism

1

The Politics of Cruelty: When the Social Fabric Unravels

The Rising Tide of Neoliberal Cruelty and Its Assault on Democracy

Neoliberalism has never been merely an economic agenda;[1] it is also a cultural and pedagogical force that corrodes social solidarity and loosens democracy at its roots. It does not merely defund public institutions like healthcare, education, and welfare, it delegitimizes them, refashioning them as burdens rather than essential public goods. As a pedagogical and ideological project, neoliberalism champions greed, unchecked self-interest, and a government devoid of social responsibility. It recodes mutual care as weakness and elevates competition to the status of nature's law. Relentless competition for survival breeds resignation, and with it, a politics in which cruelty feels ordinary.[2]

In this moment of democratic exhaustion, neoliberalism functions as a staging ground for fascism.[3] By concentrating wealth and normalizing abandonment, it lays the groundwork for authoritarian viciousness. Neoliberalism's fundamental tenet, that the market is the blueprint for all relationships, draws a parallel that connects capitalism and authoritarianism. At its core lies a colonizing logic that ranks lives, extracts value, and erases social responsibility. Privatization, deregulation, and commodification strip away practices of justice, equity, and care. In this context, cruelty has become the currency of exchange, a dominant motif of both governance and spectacle. Here, democracy is actively repurposed to serve a market indifferent to everything but profit. Its corrosive logic makes the slide toward fascism less an accident than a trajectory, one almost inevitable over time.

How Neoliberalism Normalizes Cruelty and Fractures Social Life

To understand fascist politics, we must reckon with its most visceral expression, a culture of cruelty. This cruelty is not an abstraction; it is inscribed on bodies and minds, destroying lives with calculated precision. As Brad Evans reminds us, violence must never be studied in an "objective and unimpassioned way," for it demands a reckoning that is both ethical and political.[4] This abyss of malice exposes not only how systemic injustice is endured but how the machinery of power turns the so-called American Dream into a nightmare of survival.

Since the 1980s, cultural politics has turned toxic as ruling elites seized control of dominant cultural apparatuses and new powerful technologies, transforming them into dangerous repressive pedagogical apparatuses.[5] These tools of ethical numbing unleash a torrent of degrading images, reducing the poor, immigrants, Muslims, and all labelled disposable to surplus lives slated for exclusion. Monied hoodlums and white nationalists now run the government, wallowing in corruption while destroying the public good and social bonds that "gave working Americans a sense of purpose and stability ... meaning and hope" for the future.[6]

Meanwhile, the capitalist dream machine delivers obscene profits to the ultra-rich and corporate elites. In this landscape of wealth and manufactured scarcity, a fanatical capitalism fuels a winner-take-all ethos, merging cruelty with white nationalism. The welfare state is razed; millions are consigned to precarity and anxiety. Increasingly cultural repression is matched by the violent force of the state. ICE and other federal agents have been transformed into Trump's personal army of lawless vigilantes. As J. David McSwane and Hannah Allam point out in *ProPublica*, "There are virtually no limits on what federal agents can do to achieve President Donald Trump's goal" of mass repression. They add:

> Current and former national security officials share the mayor's concerns. They describe the legions of masked immigration officers operating in near-total anonymity on the orders of the president as the crossing of a line that had long set the United States apart from the world's most repressive regimes. ICE, in their view, has become an unfettered and unaccountable national police force. The transformation, the officials say, unfolded rapidly and in plain sight. Trump's DHS appointees swiftly dismantled civil rights guardrails, encouraged agents to wear masks, threatened groups and state governments that stood in their way, and then made so many arrests that the influx overwhelmed lawyers trying to defend immigrants taken out of state or out of the country.

Writer Pankaj Mishra captures this transformation of ideology and state power with unsettling clarity. He argues that neoliberalism has so profoundly reshaped society that compassion itself is now regarded as weakness or folly, a moral failure rather than a virtue. This contempt for compassion, he suggests, has created the perfect moral climate for the normalization of state violence and systemic repression. He writes: "The puzzle of our age is how [the] essential foundation of civic life went missing from our public conversation .... the compassionate imagination was indispensable.One result of mainstreaming a bleak survivalist ethic is that 'most people .... secretly believe that kindness is a virtue of losers.'"[7]

Fascism's New Face: From Neoliberalism to Authoritarian Rule

Trumpism is the logical extension of a neoliberal system that thrives on hierarchy, disposability, ignorance, and fear. The destruction of public goods accelerates what Étienne Balibar calls "the transition from the social state to the penal state," where repression replaces care.[8]

The gutting of aid programs, the war on DEI initiatives, and the defunding of social institutions are not incidental; they are central to the neoliberal strategy of dispossession aligned with white supremacy. In the age of Trump, heartlessness becomes an organizing principle of violence, a homegrown authoritarianism that defines who counts as an American in racist terms, sanctions genocide in Gaza, promotes mass poverty, disregards the law, and embraces ecological destruction.

Under such circumstances, Pankaj Mishra notes the emergence of a culture convulsed in hatred and rancor matched by dehumanization and "grandiose fantasies of omnipotence."[9] Trump's presence in American politics appears as the endpoint of this pathology, where hate and sanctioned ruthlessness "have reached a new peak of ferocity."[10] It signals an era in which reason yields to irrationality, truth to lies, and informed argument to conspiracy, broadcast in vulgar spectacles of cruelty.[11] Under Trump, neoliberalism has been unleashed in its attack on the welfare state, justice, and the constitutional rights of both citizens and non-citizens. James Spyer is right in stating that "the Trump administration is essentially acting as a massive criminal enterprise. It lies, steals, extorts and murders—all the while cloaked in the awesome authority of the state. It is on a crime spree that puts Al Capone to shame."[12]

We are witnessing the emergence of a dangerous social formation where unchecked capitalism, Big Tech, and far-right politics conspire to dismantle the public good. They share a hatred for diversity and a belief that political power belongs to white Christian men alone.

The Toxic Politics of Capitalism: White Supremacy and the War on Democracy

The criminalization of identity has found its twin in the assault on due process, until the logic of repression, once unimaginable, has become the pulse of everyday life, shaping how people see, fear, and relate to one another. As part of their white supremacist agenda, the MAGA far-right has waged an all-out war on those they deem "other," part of a throw-away population unworthy of citizenship. This campaign of exclusion is not merely rhetoric, it is policy. The assault on DEI and the drive for mass deportations are not separate policies but expressions of the same authoritarian project, a campaign of racial purification masquerading as patriotism. Across the country, Americans are being stopped in the streets by masked ICE agents barking "Show me your papers," enacting a theater of humiliation that fuses state power with racial terror. What emerges is a new order of cruelty, where authoritarianism is no longer the exception but the rule, and dangerous myths like "white replacement theory" serve as fuel for division and domination.[13]

This brutal assault on democracy is part of a long history of capitalist-driven repression, a history that has now evolved into what I call neoliberal fascism: an alliance of economic barbarism and political repression sustained by a culture that glorifies cruelty as strength. As Robin D. G. Kelley aptly notes, the destruction wrought by neoliberalism in the United States has been both relentless and devastating, and we are now living in its catastrophic wake.

> Over the last five decades we've witnessed massive social disinvestment: the erosion of the welfare state, living-wage jobs, collective bargaining rights, union membership, government investment in education, accessible and affordable housing, health care, food, and basic democracy. In some states, Emergency Financial Managers have replaced elected governments, overseeing the privatization of public assets, corporate tax abatements, and cuts in employee pension funds in order to "balance" city budgets. At the same time, we have seen an exponential growth in income inequality, corporate profits, prisons, and well-funded conservative think tanks and lobbying groups whose dominance in the legislative arena has significantly weakened union rights, environmental and consumer protection, occupational safety, and the social safety net.[14]

Trump's Budget: A Manifestation of Cruelty and Social Disintegration

Trump's 2025 budget stands as the ultimate expression of cruelty, a blueprint for deepening inequality and desolation. It slashes healthcare for millions, guts housing and child support, and funnels billions in tax breaks to the ultra-rich while financing the largest military buildup since the 1980s. With Trump's war against Iran, even more money will go to the military-industrial complex, draining funds away from crucial social programs such as Medicaid, daycare, and education. This is not fiscal prudence but moral vandalism: the ritual sacrifice of the poor on the altar of greed and militarism. During the MAGA-driven government shutdown, this malice comes into full view. The GOP has allowed health care premiums to double and triple, casting millions of low-income Americans into medical insecurity and despair. At the same time, the Trump administration refuses to fund the Supplemental Nutrition Assistance Program, threatening to deprive 40 million people of food, a policy of starvation masquerading as governance. And while staggering levels of hunger spread across the nation, US Senator Bernie Sanders rightly condemned Trump for finding "$40 billion to bail out Argentina and $300 million for a ballroom to host dinner parties with billionaires, [while refusing] to tap emergency funds to prevent millions of American kids from going hungry."[15]

The ideology of hardness, as Adam Serwer notes, runs through American culture like an electric current, ensuring that suffering is not just tolerated but celebrated.[16] Under the grip of neoliberal capitalism, especially as Trump's second administration unfolds, the essence of politics, if not social responsibility itself, is obliterated, erasing the fundamental possibility of human community and the emancipatory power of the social, public goods, and the global commons.[17] Trump's budget mentioned above is a outstanding exercise in cruelty, if not sadism directed at the working class and the underprivileged.

Trumpism and the Weaponization of State Power

Trumpism is both a reaction to neoliberal decay, and callousness performed as ideology. Unlike past presidents who at least feigned democratic ideals, Trump openly embraces vengeance. He systematically targets adversaries, employing the state to exact retribution. He has used the machinery of government to humiliate opponents, stripping security clearances and launching politicized prosecutions.[18] The death of moral authority in politics breeds a climate of cruelty and violence in which the unimaginable is normalized. For instance, the alleged helping hand of the US has now been turned into a brutal fist, accompanied by the sneers of billionaire techno zombies, such as Mark Zuckerberg, Elon Musk, and Jeff Bezos, who endorse an anthology of proto-Nazi sentiments.[19]

What more damning illustration of his assault on global care than Trump's dismantling of the US Agency for International Development (USAID), leading to the suspension of essential services, including HIV treatment in Uganda and cholera prevention in Bangladesh, which have exacerbated global health crises? The projected number of deaths from such cuts is estimated at 14 million, a modern day genocide.[20] As Fintan O'Toole observes in *The New York Review*, the farce of Trump's first term has now transformed into the brutal and ugly realities of a second term.[21] The unchecked lust for power and the disastrous consequences of a war in Iran is now giving way to land grabs and dangerous imperial ambitions, as Trump seeks to realize his vision of a "unified Reich."[22]

Trump's drive to dismantle USAID and expel Palestinians from Gaza reveals a fascist logic in which cruelty, to borrow Balibar's phrase, "crosses the lines of extremity."[23] These actions, cloaked in the rhetoric of efficiency, dispossession, and disposability are in fact state-sanctioned terrorism masquerading as policy.

The Trump–Musk administration is not saving money in cutting foreign aid for USAID since it amounts to about 0.6 percent of total US annual government spending of $6.75tn.[24] Yet, what is at risk in eliminating USAID are "HIV medication for more than 20 million people; nutrition supplements for starving children; support for refugees, orphaned children and women battered by violence."[25] Moreover, as Ralph Nader notes, in an utter disregard for the health and spread of diseases on a global level, "Trump is also cutting monitoring for the emergence of deadly epidemics such as Ebola, drug-resistant tuberculosis, malaria and other lethal viruses and bacteria, which could come to the US like COVID-19 did."[26]

The moral emptiness and ruthlessness of politicians whose mouths drip with the blood of their actions are starkly revealed in the Trump–Musk assault on USAID which will inevitably lead to the deaths of countless millions. As Anne Applebaum observes, the deliberate purge of USAID employees, who work in the world's most dangerous conditions to deliver food and medicine to the most vulnerable, will have tragic consequences. These are the workers who "provide special meals to malnourished children."[27] Without such meals, their lives will be lost. This is nothing less than state-sanctioned terrorism cloaked in the false guise of efficiency, a regressive and heartless ideology that masks its destruction with the rhetoric of progress. A researcher from Boston University states that USAID cuts caused more than 330,000 deaths worldwide.[28] It gets worse. A 15-member research team from Spain, Brazil, Mozambique, and the United States, writing in *The Lancet*, warned that more than 14 million people could die by 2030 due to US foreign aid cuts, including 4.5 million children under the age of five.[29]

Yet, this cruelty is not limited to public health; it extends to the horrifying spectacle of ethnic cleansing in Gaza. Trump's unyielding support for Israel and the looming threat of forcibly removing over two million Palestinians from Gaza, exposes a deeper, genocidal logic. This isn't just a violation of international human rights; it is a death sentence for countless Palestinian children, women, and the elderly, those who are already enduring an unrelenting history and cycle of genocidal deprivation. This calculated disregard for the lives of nonwhite people is emblematic of a white supremacist project that views these lives as expendable, undeserving of basic human dignity or rights.

Although a ceasefire has formally begun, reports from Gaza's media office indicate that Israel has already breached the truce dozens of times since early October, resulting in 723 deaths by Israeli fire.[30] These alleged violations include shooting civilians, shelling of residential areas, and the arrest of noncombatants, evidence that Israel's campaign of aggression continues despite formal declarations of the pause in fighting.[31]

It is worth repeating that both Trump's actions at home and abroad, whether in cutting USAID or in supporting the ethnic cleansing of Palestinians, are not isolated or coincidental. They are threads in a single, cohesive political agenda that thrives on division, viciousness, and the calculated erasure of those who do not fit into the narrow, violent vision of a fascist state. These policies, far from being budgetary decisions, are part of a larger strategy that seeks to normalize a systemic policy of heartlessness, reduce lives to disposable commodities, weaken the bonds of solidarity, and manipulate violence as a spectacle of power. This viciousness extends to Trump's assault on sanctuary cities, threatening funding, prosecuting officials, and flooding communities with ICE troops. These actions weaponize fear and erode the rule of law, reducing it to a judicial hoax.

In spite of massive protests,Trump continues to flood cities governed by Democrats with military troops and ICE, which evokes fear, enables lawless violence, and violates human rights. These measures not only undermine public safety and erode trust between immigrant communities and law enforcement, but they make clear a governance style deeply rooted in vindictiveness, leveraging the apparatus of the state to intimidate and punish, thereby eroding democratic norms and fostering a climate of fear. For Trump, governance is not service but domination. His rallies are theaters of cruelty, encouraging supporters to revel in others' suffering. Whether mocking disabled people, humiliating women, or encouraging police brutality, Trump's politics transform ruthlessness into communal bonding. Trump has fully embraced the logic of state-sponsored violence and weaponized governance, ensuring that social abandonment and the politics of disappearance are not byproducts but ideology itself. This orchestrated domestic terrorism targets the marginalized and those who hold power accountable.

Manufactured Precarity and the Weaponization of Resentment

The devastation wrought by neoliberal fascism creates widespread precarity, forcing people into perpetual insecurity. When safety nets are dismantled, individuals become desperate for stability, making them ripe for demagogues who offer scapegoats. Trumpism exploits this desperation by redirecting anxiety toward manufactured enemies, immigrants, welfare recipients, and marginalized communities, rather than corporate elites. It is a pedagogy of resentment, turning victims into accomplices.

This manipulation of insecurity requires a machinery of persuasion, one that transforms fear into ideology and resentment into identity. Central to the weaponization of resentment is the takeover of both old and new cultural apparatuses that shape mass consciousness, individual and collective agency, and social values. Citizens are increasingly constructed through a mass-produced language of contempt for the vulnerable, poor, and others considered unworthy.

A constant torrent of hate and bigotry now spreads with tsunami force through podcasts, corporate controlled media, and right-wing platforms, all of which legitimate an ideology of hardness, cruelty, and lies, draining the strength from social relations and individual character, moral compassion and collective resistance. Algorithmic authoritarianism, powered by neoliberalism's "disimagination machines," has gutted the public sphere, replacing critical thought with conformity and turning truth itself into a political casualty. A very small number of firms now control the architecture of our digital reality, just a handful of tech giants that own the platforms, data pipelines, and algorithmic guts of our common life.[32] They decide what we see, what remains invisible, and what counts as reality. Their business model is not illumination but manipulation, feeding division, hatred, anger, and outrage to keep users captive and democracy anesthetized. In this new information order, emotional intensity replaces reason, spectacle displaces substance, and ignorance is weaponized as common sense. Historical consciousness becomes subversive, dissent, an act of treason.

Matters of life, death, and politics now converge in a MAGA party shaped by a social, digital, and ocular order marked by a militaristic and misogynistic notion of masculinity, the celebration of profit over human needs, and an addiction to violence. Shared values and truths have given way to political corruption and the allure of escape from moral responsibility. Trump and his corporate allies have erected a vast cultural machinery to mold individuals into subjects fit for authoritarian rule, governed by fear and seduced by certainty.[33]

Ensnared in a culture of ignorance, they drift in the fog of anti-intellectualism, where thinking is neither required nor desired. Difference becomes anathema, the Other, an enemy, a poison to be eliminated. They are prisoners of language, trapped within what Zadie Smith calls "auto-imprisonment," where words do not liberate but constrict, where thought itself is reduced to the blinding poison of manufactured ignorance and consent.[34] Their world flattens into crude binaries, good and evil, us and them, purity and contamination. Complexity is the first casualty, sacrificed on the altar of simplicity, where nuance is a threat and history is rewritten to serve power. The erasure of the ability to dissent is fascism's most insidious triumph, the engineering of subjects who no longer know they should resist.

Trump's "rancid and irredeemable character" now washes over America in pandemic-like fashion, weakening the body politic and degrading the substance of language itself.[35] His attacks on transgender athletes, his grotesque claim that a military helicopter crash was caused by hiring disabled air traffic controllers, and his lie that government agencies fund "transgender comic books" and "sex changes" abroad do more than justify toxic policy, they normalize heartlessness as common sense.[36] What is in fact at work here is an ideological crusade designed to reinforce white supremacist and patriarchal hierarchies. Balibar describes this as the "preventive counterrevolution," a strategy where extreme violence and mass insecurity are systematically used to prevent collective movements of emancipation.[37]

From Neoliberal Decay to Fascist Restoration

Neoliberalism does not simply fail; it creates the conditions for authoritarian restoration.[38] As public goods are gutted and civic life is eroded, the only function left for the state is repression. Thus, the rise of Trumpism coincides with the expansion of the police state and the criminalization of protest. The collapse of the social leaves a vacuum, and that void is filled by the authoritarian impulse to restore order through force.

Under Trump, the machinery of violence has accelerated. White supremacist groups gained confidence, political brutality seeped into everyday life, and hostility toward journalists, educators, and dissidents became a public performance of power. The January 6th attack was the clearest expression of this trajectory, exposing how quickly democratic norms can collapse when authoritarian energies are unleashed. What we are witnessing is not a series of isolated eruptions but the movement from neoliberal chaos toward an openly fascist configuration of power. Balibar's insight that globalization has carved the planet into "life zones and death zones" is starkly visible here: Trump's policies lavish protection on corporate elites while turning the poor, racialized, and dispossessed into expendable targets of state violence.[39]

From Destruction to Reclamation: The Fight for Public Goods and Democracy

We cannot fight cruelty with outrage alone; we need a radical reimagining of public goods. The call for universal healthcare, education, and living wages is not only economic policy, but also resistance against an all-encompassing authoritarian logic. In this era of resurgent authoritarianism, neoliberal capitalism must be named not as democracy's ally but as its betrayal. Étienne Balibar reminds us democracy requires an "insurrectional element," a constant struggle against exclusion and dehumanization. Rebuilding the social is not simply reversing neoliberal policies; it is reclaiming politics itself.[40]

Central to such a task is making clear to the American public that democracy cannot exist in a country in which three major tech billionaires own as much wealth as 170 million Americans. It cannot exist in a society in which as Bernie Sanders points out,

> 60% of Americans live paycheck to paycheck; millions are earning starvation wages; 85 million are uninsured or underinsured; young people are unable to afford the cost of college; 25% of seniors live on $15,000 a year or less; we have the highest rate of childhood poverty of almost any major country on earth, and we have a major shortage in low-income and affordable housing.[41]

All of this is legitimated and reproduced by a fascist political movement under Trump in which the means of communication on various platforms are controlled by the far right and their billionaire owners and backers.

Today, democracy is increasingly dominated by a toxic mix of media platforms that fuel lies, misinformation, and conspiracy theories and democracy is on life support, battered by the unchecked power of billionaire wealth who own those platforms. Donald Trump and his supporters seem to believe in neither law nor accountability; how else can we explain his appalling assertion that "He who saves his country does not violate any law,"? or his self-aggrandizing, delusional declaration, "Long Live the King?" Equally revealing are the grotesque AI-generated videos and images in which he casts himself as a messianic figure, either portraying himself as Jesus or basking in Jesus's embrace, a spectacle of unchecked narcissism and authoritarian delusion that collapses the line between political power, religious idolatry, and cult-like devotion. These statements reflect a worldview that dismisses the rule of law in favor of authoritarianism where power is unchecked, and truth is whatever those in power choose it to be.

The Battle for the Future: Can Democracy Survive in the Age of Authoritarianism?

This assault on the rule of law is deeply entwined with the broader breakdown of social structures that sustain a healthy democracy. Democracy cannot survive in a society where people are forced into constant competition for dwindling resources. Without public goods, civic life collapses, and despair takes its place. Hope, in this context, is not naive optimism but a call to organized resistance, a refusal to accept the conditions of malice as inevitable. The challenge ahead is not only to expose the logic of neoliberal destruction but to fight for a future in which public life is not dictated by profit. As later chapters show, neoliberalism's assault on public life has prepared the cultural ground for authoritarian rule.

With Trump's second term unfolding, fascism is a developing reality, accelerating the collapse of democratic institutions and expanding state violence. What is particularly dangerous in this new world order is that Trump and his rich Vichy tech stooges are not simply out to get more tax cuts. The threat they pose is much larger. It is about the resurgence of a totalitarian instrumentalism which, as Mike Brock notes in *The Plot Against America*, "is not about efficiency. It is about erasure. Democracy is being overwritten, replaced by proprietary platforms and AI regimes. This is a coup, not with guns, but with backend migrations and erased databases, a digital purge designed to rewrite history and consolidate power."[42] Under the Trump administration, this erasure will accelerate alongside acts of overt violence. Countering this new stage of state brutality requires not only understanding the deep roots of neo-fascism in the United States but dismantling the economic, political, and cultural forces that sustain it.

Writing in *The New European*, Suzanne Schneider delivers a sharp critique of far-right ideologue Curtis Yarvin's embrace of "turbocapitalism." She notes that "the engineers represent the triumph of instrumental reason in our new century. They fetishize efficiency and understand the democratic state as an impediment to the sort of 'progress' they desire."[43] This is not just about controlling information systems; it is a clear indication that education itself has become a political battlefield. In this framework, knowledge is no longer a means of enlightenment but is cast as a tool for reinforcing authoritarian power.

Only through a massive educational and political struggle can we dismantle the ethos of harshness born of turbocapitalism, a system that thrives on inequality and contempt for the public good. Its logic laid bare by Peter Thiel in 2009 when he wrote, "I no longer believe that freedom and democracy are compatible," reveals the moral bankruptcy at its core.[44] Yarvin, a celebrated darling of the right-wing media ecosystem, goes even further, insisting that American democracy be scrapped and replaced with a "monarchy" governed by a single corporate "C.E.O."—his sanitized word for a dictator.[45] Such visions, where gangster capitalism merges with techno-authoritarianism, push democracy to the brink. Yet even in this darkness, the possibility of renewal persists. It survives only if we summon the courage to fight for it, to reclaim a future that has not yet been lost.

As David Livingston warns, "We are probably living in the most dangerous time for the human species since our early origins," marked by "massive numbers of wildfires, the prospect of a nuclear winter, and historic peaks in wealth inequality alongside historic lows in public trust in government."[46]

We live in a time too urgent to abandon hope for a more just and radical future. We face an immense task in recognizing that hope is wounded but not lost, and as Alain Badiou states, what we now face is "showing how the space of the possible is larger than the one assigned, that something else is possible, but not everything is possible."[47] The task before us is not just to resist, but to widen the horizon of the possible. We must refuse the suffocating limits imposed by neoliberal fatalism and authoritarian rule, and instead, fight for a future where justice is not a dream deferred but a struggle embraced, where democracy is not a relic of the past, but the foundation of what must come next.

2

Abducting Bodies: State Violence and the Architecture of Domination

Introduction

For Americans, and for all who still believe that democracy is more than a slogan, the task is urgent: to resist the politics of disappearance and disposability now unleashed under the Trump regime, an authoritarian contagion mirrored by strongmen across the globe. Fascism is being reborn in familiar forms, where the state, cloaked in the language of security, vanishes those who dissent, branding them as terrorists, antisemites, or traitors. In the name of protecting the nation, it dismantles it. Fueled by white supremacy and fear of opposition, these disappearances are rehearsals for a darker future in which dissent itself becomes a crime and the machinery of terror operates with bureaucratic precision. The line between repression and everyday life grows thinner by the day, as the logic of disappearance seeps from the shadows of policy into the fabric of daily governance. The specter of fascism no longer hides behind rhetoric or spectacle; it steps onto the stage of power itself, turning the machinery of erasure inward, ruthlessly deciding who counts as a citizen and who does not.

Under Trump's militarization of institutions, cities, and everyday life, the meaning of who counts as an American collapses. No passport, birth certificate, or legal claim offers protection; abductions are carried out with impunity, their logic written in the color of one's skin. As of October 2025, journalist Nicole Foy reports that more than 170 American citizens have been illegally detained by ICE, many "kicked, dragged, and held for days" by immigration agents.[1] Deportation has become the twin of dispossession, working hand in hand with the destruction of citizenship itself. In this new order, people are sent to so-called "third countries," where death or torture may await them. The state is deporting bodies and erasing belonging, rendering people displaced, exiled both from the nation, and the very idea of human rights. Official disappearances also take place at home as the Trump regime populates America with immigration detention centers--prison camps which currently hold more than 73,000 people.[2]

As I noted in the Introduction, this nightmare is not speculative. It is embodied in Mahmoud Khalil's abduction, a Columbia graduate, Palestinian, and permanent US resident, seized for the "crime" of speaking against the slaughter of his people in Gaza. Without warning, ICE handcuffed him, dragged him from his apartment lobby, shoved him into an unmarked car, and disappeared him. He broke no law; his only offense was refusing silence in the face of settler colonial violence and mass killings by Israeli forces. In minutes, his rights were erased, his body rendered vulnerable, his voice targeted. Khalil became yet another casualty in the escalating war on dissent, white supremacy, and state-sanctioned cruelty.

Despite the absence of any criminal charges against Khalil, a Louisiana immigration judge ruled that he could be deported, citing that his presence in the United States posed "potentially serious foreign policy consequences."[3] The sheer shamelessness and legal absurdity of this decision became even more evident in a memo from Secretary of State Marco Rubio. He acknowledged that while Khalil's beliefs might be lawful, the Immigration and Nationality Act of 1952 grants the Secretary of State the authority to "personally determine" whether Khalil should remain in the country based on his "expected beliefs."[4] This alarming statement, with its Nuremberg-like laws and Kafkaesque horrors, reveals the essence of authoritarian regimes where punishment extends beyond actions to the pre-emptive targeting of individuals for their very thoughts. It echoes the darkest chapters of totalitarian history, where freedom is not merely stifled but eradicated at its roots. This is not a simple legal overreach; it is a blatant assault on due process and liberty, a grotesque perversion of justice that seeks to strip away the most fundamental human rights.

Defenders of American-style authoritarianism—Trump, Rubio, Miller—have turned Khalil into a high-profile political prisoner. His real "crime" is refusing to remain silent in the face of state-sponsored atrocities. He stands as part of a broader youth-led resistance that refuses to bow to the dogma of obedience, nationalism, and state terrorism. As Nawal Arjini puts it, he is one of "so many young people willing to put their bodies on the line for their beliefs." I was encouraged to witness "their outrage and pain, their understanding of the economic underpinnings of oppression, and their powerful sense of political and ethical accountability."[5]

What unnerves the powerful is that Khalil, like many others, insists on solidarity across racial and national boundaries, on refusing complicity in genocide, repression, and empire. Trump's ramping up of the targeting of immigrants, activists, journalists, and individuals and institutions deemed "enemies of the state" reflects this administration's fear and intent to destroy any form of "cross-movement organizing and solidarity combating" both the administration's war on dissent and its systemic racist attacks on immigrants and people of color.[6]

To understand Khalil's case is to grasp a deeper reality: the state now claims the power to erase those who refuse to conform. His abduction represents a dangerous precedent, not just an assault on speech, but on historical memory, civic literacy, and the very institutions that make democratic life possible. This is not simply about one protestor or one student. It is about the death of democratic possibility itself.

Another harrowing instance came on March 26, 2025, when Rumeysa Öztürk, a Turkish citizen and doctoral student at Tufts University, was walking through Somerville, Massachusetts, on her way to join friends and break her Ramadan fast.[7] Surveillance video shows five individuals in plain clothes surrounding her. They did not identify themselves; they simply grabbed her, claiming to be police, as if rehearsing a scene from the fascist playbook. She begged to call someone, but they refused. They took her phone, seized her knapsack, handcuffed her on the street, and threw her into an unmarked SUV. She vanished, only to reappear in an Immigration and Customs Enforcement (ICE) jail in Louisiana.

This was an act of political kidnapping, state-legitimated violence masquerading as law enforcement. It revived the Gestapo's logic of silencing dissent, with violence as pedagogy and terror as governance used to disappear the "undesirables," and spread fear through calculated, extrajudicial violence in Nazi Germany.[8]

Only after public outrage and press scrutiny did Homeland Security issue a statement, accusing Öztürk of having "engaged in activities in support of Hamas, a foreign terrorist organization," and stating that her student visa had been revoked. Öztürk's only "crime" was protesting Israel's brutal war on Gaza. She had helped to coauthor a March 2024 op-ed in *The Tufts Daily* titled "Try again, President Kumar: Renewing calls for Tufts to adopt March 4 TCU Senate resolutions."[9] The op-ed urged Tufts to "meaningfully engage with and actualize" resolutions passed by the Tufts Community Union Senate, which had passed three resolutions demanding that the university "divest from companies with direct or indirect ties to Israel."

ICE's violation of her right to free speech should send a chill down the spine of anyone who believes in democracy. No charges were filed. No due process offered. No hearing. Just disappearance and denunciation. She was accused, without evidence, of supporting Hamas and told she didn't belong in the country. That was enough. What makes this even more troubling is how seamlessly such actions echo Israel's system of administrative detention, where people are held indefinitely on the pretext that they might break the law. Trumpism did not invent this machinery—it draws inspiration and confidence from it. The precedent has already been set by a regime that normalizes holding bodies in limbo, criminalizing thought, and erasing due process. ICE and Israel's administrative detention system operate on the same authoritarian logic: that certain people can be disappeared not for what they have done, but for what they represent.

Both Khalil and Öztürk were released after judges ruled that neither of them was guilty of a crime or posed a threat to the United States.[10] It is worth noting that the kidnappings of Mahmoud Khalil and Rumeysa Öztürk by plainclothes agents of the state mark a terrifying threshold in the unfolding drama of American authoritarianism. These acts were not exceptional law enforcement errors but acts of political terrorism, signaling that fascism in the United States is no longer a creeping threat; it is a reality. These young scholars, legal US residents, were seized, denied due process, and imprisoned in remote detention centers for nothing more than their dissent against the Israeli American genocide in Gaza.

Khalil and Öztürk's abduction are part of a broader pattern of state violence.[11] More than 200 Venezuelan migrants were seized and sent to a notorious maximum-security torture dungeon in El Salvador run by Nayib Bukele, a ruthless dictator,[12] punished for the ink on their skin.[13] Their tattoos were read as threats, their bodies as deviant. Later, they were deported to Venezuela as part of a large-scale prisoner exchange among the United States, Venezuela, and El Salvador, an arrangement that saw ten Americans held in Venezuela freed in return for the Venezuelan deportees.

As reported in *The New York Times*, many of the men testified that while imprisoned,

> they were shackled, beaten, shot with rubber bullets and tear gassed until they passed out. They said they were punished in a dark room called the island, where they were trampled, kicked and forced to kneel for hours. One man said officers thrust his head into a tank of water to simulate drowning. Another said he was forced to perform oral sex on guards wearing hoods.[14]

What emerges here is not simply a catalog of human-rights abuses, nor merely the grotesque suspension of due process; it is the language of barbarism made policy, brutality elevated to the level of governance. These acts, carried out under the pretext of fighting terrorism, reveal themselves for what they are: the state-sanctioned machinery of a racialized war, a campaign of terror unleashed by the Trump regime against immigrants. Such violence does more than break bodies, it shreds the very fabric of a democratic society, teaching a lesson no nation should ever teach—that some lives can be debased with impunity.

This practice of cruelty and lawlessness soon found another victim, exposing how state violence feeds on impunity and bureaucratic deceit. In what became an international scandal, the US admitted that Ábrego García was mistakenly sent to El Salvador. Despite the Supreme Court's ruling ordering his return to the US, the Trump administration delayed and refused to comply, using semantics and technicalities as excuses. With the support of a dictator like Bukele, the White House allowed an innocent immigrant to languish in a brutal detention center, revealing a profound disregard for justice and due process.[15]

Ábrego García was eventually returned to the US by order of the courts and is now facing federal human smuggling charges in Tennessee. His attorneys have contested the charges, labeling them as politically motivated and an attempt to justify his wrongful deportation. A federal judge has ruled that he is eligible for release under certain conditions, and as of April 6, 2026 he is free. The Justice Department has announced that rather than proceed with the trial on human smuggling charges, they plan to deport him to Liberia before considering any deportation to a "third country," though no specific timeline has been provided.

Countless others, such as Yunseo Chung and Badar Khan Suri, have been seized without due process in violation of the law.[16] Their so-called crimes are constructed within the toxic logics of white supremacy, the fear of dissent, and a politics of disposability. At the end of September 2025, Yunseo Chung, a lawful permanent resident and Columbia student, remained in the US under a court-issued restraining order that blocked her deportation. On October 1st, Judge William Young, a Reagan appointee, ruled that the administration's actions against Chung and a number of other students "violate the First Amendment [and that] such conduct is not only unconstitutional, but a thing virtually unknown to our constitutional tradition."[17] Badar Khan Suri, a Georgetown postdoctoral scholar, was released from ICE detention in mid-May on bond and continues his legal fight in Virginia.

The disappearance of immigrants, students, Muslims, Arabs, and outspoken critics of empire marks a horrifying escalation: people are being targeted not for what they have done, but for who they are and what they symbolize. This is the politics of disappearance, a machinery of erasure that punishes dissent and issues a brutal warning to all who refuse to bow to authoritarian power. These tactics echo some of the darkest chapters of modern history, from the Gestapo's vanishing of political opponents to Latin America's Dirty Wars, where students, workers, and intellectuals were seized, tortured, and erased without a trace. Today's so-called "war on terror" reproduces this logic, collapsing protest into terrorism and dissent into subversion. The consequences are devastating in that rights are gutted, memory is expunged, and the very ground of civic and political life disintegrates. The true danger lies not only in what is destroyed, but in the futures foreclosed, the histories, voices, and possibilities that disappear with them.

The Trump administration's indiscriminate use of terrorism as a pretext for exclusion and deportation is not limited to those struggling for Palestinian liberation from settler-colonialism and genocide, but also many other activists addressing a range of social problems. For instance, Noura Erakat, writing in the *Boston Review*, warns that elements of fascism are increasingly being deployed domestically in the United States. She highlights how repressive tactics used against Palestinians are now being applied in Georgia, where "forty-two activists protesting the expansion of Cop City, a $90 million militarized police training facility ... have been charged with domestic terrorism."[18]

Erakat also points to Tennessee's HB 2348/SB 2610, passed in May 2024, which enables the state to use terrorism charges to target social movements, particularly environmental groups who express solidarity with Palestinians (i.e., Black Lives Matter). At the heart of Erakat's argument lies a crucial truth: to resist fascism, we must confront it on two fronts, both the US state's violence at home and abroad. The war against Palestinians is inseparable from the war at home against democracy, free speech, and equality. To fight one is to fight the other. As Trump sends armed National Guard units to occupy cities such as Portland, Chicago, Los Angeles, and Washington, DC and potentially more, the outlines of a police state become more evident.

The Nightmare Returns

Trump's second presidency has stripped away the last restraints on power, turning civil liberties and democratic institutions into targets rather than safeguards. No longer constrained by those who once sought to temper his worst impulses, Trump now governs with open contempt for the rule of law, emboldened by a movement that thrives on cruelty, grievance, and unrelenting violence. His language has always been a weapon, honed by fear, sharpened by menace, and wielded to incite violence against immigrants, Black Americans, and anyone who dares to challenge his rule.[19] Under Trump, the machinery of governance itself has become a battlefield, war turned inward as the organizing principle of rule. For years, the mainstream press dismissed Trump's rhetoric as nothing more than bluster, an act designed for entertainment or spectacularized provocation rather than a genuine call to power. His declaration of wanting to be a "dictator for a day" and his subsequent quote, "He who saves his Country does not violate any Law," were met with little more than a shrug, treated with barely a flicker of concern.[20] Many assumed his fascist threats were nothing but empty theatrics, comforted by the belief that handlers and legal restraints would keep him in check. That illusion has now been shattered.

By his second term, authoritarianism no longer hides in the shadows, it operates in plain sight. The punitive carceral state now boldly criminalizes dissent, weaponizes the justice system, dismantling public and higher education, abducting individuals, embracing corruption, and executing mass deportations with a cold, calculating efficiency that evokes some of America's darkest historical chapters. This legacy echoes in the Palmer Raids of 1919–1920, when thousands of leftists, anarchists, and immigrants were arrested without cause, often enduring brutal treatment.[21] The Red Scare, especially during the McCarthy era of the 1950s, marked another grim chapter, as government-sanctioned witch hunts destroyed lives and careers on the flimsiest of accusations.[22] In the wake of the Vietnam War, opposition to the conflict was labeled un-American, culminating in the tragic deaths of students at Kent State.[23] More recently, the Bush administration's post-9/11 War on Terror entrenched surveillance, indefinite detention, and the spectacle of torture at Guantánamo Bay.[24]

From McCarthyism, through the covert assaults of COINTELPRO, to the sweeping excesses of the War on Terror, US history is threaded with a recurring pattern of repression, each era criminalizing dissent and targeting the vulnerable in the name of national security. Trump has breathed new life into this legacy, adapting it to the technologies and authoritarian ambitions of our time. He has digitized repression for the twenty-first century, drawing on tactics perfected by Latin America's bloodiest dictatorships and the Gestapo's machinery of erasure. In doing so, he has revived a dangerous historical playbook and transformed it into a weapon against those who refuse submission and those who still believe in the promise of universal citizenship.

History Matters

History, and the dangerous memories it carries, matters because it illuminates the shadows where authoritarianism hides and where its ghosts still breathe. As Paul Gilroy reminds us, "Those horrors are always much closer to us than we like to imagine. Preventing their recurrence requires keeping them in mind."[25] Fascism today is not interred in the past, nor a mere replica of another age; its mobilizing passions, its cult of purity, its hatred of difference, its worship of power, are still with us, reshaped but no less lethal. Primo Levi's prescient warning echoes across our time and is worth repeating in full:

> Every age has its own fascism, and we see the warning signs wherever the concentration of power denies citizens the possibility and the means of expressing and acting on their own free will. There are many ways of reaching this point, and not just through the terror of police intimidation, but by denying and distorting information, by undermining systems of justice, by paralyzing the education system, and by spreading in a myriad subtle ways nostalgia for a world where order reigned, and where the security of a privileged few depends on the forced labor and the forced silence of the many.[26]

Under Trump, the treatment of dissenters bears what Martin Wolf has called "authoritarianism with fascist characteristics."[27] As history teaches, repression begins with language before it becomes law, and law before it becomes violence. The Nazis labeled dissenters as terrorists, with Heinrich Himmler making clear that students who defied the Reich had no place in its vision, likening them to pests that needed to be eradicated.[28] Pinochet branded universities as breeding grounds for terrorists, justifying mass arrests, torture, and executions. Argentina's military regime abducted students, hurled them from planes, and murdered over 30,000.[29] Trump's administration is assembling the rhetoric and mechanisms of such atrocities, one abduction at a time. History's warning is simple: once conditions ripen, the unimaginable returns in familiar forms.

It is crucial to emphasize that the abduction and state persecution of Khalil and other students fighting for Palestinian freedom, along with their defense of the university as a democratic public good, is not merely an assault on free speech and academic freedom, but a direct embodiment of what G. M. Tamás identifies as the fundamental feature of fascism: "hostility to universal citizenship."[30] As part of his grab for uncontested power, Trump views citizenship as something only he can grant rather than a constitutional right. Tamás rightfully views this as a central feature of what he calls post-fascism. Trump's crackdown on immigrants and international students articulates both a new speech code and a reactionary view of the rights of citizenship. As Moira Donegan observes in *The Guardian*:

> [T]he Trump administration clearly thinks of immigrants as a population with no rights that they need respect. Rather, the point is that Trump administration's promise to crack down on student protests against Israel's genocide in Gaza has the effect of articulating a new speech code for immigrants: no one who is not a United States citizen is entitled to the First Amendment right to say that Israel is committing a genocide in Gaza, or that the lives of Palestinians are not disposable by virtue of their race.[31]

This exposes a deeper cruelty: Trump's assaults on communists, trans people, immigrants, Black and Brown people, Jews, and LGBTQ individuals are not just acts of ideological aggression but calculated attempts to dehumanize them, erasing their dignity and their most basic rights. As Tamás notes, by framing them "as non-citizens," Trump casts them as non-human, relegating them to a status beneath recognition and rights.[32] This dehumanization is the very linchpin of fascism, paving the way for the violence that inevitably follows, violence framed as justified, even necessary. The barbaric actions of ICE and the wider punishing state now function as "a racial police force."[33] Their practices, illegal arrests, sensationalized kidnappings of students, and grotesque chain-gang marches of immigrants, are deliberate performances of racial terror. The defense of these actions is laced with the poison of racist police brutality and emboldened vigilantism, poisoning communities and revealing the deep, dangerous roots of racialized violence that is spreading to every corner of American society.

Domestic Terrorism as the Organizing Principle of Politics

For Trump and his sycophants, war has become the negation of democracy. Militarization moves from the margins to the heart of governance. The punitive state criminalizes dissent, weaponizes the courts, dismantles education, and executes mass deportations with cold efficiency.

As Theodor Adorno and others have illuminated, Trump's actions echo long-established patterns of domination, crystallizing into a menacing celebration of hierarchy, power, cruelty, and the cult of masculinity, all underscored by a profound disdain for those deemed weak.[34] In his alignment with authoritarian figures, Trump not only venerates dictators but also threatens to unravel alliances forged over generations, launching trade wars and territorial aggression in his wake. His regime is not merely lawless; it is a deliberate and systematic dismantling of democratic norms, reshaping the United States into a fascist order where power is consolidated, the billionaire class is enriched, and opposition is silenced through fear, repression, and the chaos he himself stirs. This is not governance, but a descent into a state of perpetual turmoil, designed to secure power and control at any cost.

This brand of authoritarian governance is most evident in its assault on higher and public education, waging a relentless campaign to ban books on gender, Black history, and courses addressing transgender issues and pressing social injustices. But it doesn't stop there. As Jason Stanley notes, Trump's plan to dismantle the Department of Education is a brazen attempt to strip funding from Title I, a program that provides essential federal support for students in underfunded urban and rural schools, as well as special education programs for disabled students, and a host of other vital educational initiatives.[35]

Weaponizing a fabricated charge of antisemitism, Trump has also threatened to withdraw federal funding from sixty colleges as a means of coercing universities into submission. In doing so, he has targeted faculty, students, and entire academic programs deemed incompatible with a white nationalist, Christian fundamentalist vision of education.[36] This is not just an attack; it is an attempt to remake education as a tool of ideological indoctrination and authoritarian control. Disturbingly, a growing number of universities are capitulating to these demands, with Columbia University among the most egregious.[37] Unfortunately, too many university presidents and academics remain silent, "refusing to make a firm public defense of democracy," rendering themselves complicit in an educational model that bears an alarming resemblance to the historical precedents of Nazi Germany and the former reality of Orbán's Hungary.[38]

The gravity of this moment demands more than the usual analyses of corruption and political overreach. What we are witnessing is not just the dismemberment of constitutional protections or the expansion of a violent state; it is domestic terrorism orchestrated from the highest levels of government. This is not simply the erosion of rights but the calculated deployment of fear, a homegrown machinery of repression that transforms governance into an instrument of terror. It is a malignant legality, waging war on the American public under the guise of law and order, where power no longer merely punishes but seeks to invoke a living death on those it marks as enemies. The arrest of Khalil and others, both Jews and non-Jews, who stood in solidarity with Palestinian freedom, has been smeared as antisemitic violence. This framing blurs the line between state repression and the broader attack on critical thought itself. Under the Trump regime, thinking is viewed as a form of moral cowardice, and as Umberto Eco insightfully observed in his critique of fascism, critical thinking is also smeared as a form of emasculation.[39]

The Politics of Annihilation and Disappearance

This is a politics of annihilation, one that does not always kill outright but keeps entire populations in a state of unrelenting precarity, caught between survival and disappearance. As Judith Butler warns, this is the logic of governance that "produces precarity, sustaining populations on the edge of death, sometimes killing its members, and sometimes not."[40] It is a form of slow violence, where existence itself is made tenuous, where immigrants, dissidents, the poor, and the racialized are left in a state of permanent vulnerability, their lives dictated not by the rule of law but by the whims of power. One of fascism's signatures is the replacement of due process and the rule of law with a judicial black hole.

Trump's ceaseless torrent of lies, his relentless branding of dissidents as "terrorists," "Hamas supporters," and "enemies from within," along with his call for brutal retribution and the imprisoning of his foes, journalists, judges, politicians, and prosecutors, forms an insidious architecture of terror and lawlessness.[41] This system is designed to silence, disappear, and annihilate those who resist. We must pause and reflect when Attorney General Pam Bondi [since removed from her position] claims that a judge supports terrorism merely because he ruled against the Alien Enemy Act's use for mass deportations. Or when Trump backs a law "that would give Congress the authority to revoke the tax-exempt status of any nonprofit organization it accuses of having terrorist affinities, without access to the evidence or the right to due process."[42]

Beyond Khalil, Trump is using ICE to intimidate, detain, and threaten the deportation of those labeled as dissidents or "others" within the fascist rhetoric of white Christian nationalism. Take, for example, Momodou Taal, a Cornell University student who was ordered by Immigration and Customs Enforcement to report to their offices after he "sued the Trump administration to block its targeting of international students protesting in support of Palestinian rights."[43] Fearing imprisonment, Taal, a dual UK–Gambia PhD student at Cornell, chose to leave the US voluntarily in early April amid threats of visa revocation and deportation.

Not long after Khalil was abducted, Georgetown University scholar Badar Khan Suri was "ambushed by masked federal agents with the Homeland Security Department and taken into custody without being charged with any crime."[44] According to filings, Suri, a professor and postdoctoral fellow in peace and conflict studies, was instead deemed a "threat to U.S. foreign policy interest" under a rarely used act passed in 1952, accused of allegedly spreading Hamas propaganda.[45] Unlike Khalil, Suri was not even a political activist, but a serious scholar.

In another instance of using immigration to harass supposed Palestinian sympathizers, Dr. Rasha Alawieh, an esteemed Lebanese kidney transplant specialist and Brown University professor with a valid H-1B visa, was illegally deported.[46] In this case, it is vital to understand the racialized and religious dimensions of the action: Dr. Alawieh, a Muslim Arab woman, is not being targeted for any criminal wrongdoing, but most likely because of her identity.

As suggested previously, the persecution of Öztürk, and that of Khalil and countless others, are not isolated acts. It is part of a wider, insidious pattern of state-sanctioned repression, one that disproportionately targets individuals of Muslim or Arab descent, not because of what they have done, but because of who they are. This is what authoritarianism looks like when it wears the face of state violence.

Trump has pledged to deport any student he claims is engaged in "pro-terrorist, antisemitic, anti-American activity."[47] But let us be absolutely clear: in Trump's rhetoric, these terms are stripped of meaning and weaponized. Supporting Palestinian rights, or merely existing as a Palestinian, is now enough to be branded a national threat. Trump has repeatedly used "Palestinian" as a slur, collapsing ethnicity, political dissent, and imagined criminality into a single category of exclusion. In a calculated insult aimed at Senator Chuck Schumer, Trump claimed "he is a Palestinian," weaponizing identity in a grotesque display of bigotry.[48] We are witnessing the legal scaffolding of a political purge, one that criminalizes identity, suppresses dissent, and lays the groundwork for mass expulsions under the guise of national security.

Weaponizing Terrorism

Trump's tendency to label any dissent as terrorism is both absurd and profoundly dangerous. His declaration on the White House lawn that people protesting at Tesla dealerships "should be labeled domestic terrorists" makes this perfectly clear.[49] He has even attempted to brand Antifa, a loose constellation of individuals united only by their opposition to fascism, as a terrorist organization, a move that exposes how his authoritarian impulse targets not violent extremists but anyone who challenges the regime's power. This punitive logic extends even to religious authority. As Owen Scott reports in *The Independent*, Trump branded Pope Leo XIV as "weak" on crime and "terrible" on foreign policy in a late-night Truth Social tirade, "which also saw him uploading an AI-generated image of himself dressed as Jesus."[50]

Such rhetoric is not simply an attack on free speech; it is the signature move of fascism, transforming critics into enemies of the state and reducing human beings to targets.

This logic rests squarely on a racialized foundation: people of color, immigrants, and those already marked as disposable become the first to be cast as internal threats, their bodies deemed expendable, their rights negotiable, their lives stripped of value.[51] White supremacy becomes the organizing principle of state power, sorting populations into those who are protected and those who can be sacrificed. As Robert Jay Lifton reminds us, we inhabit a "death-saturated age,"[52] and Trump's widening of the terrorism label hastens this condition, making room for policies of disappearance, secret detention, and racialized violence once believed impossible on US soil. The danger extends well beyond efforts to silence critics. We are witnessing the intentional resurrection of authoritarian tactics—from state-sanctioned violence to secretive carceral sites—alongside a slow, methodical destruction of the civic spaces where justice and democratic opposition might still breathe.

Conclusion: History Does not Forget

Understanding Trump's reign of terror requires moving beyond conventional political frames. We must historicize it, trace its roots, expose the cultural forces that make it possible, and refuse to look away from the totality of his repression. The normalization of fascist politics in America is not just a function of law or policy; it is a war over meaning, over memory, over agency, and over the capacity to imagine a different future. What we are witnessing in the current historical moment is the final evolution of neoliberal violence with the appearance of a criminogenic state that repackages social problems and dissent as terrorism. Salvation is now measured by blind loyalty, the normalization of social abandonment, authoritarianism, and corruption. Trump's return to the White House has unleashed a litany of lawlessness, state terrorism, and the open emergence of a police state.

State-engineered violence, cruelty, and the rise of organized terror as the governing principle of the Trump regime are not a mere aberration; they are an intentional distortion of governance, a calculated shift in how the state wields power. This is a moment when violence and cruelty are tearing at the fabric of justice and embedding terror into the very essence of democracy.

This crisis, the systemic violation of civil rights, the suppression of free speech, and the targeting of political activism, must be understood as part of a historical rupture. It is what Nancy Fraser has called "a crisis of the social totality, one in which conscience, ethics, and politics are yoked together in a struggle to retain our collective humanity."[53]

The abduction and jailing of students, journalists, and others fighting to hold power accountable is a stark warning. The use of state violence to punish dissent illuminates the brutal consequences of a society where those who challenge power find themselves not only stripped of citizenship and dignity but also disappeared into the black hole of social and political abandonment. In an era overshadowed by rising totalitarian fascism, the very fabric of American society is being redefined by reactionary ideological closures that determine who is deemed worthy of belonging, who is silenced, and who is subjected to state violence. These actions define a systemic effort to expunge history, destroy the capacity for critical thought, criminalize dissent, and disappear the bodies and identities of those deemed "other" by race, ethnicity, religion, or thought. The United States has crossed into the terrain of what was once thought unimaginable. Immigrants who have lived in the US for years are abducted and deported to other countries "where they are likely to face torture, persecution, death, or other grave harms."[54]

Trump's politics of dehumanization, terror, exclusion, and state-sanctioned violence have escalated. His vow to erect prison camps across the US, modeled after the grotesque facility he built in Florida, reveals the dark undercurrents of his authoritarian regime. This facility, dubbed "Alligator Alcatraz" by his administration, serves as a prison for political detainees, immigrants, and people of color who are deemed unworthy of their presence in a white-dominated America.[55] Thom Hartmann aptly calls it "an experiment in authoritarian governance," adding that it is "not just another immigration facility. It's a political prison engineered not merely to detain, but to humiliate, dehumanize, and broadcast terror. It's America's first open-air symbol that our democracy is not just dying; it is being dissected publicly, cruelly, and with cold calculation."[56]

Trump's expanding brand of "blood and soil nationalism" also manifests in his attempt to strip away birthright citizenship and revoke the status of naturalized citizens, particularly targeting the nearly 25 million living in the United States. This lawless assault on naturalized citizens was underscored when Trump mused about revoking comedian Rosie O'Donnell's citizenship simply because he disliked her. As Andrew Perez and Asawin Suebsaeng write in *Rolling Stone*, a more politically motivated abuse of power emerged when Trump threatened to denaturalize Zohran Mamdani, the Democratic Socialist New York mayor. Mamdani, who was born in Uganda and became a naturalized citizen in 2018, became another target of Trump's weaponization of naturalized status for political gain.[57]

This is fascist control in motion, an apparatus remaking the world in the image of dictators, leaving in its wake a landscape where justice is no longer governed by the rule of law, but by the dictates of global authoritarianism. It marks capitalism's terminal phase, governing through terror, force, reactionary culture, and the politics of death. The promises of equality, social mobility, the redistribution of rights, and justice have crumbled, facing a legitimacy crisis and are all but dead in their appeal. What remains is a brutal form of gangster capitalism, a technofascism where the ideologues of Trump and Musk boldly and unapologetically proclaim not merely that the US has become a more recognizably authoritarian state, but that an endpoint has been reached where the US, if not the world, "can belong only to a few." This is no longer the promise of democracy, but its death knell.

Trump's assault on civil rights, his war on free speech, and his crackdown on political activism do not mark the beginning of authoritarianism in America; they are its continuation, its escalation. This playbook is not new. It echoes the brutal tactics of countries such as Saudi Arabia, Israel, and India, where dissent is silenced, resistance is rebranded as terrorism, and critics of the state disappear without consequence. What we are witnessing is the slow but deliberate dismantling of the legal and democratic guardrails that once restrained power.

Arwa Mahdawi's warning in *The Guardian* is both urgent and undeniable: "We are sliding toward an authoritarian future at alarming speed."[58] But this is not some distant horizon. Repression is not creeping; it is here. Freedoms are not eroding; they are being stripped away in real time before our very eyes. And as Mahdawi reminds us, "All of our freedoms are intertwined."[59]

To defend one is to defend all. The fight for justice cannot be compartmentalized, parceled out to the persecuted few. When one of us is silenced, shackled, imprisoned, deported, or erased, it is not just a student, an activist, or an immigrant who suffers; it is the body of democracy itself that is wounded. The struggle is not solitary; it is shared. The stakes are not theoretical or abstract; they are existential, lived, and drenched in a painful assault on the body politic. Resistance is an imperative; it is the fault line between democracy and tyranny, between freedom and subjugation, between life and death. Silence is complicity. Now is the time to rise. This is not a moment for half-measures or polite appeals; it is a battle that must be waged collectively by workers, educators, students, cultural workers, unions, and minorities of color and class, and all those who refuse to live under the yoke of gangster capitalism and its brutal machinery of exploitation. This is not a plea for reform; it is a call for radical transformation, a decisive break from the obscene inequalities, entrenched power, and the suffocating grip of financial elites. The future cannot be a mirror of an authoritarian present; it must be seized, forged in struggle, and built from the ruins of a system that has long served only the powerful. The shadows of fascism are thickening, spreading across the globe. We either resist or we are consumed.

The struggle against a capitalist future will be difficult, but there are no other options as the death march of fascism increasingly encircles the globe.

History does not forget, nor should we. The question is not whether we recognize these warning signs, but whether we act before it is too late. The past is not past; it is knocking loudly at our door, demanding our attention. The time to act is now, or we risk being ushered into a world that is as dangerous as it is unthinkable.

3

Trump's America: Ghosts of the Past, Shadows of the Future

The irony is piercing. Trump has flooded public life with orchestrated falsehoods, turned immigrants and Black communities into political targets, and made corruption and intimidation the operating system of his rule. His devotion to dictators, his retinue of loyalists and enforcers, and his steady use of state power against the vulnerable reveal a worldview in which cruelty is not incidental but essential. Abducting foreign students, persecuting immigrants, suppressing dissent, he has transformed public institutions into mechanisms of punishment.[1]

Even grief is conscripted into his politics of vengeance. Instead of mourning Charlie Kirk, he rushed to vilify the Left before the alleged suspect, Tyler Robinson, had even been arrested.[2] A moment that should have summoned compassion was staged as a spectacle of blame, designed to inflame resentment, tighten control, and deepen the atmosphere of fear.

This is the voice of authoritarianism. Each action signals a country in free fall: state power turned inward against those without protection, dissent modified as betrayal, violence granted the aura of legitimacy. The United States is already living within the architecture of fascism, where truth yields to manufactured fantasy, reason collapses under conspiracy, and civic life shrinks beneath the weight of fear.

Trump Blames the Left

As Jeffrey St. Clair observed, "Leaders of the Right didn't waste much time counseling their ranks to restrict themselves to 'thoughts and prayers' over the murder of Charlie Kirk. Even before the assassin had been identified or a motive uncovered, they blamed the 'violent rhetoric' of the Left for Kirk's death."[3] This is not mourning, it is the oldest trick in the authoritarian playbook: accuse first, investigate never, and weaponize tragedy to consolidate power. This strategy reached its clearest expression at Kirk's funeral.

In a speech steeped in resentment and vengeance, Trump stated that the violence that took Kirk's life "largely comes from the Left," offering no evidence and conveniently ignoring the accelerating surge of far-right extreme violence. His words were not idle; he framed progressives as enemies of the nation and signaled his willingness to wield state power against them, branding antifascist resistance as terrorism. Within days, he declared "Antifa" a "domestic terrorist" organization, a cynical distortion, since Antifa is not a structured entity but a decentralized, leaderless movement of antifascist resistance. Soon after, Trump signed a presidential memorandum on "domestic terrorism" titled the National Security Presidential Memorandum designed to unleash the machinery of government against left-wing dissent. Trump even named centrists and venture capitalists like George Soros, Reid Hoffman, and the Democratic Party as supposed funders of radical violence.[4]

C. J. Polychroniou and Alexandra Boutri rightly argue that "this memorandum, which is far more dangerous than the Antifa order, is a truly fascist blueprint that directs the federal government to go after 'anti-fascist,' 'anti-capitalist' movements in the US."[5] It basically targets anyone who is opposing Trump and his MAGA ideology. As Rebecca Falcone warned in *Axios*, what is unfolding is nothing less than the institutionalization of politically motivated repression, a calculated campaign to delegitimize opposition and muzzle anyone daring to hold Trump to account.[6] Yet Falcone stops short. What looms before us is far more ominous: the resurrection of fascist specters, refashioned for our time, threatening to darken the future with the familiar stench of authoritarianism reborn.

If Trump's words voiced and legitimated the law of repression, Stephen Miller's rhetoric gave it the blaring rhythm of menace. At Kirk's eulogy, Miller delivered what Jonathan Chait in *The Atlantic* called "a jarring piece of rhetoric," cloaking his speech in the grandeur of Western civilization while invoking a cosmic struggle between light and darkness, good and evil.[7] Yet beneath this language of moral purity lurked the toxic dogma of white nationalism: those deemed evil and disposable were immigrants, people of color, and dissenters, while those deemed worthy were white Christian nationalists. In exalting vengeance over forgiveness, even ignoring the widow's call for compassion, Miller and Trump sanctified cruelty as a civic virtue. More ominously still, they fused mourning with menace, presenting dissenting speech as violence and repressive power as justice, openly declaring that the state itself would become the weapon that crushes opposition.

In this poisonous narrative, the real "enemies within" are not the racists, insurrectionists, corrupt corporations, neo-Nazi militia, and right-wing extremists who stormed the Capitol, but the critics of authoritarian power and groups designated as "other." Against them, Trump and his allies wage war on the First Amendment, turning freedom of speech from a bulwark of democracy into its enemy. The consequences of such distortions extend beyond rhetoric. This warning is urgent, for Trump's wilful ignorance unleashes predatory passions that nourish a culture of authoritarian violence.

Dissenting Voices

From comedians and journalists to students, educators, and independent groups, every dissenting voice is branded a conspirator in imagined crimes, their real offense nothing more than speaking against cruelty when silence was demanded. As Hannah Arendt once warned, under totalitarianism thinking itself becomes dangerous.[8] Authoritarianism in its many forms arises in part from the failure to think, a prescient warning in the age of manufactured ignorance.[9] As Arendt observed, totalitarianism depends on the fusion of propaganda and reality. The goal is not merely to lie but to annihilate the distinction between truth and falsehood. The normalization of illiteracy, thoughtlessness, and moral blindness in the age of Trump is foundational to creating fascist subjects who cannot tell right from wrong, truth from lies, or justice from evil. When all narratives become possible, the only truth that remains is power itself. Wendy Brown is right in arguing "that democracy ... cannot survive the people's wholesale ignorance of the forces shaping their lives and limiting their futures."[10]

This warning is even more urgent today, because there is a horrifying ignorance in Trump that unleashes predatory passions, stretching from his embracing of war criminals and historical amnesia to the fatal strikes he ordered on four unproven drug-smuggling boats. Not only has he waged an internationally illegal war on Iran, he has embraced the language of genocide and mass extermination, openly threatening the destruction of a nation of 93 million people. In a Truth Social post, he declared, "A whole civilization will die tonight, never to be brought back again." This is not rhetorical excess or careless hyperbole. It is the explicit language of annihilation, the discourse of a war criminal, stripped of moral restraint. It names, without ambiguity, a willingness to erase an entire people, to sanction the deaths of children, the elderly, the sick, and countless civilians. Such words do not merely describe violence; they authorize it, normalize it, and render genocide thinkable, even permissible. For Trump, the legality of such acts is irrelevant. Violence, coupled an utter disregard for the law, human life, and morality, is central to the logic of annihilation that engenders fascist politics.

This genocidal imaginary does not remain confined to foreign policy. The same logic that renders entire populations abroad disposable returns home, where it is refashioned as a war against dissent. Violence, once normalized on the global stage, becomes a governing principle of domestic politics, recoding opposition as an existential threat and elevating repression into a form of patriotic duty. The war abroad thus bleeds into a war at home, fusing militarism with authoritarianism and transforming the language of national security into a weapon against critics, protesters, and all those who refuse to submit.

The erosion of criminality into politics is one of fascism's oldest and most reliable maneuvers.[11] In 1933, Hitler seized on the Reichstag fire, blaming communists and invoking emergency powers to suspend civil liberties and dismantle democratic institutions.[12] Five years later, Joseph Goebbels exploited the assassination of a Nazi diplomat in Paris by Herschel Grynszpan to unleash Kristallnacht, a state-orchestrated orgy of violence that "became a turning point in German policy, setting into motion the Nazis' systematic extermination of Jews, the Romani people, Communists, Christians, homosexuals, and the mentally ill."[13] Francisco Franco followed a similar script in Spain, fabricating tales of "red violence" and "red terror" in order to unleash the White Terror, a campaign of mass executions, disappearances, and the ruthless liquidation of political opponents.[14] In our own era, Viktor Orbán, denied another mandate in the 2026 election, perfected the tactic in Hungary, scapegoating "Soros-funded leftists" to dismantle universities, criminalize protest, and eviscerate the press.[15]

Trump is no exception. He exploits Kirk's death not to grieve but to consolidate power. His message is blunt: dissent is violence, criticism is terrorism, disloyalty is a crime, and free speech itself is a threat to Trump's ideological panopticon. The vicious amplification of this line of toxic thinking is evident in the rhetoric of Trump's consigliere Laura Loomer, who, following Kirk's assassination, demanded the state "shut down, defund, and prosecute every single Leftist organization."[16] The rhetoric reached hysterical heights with Christopher Rufo, a leading far-right critic of higher education, who declared, "The last time the radical Left orchestrated a wave of violence and terror, J. Edgar Hoover shut it all down within a few years. It is time, within the confines of the law, to infiltrate, disrupt, arrest, and incarcerate all of those who are responsible for this chaos."[17] The rhetoric is sobering not only for its cruelty but for its naked embrace of repression and the threat of violence as state policy.

Trump's Chilling Message

The consequences of Trump's assault on dissent are impossible to ignore, flashing like an oversized neon sign in Times Square. Under his lawless reign, even satire is refashioned as "un-American" and branded a "hate crime," as though laughter itself had become treason. Academic institutions that preserve the memory of history and the struggles for freedom are targeted with mob-like threats, extortion disguised as patriotism, and intimidation presented as loyalty. Meanwhile, media outlets and law firms are threatened and pressured into paying Trump exorbitant sums. The corruption on display, highlighted by his blatant violations of the emoluments clause and his demand that the Justice Department compensate him $230 million of taxpayer money for federal investigations, reaches new extremes.[18] To make matters worse, Canadian citizens are now threatened with visa revocations simply for making critical comments about Kirk. This sends a disturbing message: Trump's authoritarian reach now extends beyond US borders, wielding its silencing power internationally.

This distortion of critique reflects a broader pattern of silencing dissent, where even the most measured opposition is manipulated into something far more sinister. In this twisted logic, even a measured critique of Charlie Kirk is defined as a "celebration of his death," a grotesque distortion divorced from reality. His passing should alarm us, but this must not be conflated with silence about his far-right ideology of vitriol.[19] To condemn those beliefs is not cruelty, it is moral clarity. What emerges is a pattern both unmistakable and chilling: intimidation at the top reinforced by institutional complicity. Universities and workplaces mask this capitulation as neutrality, but it is in truth a collapse of ethical responsibility, a dark echo of the accommodations that enabled fascism in another era. The price of speaking out has become brutally clear. As *The New York Times* reports, more than 145 individuals have faced workplace reprisals, including firings, for criticizing Kirk's ideology, even when they simultaneously condemned the shooting as horrific.[20] In some cases, individuals have been arrested and punished for a comment on Kirk that is vastly disproportionate to what might be considered a criminal offense.[21]

Raphael Satter and A. J. Vicens, in a eye-opening special report for Reuters, revealed that more than 600 Americans were punished simply for speaking about the Kirk murder, despite the overwhelming majority remaining firmly within the bounds of protected speech, neither endorsing violence nor celebrating Kirk's death.[22] What unfolded was not merely a right-wing backlash; it was a state-sanctioned purge, a government-backed campaign to intimidate, silence, and ultimately criminalize dissent. In targeting those who merely disagreed with Kirk's reactionary views, the state made unmistakably clear that the line between criticism and criminality is being deliberately erased.

These acts of silencing are never isolated. They are instruments of power that legitimate broader forms of state violence. Censorship, propaganda, and the glorification of cruelty converge to normalize repression as both necessary and inevitable. It is worth repeating that corporations and universities bow in fear and greed, sacrificing every shred of public responsibility to feed an unending hunger for power and capital. Nowhere is this surrender more shameful than in higher education, where universities crush dissent and betray their own students by handing over the names of those protesting genocide to the Trump administration, repeating the cowardice of fascist-era campuses.[23] Even worse, Ken Klippenstein reports that the Trump administration is preparing to designate transgender people as "violent extremists" in the wake of Charlie Kirk's murder, and is considering compiling a watchlist of trans people to surveil.[24]

It is a terrifying echo of fascist-era complicities, a moral collapse masquerading as institutional neutrality. The reverberations are unmistakable: we are witnessing a new McCarthyism, one not confined to the narrow persecutions of the 1950s but amplified into a far more expansive and punitive machinery of repression. As Ellen Schrecker reminds us, the earlier McCarthyism "attacked only individual professors and only about their sort of extracurricular political activities on the left." By contrast, she warns, "the repression that's coming out of Washington, DC ... attacks everything that happens on American campuses," adding that "the damage that the Trump administration is doing is absolutely beyond the pale and has never, never been equaled in American life with regard to higher education."[25]

This is not merely an institutional failure, it is a moral unraveling, a repudiation of knowledge, conscience, and the democratic commitments that once anchored the mission of the university. Higher education has long unsettled the right, especially since the democratizing upheavals of the sixties. Today that fear has hardened into something darker: not merely efforts to weaken the university's critical role, but the imposition of pedagogical tyranny intent on transforming campuses into laboratories of indoctrination.[26]

It gets worse. Trump, Rubio, and then Bondi and their cohort of democracy's enemies now threaten to strip dissenting Americans of their passports, revoke citizenship, and criminalize free speech. They howl in outrage at being compared to fascists, even as their actions mirror the same grim playbook: militarizing society, crushing dissent, concentrating power in the hands of a cult leader, and reanimating the legacy of white supremacy and racial cleansing.

Trump hails Netanyahu, a war criminal, as a war hero. With grotesque irony, he denounces the Left as the true perpetrators of violence. At home, his vindictiveness is just as corrosive, boasting of pressuring ABC to fire Jimmy Kimmel, now back on the air. This petty act of vengeance amounts to his own assault on the First Amendment and is a ominous reminder of how fragile free speech becomes under authoritarian whim. Yet no alarm is sounded when Fox News host Brian Kilmeade casually suggests exterminating the homeless through "involuntary lethal injections."[27] Nor does outrage rise in the Trump administration, or much of the mainstream press, over the United States' complicity in Israel's genocidal assault on Gaza, where children are being slaughtered daily and entire families erased from the face of the earth. Silence here is not neutrality; it is complicity in barbarism.

When the conduct of comedians is criminalized, it is not simply a matter of taste, decorum, or even misplaced moral outrage, it is a direct assault on the principle of free speech. Comedy has always served as a space where hypocrisy is unmasked, abuses of power are ridiculed, and the absurdities of authoritarian politics are laid bare. In fact, when Vladimir Putin first came to power in 2000, one of the early targets of his cultural crackdown was the satirical television show "Kukly" (Куклы, meaning *dolls*), a puppet show produced by the independent channel NTV. Apparently being called the *little Tsar puppet* was too much for him to tolerate.[28] This ruthless act of censorship was widely seen as a watershed moment in Putin's consolidation of power. The real issue is that policing or punishing comedians signals the state's desire to control even the spaces of laughter and satire.

Canary in the Coal Mine

This criminalization is more than censorship; it exposes how swiftly the machinery of repression is moving toward fascism. When jokes are reclassified as crimes, the warning could not be clearer: what begins with comedians will not end with them. It marks the testing of boundaries, the normalization of repression, and the silencing of one of the oldest and most effective forms of dissent. The move reveals the fragility of regimes that cannot tolerate critique, no matter how playful or irreverent, and it signifies a broader project to narrow public space until only official voices remain.

In this sense, the attack on comedy should not be dismissed as a trivial or secondary issue. It is a symbolic and practical escalation of authoritarian politics, one that exposes the contempt fascist movements hold for humor, irony, and dissenting speech. If laughter is made a crime, then resistance itself is already under indictment. Repressing dissent has a long history in the US extending from the Red Scare of the 1920s to the domestic repression that followed Bush's war on terrorism. Today's attacks on dissent are more widespread, damaging, and unchecked than much of what we have seen in the past. To borrow a phrase from Terry Eagleton, Trump and his MAGA stooges are drunk "on fantasies of omnipotence" and revel in acts of violence, destruction, and the exercise of boundless state power.[29]

Violence in America's militarized streets now fuses with what John Ganz calls a "sanctimonious hue and cry ... over the martyred dead, hysteria, [whipped] up about terrorism and public disorder, [as] the power of the state is brought to bear against public figures who oppose and criticize the regime."[30] Fear has become the regime's preferred weapon, wielded alongside a politics of erasure, historical amnesia, and ruthless denial.

Jeffrey St. Clair noted with grim precision that Kirk's killing is "awful, disgusting and about as American as it gets," but the hypocrisy lies in Trump's silence after earlier acts of MAGA violence: "When two Democratic legislators and their spouses were assassinated by a Trump supporter in Minnesota a few weeks ago, Trump said nothing. Nada. Zilch."[31] As St. Clair recounts, the ledger of right-wing violence between 2018 and 2025 reads like a requiem: the assault on CDC headquarters, the murder of Officer

David Rose, the plot to seize Governor Gretchen Whitmer, the massacre of twenty-three souls in an El Paso Walmart, and the slaughter of eleven worshippers at Pittsburgh's Tree of Life synagogue. Every act carried the rhythm of cruelty; every atrocity struck like a warning written in fire and blood.

In spite of the nefarious claims by Trump, Miller, Bondi, and other officials that the Left bears responsibility for Charlie Kirk's death, the facts tell a different story. NBC News reports that "the federal investigation into the assassination of conservative activist Charlie Kirk has yet to find a link between the alleged shooter, 22-year-old Tyler Robinson, and left-wing groups on which President Donald Trump and his administration have pledged to crack down."[32] The Trump regime refuses to acknowledge this, substituting evidence with a narrative designed to demonize its critics. This distortion follows a familiar historical pattern, yet what the Trump administration refuses to admit and desperately hide is that "right-wing extremist violence has been responsible for the overwhelming majority of fatalities, amounting to approximately 75 to 80 percent of US domestic terrorism deaths since 2001."[33]

It should be noted, once again, that Kirk's assassination, an utterly deplorable and indefensible act, was also seized upon to silence critics across the political spectrum, from journalists to professors, who expressed sorrow over his death while making clear they rejected his ideology. To mourn a life lost is not to endorse the ideas he espoused, and conflating criticism of those ideas with a cruel festive endorsement of his death is a dangerous distortion. As Saida Grundy brilliantly and powerfully observes in an essay in *The Guardian*, Kirk's ideology was hardly something to be memorialized in a democracy. He "ruled over an online fiefdom peddling his signature brand of rage-baiting racist, xenophobic, Islamophobic and misogynistic commentary."[34] She adds that his appeal came not from reasoned persuasion, but from the "popularization of cruelty, humiliation and dehumanization of political opponents, especially college students," which he orchestrated into a political style that attracted millions. He once dismissed empathy itself as "a made-up, new age term that does a lot of damage," a sentiment that encapsulates his contempt for compassion and solidarity.

Grundy further notes that the state-sanctioned memorials for Kirk are designed to fuse his far-right worldview with the interests of the federal government, elevating white nationalist, homophobic, and misogynistic convictions as though they were national priorities. These memorials, she argues, echo the logic of Confederate monuments: they are not neutral commemorations but instruments of power, constructed to shield their subjects from scrutiny and to sanctify an ideology of exclusion. In this sense, Trump's use of Kirk's death is not only a tribute but also a strategy, a way to build Kirk's extremism into a national narrative that legitimizes repression and white supremacy.

Celebrating Kirk's hard-right extremism thus becomes a political weapon. This is more than denial or misrepresentation; it is calculated deceit. By inverting reality, by blaming dissenters for violence overwhelmingly stoked by their own ideological allies, the administration wages war on truth itself. Lies are weaponized to justify the silencing of critics and the tightening of state repression. It is the oldest tool of authoritarianism, a well-worn script from the fascist playbook in which regimes invent internal enemies to mask their own violence and consolidate their power.

Machinery of Fascism

This is the machinery of fascism: scapegoating, historical amnesia, and the fabrication of a "threat within" to mobilize fear and erase accountability. To be quiet or indifferent in the face of such lies is to allow history's darkest patterns to repeat. The ominous rattling of boxcars is no longer mere metaphor; it is rehearsal. The same trains that once ferried enemies of the state—Jews, communists, Roma, and others—to concentration camps echo in today's discourse of surveillance, detention, and deportation. These echoes abroad make the danger at home impossible to ignore. The first targets are always the vulnerable, including immigrants, refugees, students, and the homeless. But the machinery of repression, once primed, sweeps wider. What begins at the margins always moves to the center. As history shows, repression rarely halts at its first targets.

First the masked thugs of state-sponsored terror descended on immigrants, then on student protesters, and they occupied neighborhoods, turned cities into militarized staging grounds, and normalized violence as the language of lawless rule. Now the machinery of repression is tightening its grip, moving ever closer to ordinary citizens. Peaceful protesters are subject to repeated acts of violence by ICE. Jeffrey St. Clair, in an article documenting such violence, states that ICE "is committing new acts of barbarity and stupidity in real-time on an almost hourly basis."[35] A shadow from an authoritarian past has fallen across the republic, and unless it is confronted, the future will echo the grim theaters of repression already unfolding in Turkey, India, and Argentina.

In all these countries, including the United States, leaders of the new fascism speak with bile in their mouths and blood on their hands. They share a language that Toni Morrison calls an "oppressive language, [which] does more than represent violence; it is violence."[36] Trump and his minions traffic in a repressive language infused with power, censored and censoring. Ruthless in its policing duties, it has no desire or purpose other than maintaining the free range of its own narcotic narcissism, its own exclusivity and dominance. It offers mass spectacles in place of thought, moral somnambulism, and a psychotic infatuation with those who seek refuge in unchecked power. It forges a community built on greed, corruption, and hate, steeped in a scandal of hollow fulfillment.

Conclusion: Ghosts and Futures

Trump's America stands as both symptom and warning, a mirror of the past and a prophecy of what may come. Fascism has returned not in jackboots but in hashtags, not in torchlight but in data streams. Yet history is not destiny. The same forces that made fascism possible, fear, ignorance, and cruelty, can be confronted by their opposites: memory, reason, and solidarity. To fight the ghosts of the past, we must build a politics of the living, a democracy animated by truth, justice, and collective care. The future depends on whether we choose to remember.

Both in the United States and across the globe people are showing what collective resistance looks like. Across the US wave of strikes, from auto workers to nurses to grad students, signal a widening refusal of neoliberal disposability and state violence. Grassroots networks, from sanctuary cities to legal defense funds, have mobilized to protect immigrants against raids, family separations, and the revival of detention and deportation regimes. Across the globe opposition is building against war mania of Israel and the Trump regime. In Italy, mass strikes have confronted the government's support for Israel's genocidal war.[37] In Argentina, hundreds of thousands have mobilized against austerity and creeping authoritarianism. Women in Iran continue to risk prison and death to reclaim public space; Indian farmers have forced a powerful regime to retreat; and students across the United States have turned campuses into front lines of democratic struggle. These movements, different in scale and history, share a common truth: ordinary people can interrupt the machinery of repression and expose the moral bankruptcy of those who wield power through fear. The lights are going out fast, but they are not yet extinguished. Political anger, populist education and cultural politics are building new forms of direct action in the service of democracy. Resistance is no longer optional; it is the urgent political and moral task of our time.

SECTION TWO

The Assault on Memory, History, and Education

4

Erasing History, Erasing Democracy

In the first days of his second term, Trump issued executive orders to control how schools teach race and gender, diverted public dollars to private schools, and threatened dissent with deportation.[1] On January 29, 2025, he signed "Ending Radical Indoctrination in K-12 Schooling," mandating the removal of curricula deemed "anti-American."[2] This is not curriculum reform; it is ideological enforcement, an effort to suppress historical truth, strip educators of autonomy, and convert schools into zones of obedience.

Masquerading as a crusade against "divisiveness," it wages a wider war on education as a democratic force, turning schools into barren zones of the imagination. By weaponizing federal funding to enforce conformity, this policy becomes an instrument of ideological indoctrination, enforcing a sanitized, nationalistic narrative that erases histories of oppression and resistance while deepening a culture of ignorance and compliance.

Concurrently, President Trump issued the "Expanding Educational Freedom and Opportunity for Families" executive order, aiming to enhance school choice by redirecting federal funds to support charter schools and voucher programs.[3] This policy enables parents to use public funds for private and religious school tuition. Though marketed as parental empowerment, the measure is a calculated effort to defund and privatize public education, selling it as a democratizing public good. As part of a broader far-right assault on education, this policy redirects essential resources away from public schools, deepening educational inequality and advancing an agenda that seeks to erode public investment in a just and equitable society.

In the name of eliminating alleged radical indoctrination in schools, a third executive order, which purportedly aims at ending antisemitism, threatens to deport pro-Palestinian student protesters by revoking their visas, warning that even those legally in the country could be targeted for their political views.[4] In a stark display of authoritarianism, Trump's executive order unapologetically stated that free speech would not be tolerated.

Reuters made this clear in reporting that one fact sheet ominously declared: "I will … quickly cancel the student visas of all Hamas sympathizers on college campuses, which have been infested with radicalism like never before. To all the resident aliens who joined in the pro-jihadist protests, we put you on notice: come 2025, we will find you, and we will deport you."[5]

Trump's pledge to eliminate the Department of Education is a direct attack on the last national lever capable of defending equity, civil rights, and the public mission of schooling. By gutting federal oversight, Trump is handing the fate of education to reactionary state legislatures and corporate interests, ensuring that knowledge is shaped by a state captive to billionaires and far-right extremists. This is the logic of authoritarianism: to hollow out democratic institutions, replace education with white Christian nationalist propaganda, and mandate a pedagogy of repression. At stake is an attempt to leave an entire generation defenseless before the very forces bent on dominating them. What we are dealing with is not merely an educational crisis but a full-scale war on the very institutions that defend and sustain democracy.

These executive actions represent an upgraded and broader version of McCarthyite and apartheid-era education that seeks to dictate how schools teach about race and gender, funnel more taxpayer dollars into private institutions, and deport Palestinian protesters. The irony is stark: the White House defends these regressive measures, sanitizing history, denying transgender rights, and erasing the study of oppression, as a crusade to "end indoctrination in American education." In truth, this is not about the pursuit of freedom or open inquiry, nor is it about fostering an education that cultivates informed, critically engaged citizens. At its core, this agenda is a deliberate attack on education as a public good, one that threatens to dismantle not only public institutions, but the very essence of public and higher education and its culture of criticism and democracy. The urgency of this moment cannot be overstated: the future of education itself is at stake.

Amid today's surging political and cultural currents, where fascist ideologies again rise, one of the most insidious forces is the violence of forgetting, a plague of historical amnesia. This phenomenon, which I have referred to as "organized forgetting," describes the systemic erasure of history and their violent consequences, particularly in the public sphere.[6] This is especially evident in the current historical moment, when books are banned in libraries, public schools, and higher education across several countries, such as the United States, Turkey, India, China, and Russia.[7] To ignore past atrocities and uncomfortable truths is not an oversight but an active violence that shapes both our collective consciousness and political realities. What we are witnessing here is an assault by the far-right on memory that is inseparable from what Maximilian Alvarez describes as a battle over power, over who is remembered, who is erased, who is cast aside, and who is forcibly reduced to something less than human. This struggle is not only over history but over whose stories will shape the present and future. He captures this reality with striking clarity and is worth quoting at length:

> Among the prizes at stake in the endless war of politics is history itself. The battle for power is always a battle to determine who gets remembered, how they will be recalled, where and in what forms their memories will be preserved. In this battle, there is no room for neutral parties: every history and counter-history must fight and scrap and claw and spread and lodge itself in the world, lest it be forgotten or forcibly erased. All history, in this sense, is the history of empire, a bid for control of that greatest expanse of territory, the past.[8]

Organized forgetting helped fuel Trump's rise, as truth and reason give way to lies, corruption, denial, and the weaponization of memory itself. A culture of questioning, critique, and vision is not simply disappearing in the United States—it is actively maligned, disparaged, and replaced by a darkness that, as Ezra Klein observes, is "stupefyingly vast, stretching from self-destructive incompetence to muddling incoherence to authoritarian consolidation."[9]

This erosion corrodes institutions of law, civil society, and education, pillars that depend on memory, informed judgment, and evidence to sustain civic life. The attack on the common good goes beyond the distractions of an "attention economy" designed to distort reality; it reflects a deliberate effort to sever the ties between history and meaning.[10] Time is reduced to fragmented episodes, stripped of the shared narratives that connect the past, present, and future.

This crisis embodies a profound collapse of memory, history, education, and democracy itself. A culture of manufactured illiteracy, rooted in the rejection of history, facts, and critical thought, erases accountability for electing a leader who incited insurrection and branded his opponents as "enemies from within." Such authoritarian politics thrive on historical amnesia, lulling society into passivity, eroding collective memory, and subverting civic agency. This is epitomized by Trump's declaration on "Fox & Friends" that he would punish schools that teach students accurate US history, including about slavery and racism.[11] The call to silence dangerous memories is inseparable from the violence of state terrorism, a force that censors and dehumanizes dissent, escalating to the punishment, torture, and imprisonment of truth-tellers and critics who dare to hold oppressive power accountable.

At its core, this violence of organized forgetting works through denial and distortion of historical events that threaten dominant power. From the struggles for civil rights to the history of settler-colonialism, many of the most significant chapters of history are either glossed over or erased altogether. This strategic omission serves the interests of those in power, enabling them to maintain control by silencing inconvenient truths. As the historian

Timothy Snyder reminds us, by refusing to acknowledge the violence of the past, society makes it far easier to perpetuate injustices in the present.[12] The politics of organized forgetting, historical censorship, and the attack on historical consciousness underwrite the rise of far-right forces in the US and across the world.

With the rise of regressive memory laws, designed to repress what authoritarian governments consider dangerous and radical interpretations of a country's past, historical consciousness is transformed into a form of historical amnesia. One vivid example of a regressive memory law was enacted by Trump during his first term. The 1776 Report, which right-wingers defended as a "restoration of American education," was in fact an attempt to eliminate any reference to a legacy of colonialism, slavery, and movements which highlighted elements of American history that were unconscionable, anti-democratic, and morally repugnant from history curricula. Snyder highlights the emergence of memory laws in a number of states. Snyder writes in a 2021 *New York Times* article:

> As of this writing, five states (Idaho, Iowa, Tennessee, Texas and Oklahoma) have passed laws that direct and restrict discussions of history in classrooms. The Department of Education of a sixth (Florida) has passed guidelines with the same effect. Another 12 state legislatures are still considering memory laws. The particulars of these laws vary. The Idaho law is the most Kafkaesque in its censorship: It affirms freedom of speech and then bans divisive speech. The Iowa law executes the same totalitarian pirouette. The Tennessee and Texas laws go furthest in specifying what teachers may and may not say. In Tennessee teachers must not teach that the rule of law is "a series of power relationships and struggles among racial or other groups." ... The Idaho law mentions Critical Race Theory; the directive from the Florida school board bans it in classrooms. The Texas law forbids teachers from requiring students to understand the 1619 Project. It is a perverse goal: Teachers succeed if students do not understand something.[13]

A major aspect of this forgetting and erasure of historical memory is the role of ignorance, which has become not just widespread but weaponized in modern times. Ignorance, particularly in US society, has shifted from being a passive lack of knowledge to an active refusal to engage with critical issues. This is amplified by the spectacle-driven nature of contemporary media and the increasing normalization of a culture of lies and a language of violence. In addition, the mainstream media's obsession with theater, be it political drama, celebrity culture, or sensationalist stories, often overshadows the more important, yet less glamorous, discussions about historical violence and systemic injustice. This cocktail of normalizing ignorance and distraction rather than reflection has become a powerful force for spreading bigotry, racial hatred, and right-wing lies.

Organized forgetting is one of the most brutal weapons in the authoritarian arsenal. As earlier chapters make clear, fascism thrives on erasure, of people, histories, struggles, and the very possibility of truth. When a society abandons its memory, it abandons those who have suffered under Jim Crow, imperialist violence, economic dispossession, and state terror. This cultivated amnesia is not an accident; it is the mechanism by which systems of power shield themselves from accountability and rebrand old violences as new necessities. By severing the present from the past, the powerful are free to recycle the same racialized fantasies, the same hierarchies of disposability, and the same narratives of threat that justified previous rounds of repression. Without historical consciousness, societies lose the capacity to recognize patterns of domination and systems of resistance, making it far easier for far-right movements to normalize cruelty and redefine dissent as treason.

The cultural damage is catastrophic. Organized forgetting hollows out public memory, stunts collective imagination, and strips people of the intellectual resources necessary to resist. In this void, the assaults on democracy detailed earlier, criminalizing immigrants, branding protesters as terrorists, disappearing dissidents, gain legitimacy by default. Forgetting is not passive; it is an active collusion with power. It is the permission slip that allows the state to disappear the present as ruthlessly as it erases the past. By erasing histories of suffering and resistance, society not only condones ongoing oppression but also silences those who dare confront contemporary atrocities, from communities resisting police violence to critics of Israel's US-backed genocide in Gaza. In this death-saturated age, to forget is to participate in the machinery of disappearance; it is to join the chorus that buries truth, memory, bodies, and the fragile possibility of democratic life.

Equally dangerous is the form of historical amnesia that has come to dominate our contemporary political and cultural landscape. This organized forgetting feeds into a pedagogy of mass-produced ignorance and tyranny that prioritizes emotion over reason and spectacle over truth. In this process, history is fragmented and distorted, making it nearly impossible to construct a coherent understanding of the past. As a result, public institutions, particularly education, are undermined, as critical thinking and social responsibility give way to shallow, sensationalized narratives. Higher education, once a bastion for the development of civic literacy and the moral imperative of understanding our role as both individuals and social agents, is now attacked by forces seeking to cleanse public memory of past social and political progress. Figures like Trump embody this threat, working to erase the memory of strides made in the name of equality, justice, and human decency. This organized assault on historical memory and intellectual rigor strikes at the heart of democracy itself.

A democracy cannot thrive in the absence of informed and engaged agents that can question, challenge, and reimage a future different from the present. Without such citizens, the very notion of democracy becomes a hollow, disembodied ideal, an illusion of freedom without the substance of truth or responsibility. Education, in this context, is not merely a tool for transmitting knowledge, but the foundation and bedrock of political consciousness. To be educated, to be a citizen, is not a neutral or passive state, it is a vital, active political and moral engagement with the world, grounded in critical thinking and democratic possibility. It is a recognition that the act of learning and the act of being a citizen are inextricable from each other. To strip education of its critical power is to rob democracy of its transformative potential.

Confronting the violence of organized forgetting requires a shift in how we engage with history. Intellectuals, educators, and activists must take up the responsibility of reintroducing the painful truths of the past into public discourse. To break the cycles of violence, society must commit to remembering, not just for the sake of memory, but as a critical tool for progress.

Moreover, engaging with history honestly requires recognizing that the violence of erasing historical memory is a continual process. Systems of power don't simply forget; they actively work to erase, rewrite, and sanitize historical narratives. The fight to remember is ongoing and requires constant vigilance; it's not enough to simply uncover historical truths; society must work to ensure that these truths are not forgotten again, buried under the weight of media spectacles, ideological repression, and political theater.

In an era where the scope and power of new pedagogical apparatuses such as social media and AI dominate our cultural and intellectual landscapes, the challenge becomes even more complex. While they hold potential for education and connection, these technologies are controlled by a reactionary ruling class of the financial elite and billionaires, and they are increasingly wielded to perpetuate disinformation, fragment history, and manipulate public discourse. The authoritarian algorithms that drive these platforms increasingly prioritize sensationalism over substance, lies over truth, the appropriation of power over social responsibility, and, in doing so, reinforce modes of civic illiteracy, while attacking those fundamental institutions which enable critical perspectives and a culture of questioning.

The need to reclaim historical truth, critical thinking, and social responsibility has never been more urgent. We live in a perilous interregnum, a moment when the old order, exhausted but still vicious, refuses to die, and the new, struggling to be born, is besieged by reactionary monsters who thrive in the chaos between worlds. Authoritarians such as Trump seize upon this crisis not simply to govern, but to remake civic life itself, hollowing out public and educational institutions and refashioning them into laboratories of historical erasure and engines of ideological indoctrination. In this project, white supremacists and Christian nationalists do not linger at the margins of power; they occupy its commanding heights, waging a relentless assault on the very conditions that make democracy possible, the capacity to remember, to think critically, and to act with informed judgment. What is under siege, in other words, is not only the infrastructure of democratic life, but the formative cultures and pedagogies that sustain it.

Under such circumstances, democracy is not merely weakened or wounded; its animating spirit is being methodically stripped away. Across the globe, this assault takes the form of a deepening literacy crisis, one that cannot be reduced to declining reading skills alone.[14] As communication proliferates across an expanding landscape of digital platforms, spectacles, and algorithmic regimes, power consolidates its grip through the production of manufactured ignorance, substituting noise for knowledge and sensation for understanding. This is not simply a crisis of knowing, of the inability to connect reading the word to reading the world; it is a crisis of agency, conscience, truth, and politics itself, a crisis in which the very capacity to name injustice, to imagine alternatives, and to act collectively is eroded. In such a moment, the struggle over literacy becomes inseparable from the struggle over democracy's survival. In the face of a deepening crisis of literacy, history, memory and agency, any meaningful resistance must be collective, disruptive, and unapologetically unsettling, challenging entrenched orthodoxies and dismantling the forces that perpetuate ignorance and injustice. This struggle needs to be both radical in its essence and uncompromising in its demands for social change, recognizing education as inseparable from politics, and the tangible challenges people face in their everyday lives. In this collective effort lies the power to dismantle the barriers to truth, rebuild the foundations of critical thought, and shape a future rooted in knowledge, justice, and a profound commitment to hold power accountable. Central to this vision is the capacity to learn from history, to nurture a historical consciousness that informs our present, and to reimagine agency as an essential force in the enduring struggle for democracy. This call for a radical imagination cannot be confined to classrooms but must emerge as a transformative force embedded in a united, multiracial, working-class movement. Only then can we confront the urgent crises of our time.

5

When Memory Dies, the Future Disappears

The MAGA War on Memory

A democracy cannot live without memory. The task is to teach dangerous histories, not to wound the nation, but to make it accountable. Education must be reclaimed as a public good and a practice of freedom. William Faulkner's warning still resonates: "The past is never dead. It's not even past."[1] In America today, history itself has become a combat zone. The ghosts of slavery, Jim Crow, and white supremacy remain with us, shaping institutions and social life. As Angela Davis reminds us, we live with these ghosts every day. The real question is whether we choose to acknowledge them, or to erase them.[2] When a society turns away from its own horrors, it normalizes the politics that produced them.

As Yosef Hayi Yerushalmi observed, our era is defined not by fading memory but by "an aggressive assault on whatever memory remains."[3] That assault takes the form of book bans, curriculum purges, intimidation of educators, and the replacement of critical history with patriotic myth. Kimberlé Crenshaw has noted that the panic over "critical race theory" was never about pedagogy; it was an attempt to whitewash slavery and racism from the national narrative. The suppression of historical memory breeds not only ignorance but moral paralysis.[4] As Robert Jay Lifton warned, erasure of the past creates a psychic numbing, a diminished capacity to feel and act against injustice. Forgetting is never neutral. It is a political strategy.[5] Under the Trump regime, it has become a central weapon in a war against democracy, knowledge, truth, and reason. Put bluntly, it has become a central tool in the weaponization against literacy, knowledge, consciousness, and critical agency.

This is a form of domestic terrorism, rooted not only in incendiary words but in their violent translation into state policy. It is the organized weaponization of fear, the calculated deployment of intimidation and cruelty to hollow out democratic life and silence dissent. It is a deliberate assault on citizens, on institutions, and on every idea that refuses to bow before authoritarian power. Drawing on Achille Mbembe's notion of necropolitics, domestic terrorism reveals how power thrives by reducing human life to disposable matter.[6] Under the Trump regime, this takes the form of a violent, racialized project that merges the accumulation of capital with the subjugation of marginalized groups. His policies, driven by a toxic mix of racial hierarchy, xenophobia, and the celebration of violent histories, create a society where certain lives are deemed unworthy of protection or consideration. This regime operates on a death drive, relentlessly attempting to eliminate both the lives and futures of those who resist or defy its vision. In this environment, the space for dissent shrinks, historical amnesia thrives, leaving room only for those willing to submit to the dominance of a fascist, authoritarian regime.

This war on memory is not just theoretical; it takes concrete form in the attacks on institutions that hold our collective history. Under Donald Trump and the MAGA movement, memory, let alone history itself, is under siege. What we are confronting is not neglect but an orchestrated assault, fueled by the systemic violence of forgetting and the whitewashing of the past, which echoes fascism's darkest traditions. For Trump, any reckoning with slavery, Jim Crow, or the long arc of racial violence is treated as an unforgivable stain on America's story. Equally intolerable are the histories of resistance, by workers, Black communities, women, immigrants, and LGBTQ people, all of which Trump and his allies disparage as "woke" ideology.

Censoring the Smithsonian

In March 2025, Trump signed an executive order targeting the Smithsonian Institution, declaring its exhibits were corrupted by "improper ideology."[7] Trump argued that the Smithsonian museums were "out of control" and "painted the country in a negative light, including about slavery."[8] The language of the order feigned neutrality, but the intent was unmistakably authoritarian: to sanitize the nation's cultural memory. For Trump, as the White House "focused on seven museums for their exhibits and messaging," the foreboding effect was immediate. References to Trump's two impeachments quietly vanished from an exhibit on the "Limits of Presidential Power." A straightforward record of checks on executive abuse was erased in real time, as if history itself could be bent to serve power's whims.

By targeting the Smithsonian for "improper ideology," the administration pressures museums to sanitize slavery and erase constraints on presidential power. This is not curation; it is censorship. As journalist Dean Blundell observed,

> In recent days, he has attacked the Smithsonian Institution as "out of control," insisting its museums focus too much on "how bad slavery was." His administration has ordered a 120-day review of eight Smithsonian museums and hinted that funding could be used as leverage to "get the woke out." The message lands with the subtlety of a hammer: make the story brighter, or else. This is not a debate about one label or a curatorial tone. It's an attempt to police memory.[9]

The policing of history is no side issue; it a basic feature of Trump's authoritarian project, evident in his assault on the Smithsonian.[10]

Trump has repeatedly sought to bend the past to his will, pardoning the violent January 6th insurrectionists he labeled as "hostages," stripping diversity and equity programs of content that celebrated Black history, and encouraging allies to push bills that would defund schools for teaching that the nation's founding documents were entangled with slavery. The common thread uniting these assaults is unmistakable: the authoritarian logic of erasure. Memory is to be disciplined, history domesticated, and truth subordinated to the spectacle of Trump's political theater. What is at stake is not simply the content of museum exhibits or school curricula, but whether democracy itself can survive without an honest reckoning with its past. As history warns us, fascist regimes, from Hitler's book burnings to Franco's cultural purges, have always begun their reign of terror by waging war on memory. The thread uniting these efforts is the logic of erasure: history must serve power, never truth.

From Nazi Germany to Trump's America

The Trump era's assault on memory recalls, in alarming ways, the memory politics of Nazi Germany.[11] In 1933, Nazi officials staged massive book burnings, consigning to the flames the works of Jewish authors, feminists, Marxists, and anyone deemed "un-German." These were not just acts of censorship, they were spectacles of purification. Fire was the ritual through which dissent was eradicated and mythic unity forged. Schools and universities were purged of Jewish and oppositional voices, textbooks rewritten, and history transfigured as propaganda for the racial state.

The United States has not yet replicated those bonfires, but the spirit of erasure is unmistakable. Books by Maya Angelou, James Baldwin, and Margaret Atwood are being pulled from libraries. Governors stage press events around banned books, turning censorship into political theater. Viral videos of parents denouncing "divisive concepts" in classrooms circulate widely, feeding the illusion that banning history is an act of protection.

As the Trump presidency unfolds, the politics of erasure and historical amnesia increases with shocking intensity. For instance, the Trump administration has ordered the removal of signs and exhibits related to slavery at multiple national parks. One of the latest removals included "a photograph at one national park illustrating violence against slaves, known as 'The Scourged Back.' The photograph, taken in 1863, shows scars on the back of a man probably named Peter Gordon from wounds inflicted by his masters before he escaped slavery."[12] In addition, it has ordered the removal of exhibits deemed as reflecting a "corrosive ideology" at the Smithsonian. More is at stake here than the Trump regime's control over what Americans learn; it is also an attempt to govern how we think, act, and learn from history.

The attack on the Smithsonian, the banning of books, the silencing of universities, and the stigmatization of "woke" as a code word for racial justice and historical truth all make visible how white supremacy fuels the cleansing project of authoritarianism. In one particular instance, this project takes a particularly grotesque form, as Oklahoma's Ryan Walters (since fired) required applicants from "liberal states" to pass an anti-woke test before teaching. These assaults on memory are also an assault on critical thinking, critical pedagogy, and civic literacy. It is crucial to view them as anything but isolated. They form part of a systematic effort to weaponize education, culture, and memory, to produce individuals who are passive, obedient, stripped of critical thought. Primo Levi warned that "wherever you begin by denying the fundamental liberties of mankind and equality among people, you move towards the concentration camp system."[13] Forgetting, he argued, is the first step toward barbarism. The lesson of Nazi Germany is that erasing memory is not collateral to authoritarianism, it is central to it.

Conclusion: The Burden and Duty of Memory

At the heart of Trump's war on memory lies an act of pedagogical terror, a poisoning of history and the transformation of culture into a blunt instrument of indoctrination. To resist this death of memory is to recognize that the fight for democracy cannot be separated from the fight over history, over culture, and over the economic forces that shackle both under neoliberal capitalism. Culture is never simply a mirror of society; it is a battlefield that shapes how we imagine the world and our place within it. In a time when neoliberalism and fascism bleed into each other, culture becomes the decisive ground where narratives of domination collide with possibilities of resistance. Authoritarians seek to turn it into a machinery of obedience, silencing dissent and numbing consciousness. Yet culture also holds the fragile, indispensable power to ignite memory, nourish critical thought, and keep alive the hope of resistance.

At the heart of this lies a war over culture and consciousness. Antonio Gramsci, in the *Prison Notebooks*, warned that every political struggle is also a struggle over pedagogy, over who shapes the common sense of a society.[14] For Gramsci, culture and education are the true battlegrounds of democracy. Paulo Freire reminded us that education is never neutral—it either nurtures liberation or reinforces domination.[15] Trump's pedagogy of repression seeks nothing less than a populace severed from memory, stripped of critical thought, and rendered compliant to authoritarian power. The United States has become a warfare state, where the instruments of militarization and the machinery of control no longer remain at the edges of empire but are turned inward, disciplining culture, stifling memory, and colonizing everyday life under the banner of "law and order." What was once unleashed abroad in the name of empire now turns inward, producing citizens as enemies and culture itself as a battlefield.

If democracy is to endure, memory must be defended with the same ferocity as freedom itself. Yet remembrance alone is not enough; what is required is a critical culture that binds past and present, a pedagogy that transforms historical consciousness into sustained resistance. The ghosts of Auschwitz, of Jim Crow, of January 6th, remain with us, not as abstractions but as urgent reminders of the abyss that awaits when memory is erased. Our responsibility is to teach, to narrate, and to reimagine, so that memory itself becomes an act of resistance. Only by transforming remembrance into struggle can we halt the return of barbarism and reclaim democracy as a living, unfinished experiment in freedom. Only a sustained educational and political struggle can reverse the damage; the future is imperiled, but not foreclosed.

In the end, culture remains the decisive ground where radical democracy either withers under authoritarian rule or is reborn as the terrain of resistance and hope. What is clear is that the Trump regime does not merely flirt with fascism, it embodies it, hurling the United States over the abyss. And that abyss stretches far beyond American borders. Trump arms Netanyahu, an indicted war criminal who wages genocide against the Palestinian people with impunity; he aligns himself with dictators like Russia's Vladimir Putin, India's Narendra Modi, Argentina's Javier Gerardo Milei, El Salvador's Nayib Bukele, and others who traffic in repression, violence, and cruelty. The warfare state is drenched in blood. War should be a warning; under Trump it has become theater, a grotesque spectacle where cruelty parades as civic virtue. Resistance is a necessity that sears the conscience, demanding action.

Charlotte Delbo, an Auschwitz survivor, pleaded in *A Prayer to the Living to Forgive Them for Being Alive:* "You who are passing by, I beg you, do something ... to justify your existence ... because it would be too senseless after all for so many to have died while you live doing nothing with your life." Her words reverberate through time, transcending the horrors of a specific moment in history, and call us to a moral reckoning we cannot ignore. The burden of memory is a democratic duty. To defend truth is to defend freedom; to erase history is to pave the road to authoritarianism. The enduring conditions that make fascism possible at home and abroad in the past are with us again, though in different forms. The choice before us is stark: silence or resistance, complicity or memory, barbarism or democracy. The weight of this decision cannot be overstated.

6

Cleansing the Body Politic: Forgetting, Violence, and the Struggle for Democracy

The Death of Responsibility

All across the United States, people are increasingly rising up, refusing complicity in the slow-motion annihilation of democracy. They march against a regime that strips public goods, criminalizes dissent, disappears students, and hollows out the very institutions meant to protect civic life. But these assaults are not new; they culminate in what I once called the scorched-earth politics of America's four fundamentalisms: market worship, ideological conformity, religious zealotry, and educational repression.[1] These fundamentalisms have steadily laid the groundwork for a society governed by violence, cruelty, and unaccountable power—where the market is sacrosanct, history is erased, justice is inverted, and knowledge is policed.

Today these forces erupt in a violent crescendo, a cleansing politics aimed at stripping democracy of its ethical core and moral vocabulary. The state is hollowed out from within; its institutions emptied of meaning. Both the Democratic and Republican parties, though in different ways and to different degrees, have embraced the magical thinking of a death-dealing capitalism and the myth of American exceptionalism, hollowing out the very foundations of democracy in the United States. The result is a society in which civic life is emptied of democratic substance, state violence becomes normalized, and moral responsibility gives way to the dark and pathological sickness of fascist politics. History is criminalized; legal structures once meant to protect rights are now repurposed to legitimize state violence; power is no longer restrained by justice. Racialized groups are cast aside as surplus populations, their lives treated as unnecessary to the nation's moral economy. Considered disposable, they are abducted in plain sight though guilty of no crime, while the public sinks deeper into a fog of social and historical forgetting. What emerges is not merely authoritarianism but a theater of terror, where cruelty becomes policy, social abandonment the norm, and consent dangerously masquerades as neutrality.

Politics has become the extension of crime itself, with governance morphing into organized barbarism. At every level of society, militarization and repression have taken root, aimed not only at critics but at entire communities. This is a state-sponsored culture of fear aimed at immigrants, international students, dissenters, and marginalized populations. It manifests in overt abductions, including US citizens, targeted for their race, their dissent, or their opposition to Trump's domestic and foreign policies. As the fabric of democratic life unravels, the groundwork is laid for the rise of authoritarian rule, where resistance is met with violence, and the very principles of freedom and justice are reduced to a brittle facade.

What better proof of his contempt for law and humanity than Trump's willingness to abduct and deport legal residents, men, women, and children who have committed no crime, seized from streets, schools, homes, and even houses of worship, turning terror itself into an arm of the state? Meanwhile, extremists who stormed the US Capitol in violent insurrection are pardoned and walk free. In this inverted moral universe, the government deported an American citizen, Ábrego García, to a foreign gulag in El Salvador without due process, and those who dare to challenge this lawlessness are accused of "aiding and abetting terrorism."[2] This is not simply cruelty or overreach; it is the architecture of fascism itself, where law becomes a weapon, truth is treated as treason, and resistance is rebranded as terrorism. The sheer horror of this organized barbarism was laid bare when El Salvador's dictator, Nayib Bukele, met with Trump and callously refused to return Ábrego García to the United States, dismissing him as a "terrorist" he would not "smuggle" into the country. The government admitted he was mistakenly deported; yet it gets worse. As Hafiz Rashid reports in *The New Republic*, despite the Supreme Court's order for Garcia's return to the US, "the Trump administration has stalled and refused, hiding behind semantics and technicalities. And with the backing of a dictator like Bukele, the White House seems content to let an innocent immigrant languish in a gulag," showing a complete disregard for justice and due process.[3]

Even after courts forced his return to the United States, Ábrego García was placed in legal limbo, facing contested criminal charges while federal judges questioned the government's conduct and repeatedly intervened to prevent further abuses. Rather than rectify its error, the Trump administration pursued a new strategy, attempting to deport him to a third country, Liberia, a place with which he has no connection. This effort, widely criticized as arbitrary and retaliatory, has again been met with judicial resistance, with courts warning that such actions violate the most basic principles of due process. What emerges is a horrifying pattern, a state willing not only to exile an innocent man into a notorious prison abroad, but, when forced to reverse course, to continue seeking new avenues of disposability, revealing a cruel and punitive machinery of power unbound from law, accountability, and any enduring commitment to justice.

What passes for governance increasingly resembles a manual for authoritarian rule, a theater of governance masking lawlessness. The dismantling of public institutions, suppression of historical memory, erosion of legal protections, assault on higher education, abduction of students, and demonization of dissent all signal a new mode of state terrorism. This machinery of domination no longer hides its contempt for democracy; it mimics, manipulates, and ultimately discards democracy. It channels the darkest moments of the past, echoing the brutality of slavery, the violence of the police state, and the horror of the concentration camps. In this rising authoritarian landscape, the state no longer serves the people; it abandons them to a ruthless order where solidarity shatters, justice is privatized, and hope is exiled to the margins. This is fascism on steroids.

Resistance is rising, fierce, luminous, and charged with hope. Across the nation, people are pushing back against a regime that robs them of life's very essence: security, care, sustenance, and dignity. On campuses, a new front of defiance is emerging. Faculty, students, and even courageous administrators are organizing Academic Mutual Defense Compacts, collective pledges to resist Trump's escalating assault on higher education. In this darkening moment, these alliances embody a pedagogy of courage, a refusal to let learning be conscripted into the machinery of authoritarianism. They signal that education, at its best, is not a passive institution but a living act of resistance.

From city streets to university campuses, this defiance while slowing continues to challenge the rising lawlessness of the Trump regime. Workers, educators, artists, federal employees, and students, among others, are revolting against the erosion of their rights, the violence inflicted upon their bodies, and the vicious onslaught on their sense of justice and agency. As fears mount over the collapse of retirement funds, immigration status, and job security, the crushing weight of scarcity, poverty, police violence, and powerlessness takes a toll, both emotionally and physically. With food prices soaring and consumer goods becoming more elusive, the misery deepens. Yet, in the face of this darkness, resistance, however sporadic, continues to grow, an act of bold defiance against what Rob Nixon calls the "slow violence" of policies that crush daily life, erase memory, and hollow out the very meaning of agency.[4]

Millions of people have taken to the streets in the No Kings demonstrations, transforming scattered outrage into a collective refusal of authoritarian rule. These protests are not merely episodic expressions of dissent; they represent a broad-based democratic uprising against a governing logic rooted in state violence, corruption, and the unchecked concentration of power. Participants are protesting wars waged without accountability, the normalization of cruelty as public policy, the expansion of systemic racism, and the ongoing violation of constitutional rights. They are also resisting the dismantling of public goods, from higher education to environmental protections, institutions essential to any viable democracy but increasingly targeted under Trump's authoritarian project.

What gives the No Kings movement its urgency and significance is its recognition that these issues are not isolated crises but interconnected elements of a deeper transformation, one in which democracy is being hollowed out from within. The language of kingship is not rhetorical excess; it names a form of rule that elevates executive power above the law, erases the distinction between public office and private gain, and treats dissent as a threat to be punished rather than a right to be protected. In this context, the movement signals more than protest, it embodies a pedagogy of resistance, educating the public about the conditions of their own dispossession while insisting that democracy must be defended not only in courts and legislatures, but in the streets, in institutions, and in the collective imagination of the people.This tide of defiance confronts a politics of cleansing and erasure, spreading like wildfire through the body of democracy: a state stripped to serve the market; memory razed and rewritten; dissent smothered beneath ideological obedience; law twisted into a weapon of vengeance; racial others cast beyond belonging. This is a multi-front cleansing campaign that demands unrelenting mass resistance. These protests are not symbolic gestures; they are insurgent affirmations that the promise of a radical democracy is not dead, only endangered, and still worth fighting for. Yet they unfold under an ominous horizon: governmental, ideological, legal, racial, and historical cleansing intensifies in the US and metastasizes globally, threatening to become the blueprint for a brutal new world order.

Governmental Cleansing and the Collapse of the Social

Governmental cleansing begins with a calculated assault on governance as an instrument of the public good. In Trump's America, the state is no longer envisioned as a guardian of collective well-being, a fact made clear under the Bush–Cheney war on terror.[5] It no longer offers vital protections like Medicare, Social Security, affordable housing, and public education; instead, it is viewed as an obstacle to unfettered capitalism. As explored earlier, neoliberal cruelty provides the architecture for this transformation, turning freedom into a mask for domination and social responsibility into a casualty of market rule. In this worldview, there are no social problems, only personal failures, no public goods, only private investments. This is politics with closing horizons, one that blocks the translation of private troubles into larger structural issues.

Milton Friedman's infamous assertion that "the social responsibility of business is to increase its profits" epitomizes a worldview where social justice is seen as heretical and public welfare is synonymous with socialism.[6] Friedman's contempt for collective responsibility and his sanctification of profit as moral imperative reveal the ideological foundation of this new horizon of barbarism and cruelty. He writes:

> But the doctrine of "social responsibility" taken seriously would extend the scope of the political mechanism to every human activity. That is why, in my book *Capitalism and Freedom*, I called it a "fundamentally subversive doctrine" in a free society, and have said that in such a society, "there is one and only one social responsibility of business to use its resources and engage in activities designed to increase its profits so long as it stays within the rules of the game, which is to say, engages in open and free competition without deception or fraud." Talk about social responsibility by businessmen is nothing more than pure and unadulterated socialism. Businessmen who talk this way are unwitting puppets of the intellectual forces that have been undermining the basis of a free society these past decades.[7]

Friedman was not alone. Friedrich Hayek warned that even modest social protections would slide toward tyranny; Margaret Thatcher took it further, declaring, "there is no such thing as society, only individuals and their families";[8] and Ronald Reagan, the affable face of rollback, sealed the message in 1981: "Government is not the solution to our problem; government is the problem." With that, the ideological war on the social state was no longer whispered, it became national doctrine. Where earlier chapters traced the erasure of history and the politics of forgetting, this chapter turns to a different kind of amnesia, the moral forgetting born of neoliberal privatization, where civic responsibility dissolves into the marketplace and social bonds are despised and rendered obsolete.

In Trump's authoritarian worldview, this moral forgetting becomes weaponized. Social responsibility is no longer a democratic obligation but a fatal weakness, a check on market supremacy and unfettered executive power. Any commitment to equality, inclusion, justice, or the common good is cast as a liability to be eliminated.

Trump's policies do not merely echo this neoliberal logic; they radicalize it. Federal employees are purged, regulatory agencies dismantled, and essential public services auctioned off to private interests. The poor are denied meaningful health care, and their basic benefits are systematically undercut. Children's programs such as Head Start are eliminated. What emerges is not a government of, by, and for the people, but a privatized state of exception where cruelty becomes policy, social need is criminalized, and governance serves only wealth and power.

This is not merely the rollback of the state; it is the consolidation of market-driven authoritarianism. Under Trump, democracy is gutted of its moral core and replaced by an apparatus of terminal exclusion, an empire built on profit, punishment, and the erasure of history to conceal its cruelties. What we are witnessing is the normalization of a criminalized regime of terror. As Issie Lapowsky reports in *Vanity Fair*, Trump has already begun deporting immigrants and green-card holders to El Salvador's vast, dehumanizing mega-prison, CECOT, a carceral monument to state brutality. Noah Bullock, executive director of Cristosal, calls CECOT a "judicial black hole."[9] David Levi Strauss deepens this picture, describing a prison built to hold up to 40,000 inmates "stacked up like cordwood," stripped of visitation, recreation, exposure to daylight, reading material, or even bedding, and condemned to remain there indefinitely.[10] At the same time, Trump expands the domestic carceral apparatus, building new prisons such as the Alligator Alcatraz complex in Florida, transforming cruelty into policy and incarceration into the organizing principle of governance. Such violence is inseparable from a deeper form of erasure, the cleansing of memory itself. The same forces that criminalize bodies also police history, transforming forgetting into a political weapon.

Memory Cleansing and the Plague of Historical Amnesia

As I mentioned in chapter 4, across the country, "memory laws" are emerging to ban critical histories, narratives that challenge dominant renderings that whitewash, censor, and exclude the oppressed; slavery, cruelty, and war; and any account that gives voice to those written out of history. The suppression of memory and curriculum bans do not correct excesses; they criminalize complexity. Amnesia is more than absence, it is strategy. When memory is exiled from politics, tyranny fills the void. The Trump regime wants to police history and produce amnesia that power can exploit.

Memory matters because it gives people the language not to overlook or dissolve, as Timothy Snyder notes, "the historical consequences of slavery, lynchings ... voter suppression,"[11] and other acts of injustice. Trump and his MAGA blackshirts are doing more than creating a national effort to suppress historical knowledge; they are turning history into a racist weapon. History cleansing is part of a broader backlash against inclusive narratives; it is central to authoritarian regimes that make people disappear by erasing their histories, memories, institutions of learning, and, ultimately, their dignity, agency, and collective identities.[12]

Historical cleansing, as Maximillian Alvarez aptly describes it, is a "twenty-first-century political warfare on long-term historical consciousness."[13] Books are censored and banned, libraries defunded, and curricula rewritten to sanitize colonialism, slavery, and state violence. This is manufactured ignorance is policy.[14] In this form of ideological cleansing, the brutality of racism is obscured. The horrifying truth that "between 1877 and 1950, more than 4,000 Black men, women, and children were lynched in cities and towns across the country," and the fact that the lynching of Black men and boys continues, though no longer as public spectacles, are systematically erased from the historical record.[15] This racial terror has deep roots in history, yet it is now being deliberately erased from memory.

In its place, a new spectacle has emerged, one defined by mass deportations and the rise of the prison as a central instrument of fear, lawlessness, and punishment. David Levi Strauss aptly characterizes this intensified fixation on the punishing state as "carceral porn," a powerful reflection of our times. His words are worth quoting at length:

> Carceral porn reached a new level of depravity on March 26, when Homeland Security Secretary Kristi Noem (aka ICE Barbie) channeled Kafka in the penal colony and Lynndie England at Abu Ghraib and shook her ass in front of rows of caged, bare-breasted tattooed prisoners in El Salvador's CECOT prison. She was wearing a blue cap with a badge and an 18-karat gold Rolex Cosmograph Daytona watch worth about $50,000. Noem has made a cottage industry out of parading around in swat or combat gear in the midst of disasters, with a make-up person and hairstylist in tow. Of the above image, she said, "People need to see that image."[16]

As David Levi observes, cruelty today has become a form of civic entertainment, a ritualized pleasure that transforms the suffering of others into a spectacle of moral anesthesia. Such displays of cruelty constitute a kind of carceral pornography, turning punishment into entertainment and erasing the boundary between justice and vengeance. This perverse delight in punishment prefigures the fascist aesthetic of spectacle examined in Chapter 8.

The spectacularizing of politics cannot be separated from the whitewashing of history, another potent form of depoliticization, in which censorship not only obliterates the struggles of the marginalized and oppressed but also dismantles critical thinking, the rule of law, and the very notion of justice. Under Trump, this deliberate politics of organized forgetting extends into the mechanisms of state violence, where those erased from the historical narrative are disposed of through detention centers, prisons, and the brutalities of a police state.

Crimes against memory enable the return of unthinkable acts as legitimate state policies. As Rebecca Gordon points out, the "war on terror,"[17] forged during the Bush–Cheney years, ushered in an era of lawlessness, where the federal government operated with unchecked impunity. It was during this period that "vast new detention and surveillance powers" were enacted, and torture, once unthinkable, became normalized in the United States. Lawlessness became an ingrained "American habit." This culture of impunity has resurfaced under Trump, with the sins of the Bush–Cheney era conveniently erased from the national consciousness, allowing their devastating legacy to persist unchecked.

Memory cleansing is not merely a distortion of history; it transforms politics into a lie, legitimizing the exclusionary acts that silence people's voices and erase their histories, desires, and identities. Like all authoritarian regimes, the Trump administration seeks to turn the public into historical amnesiacs, obscuring the violence, corruption, and exploitation woven into the fabric of a ruthless capitalism and authoritarian power. It denies the lessons of the past that show us that what happened before need not happen again.

Ideological Cleansing and the Rise of Indoctrination Factories

Fascism endures not merely through brute force, but through the systematic erasure of memory, critical knowledge, and informed judgment. It intertwines historical amnesia with ideological cleansing, preventing the public from accessing past catastrophes so that, as Maria Pia Lara powerfully observes, they are unable to "exercise judgments whose results can give rise to disconcerting truths."[18] This process of historical cleansing inevitably leads to moral cleansing, which prepares the stage upon which other violent dramas can unfold. Fascism flourishes in a world where lies replace truth, spectacles drown out critical thought, and fear serves to justify and legitimize the apparatuses of indoctrination.

Across the United States, universities and public institutions have become contested zones where authoritarian politics increasingly dictates the terms of intellectual life. Books that examine racism, gendered violence, or the history of colonialism are being stripped from shelves. Faculty who critique the Trump regime, address pressing social injustices, or express solidarity with Palestine are met with harassment campaigns and, in many cases, punitive dismissals. As Zane McNeill notes in *Truthout,* international students now find themselves at heightened risk as well, subjected to surveillance and intimidation for participating in political debate, targeted because they fail to conform to the White House's rigid definition of what counts as a "patriotic" presence in the country.[19]

Revisiting the issue of visa revocations, it is worth noting that over 600 international students across more than a hundred institutions have had their visas revoked, with social media monitored by US Citizenship and Immigration Services for supposed "antisemitic content."[20] This pattern of ideological repression extends beyond the classroom, where entire academic departments, especially those focused on Middle Eastern Studies, are systematically dismantled, branded as havens of "ideological capture," and accused of fueling "antisemitic harassment" through targeted legislation. Faculty members are being stripped of jobs, tenure, and dignity, subjected to a surveillance state that calls to mind the darkest chapters of history, echoing the purges of Hitler's Germany and Augusto Pinochet's Chile.[21]

Ron DeSantis, the self-proclaimed anti-woke governor of Florida, embodies this crackdown with frightening precision. In a brazen act of ideological shadowing, pedagogical repression, and an intricately planned assault against all levels of critical education, DeSantis issued an executive order demanding that Florida's colleges and universities submit detailed records of faculty research grants over the last six years, including lists of papers published by faculty.[22] This sends a clear, sinister message to those faculty and others researching topics related to critical race theory, which Donald Trump has vilified as "a hateful Marxist doctrine that paints America as a wicked nation ... rewrites American history ... and teaches people to be ashamed of themselves and their country."[23]

Columbia University's shameful acquiescence to the Trump administration's demands for ideological purification signals a wider failure to defend academic freedom. Columbia's tightened security, empowered arrests, and monitoring of regional studies starkly underscore the broader collapse of American higher education's commitment to justice, truth, and student rights. In her searing critique, Fatima Bhutto captures the spirit of Columbia's capitulation to authoritarianism. She writes:

> Trying to prove that they are a university the government can rely on, Columbia has ... agreed to ban certain masks, empowering new campus security personnel to arrest students, and appointed someone to oversee the Middle Eastern, South Asian, and African studies department and the Palestine studies center of study. "Vichy on the Hudson," Professor Rashid Khalidi called them recently, referring to France's Vichy regime that collaborated with Nazi Germany.[24]

Ideological cleansing is not confined to public and higher education. Trump's recent executive order targeting the Smithsonian Institution for promoting "anti-American ideology" echoes the notorious Degenerate Art Exhibition organized by Hitler in July 1937 to condemn any cultural expression that defied state doctrine. The intent then, as now, was to impose a singular, monolithic national narrative and criminalize complexity and artistic dissent.

Fascism thrives on political theater that celebrates cruelty, militarism, sanctioned ignorance, and a multitude of fundamentalisms, whether rooted in neoliberalism, religious tyranny, white supremacy, ultra-nationalism, or settler-colonialism. As Donalyn White and Anthony Ballas rightly argue, ideological cleansing and historical amnesia are central to today's capitulation to fascism.[25] The politics of historical oblivion embrace not only ideas but also bodies, leading directly to concentration camps, prisons, and modern-day gulags.

The White House's deliberate erasure of history reaches its nadir with the removal of anti-slavery icon Harriet Tubman's image and biography from the US Park Service website, an ideological lynching that seeks to wipe away the legacy of slavery while diminishing the profound contributions of African Americans to the nation's story.[26] This is no oversight; it is a calculated assault on memory, a form of aesthetic assassination in which icons like Tubman are consigned to the dustbin of history alongside Jackie Robinson, Colin Powell, and the Tuskegee Airmen. In this act, the far right not only rewrites history but attempts to reimagine the very identity of America itself, one that can no longer acknowledge the brutal truths of its past or the resistance, courage, and brilliance of its Black citizens.

This is the dangerous terrain upon which we now tread. To allow this cleansing to continue is to abandon the very essence of democratic life and the moral imperatives that should guide us. We must recognize that the erasure of history, both in the mind and in the body, is not a neutral act, it is an invitation to totalitarianism.

Legal Cleansing and the End of the Rule of Law

Legal cleansing refers to the systematic dismantling of the law as a democratic safeguard and its conversion into a tool of authoritarian rule. This pattern of legal cleansing replaces the rule of law with the rule of power. It is not about justice but about domination, turning the law into an instrument of exclusion, vengeance, and control. Under Trump, the law is no longer designed to protect rights; it is wielded to enforce loyalty.

Federal employees are fired en masse to make room for partisan loyalists. Trump has threatened elite law firms, many of which have capitulated to his demands, smeared judges who rule against him, and promised to pardon those convicted of political violence. He has vowed to revoke Social Security numbers from immigrants and to carry out mass deportations without due process, extending punishment beyond the boundaries of the law. The Trump-aligned Congress has passed laws restricting judicial independence and weakening the power of the courts. The administration is relentless in its efforts to purge experienced, nonpartisan civil servants and replace them with political loyalists who will enforce his agenda without question.

In the process, legal protections collapse, regulatory agencies are gutted, and dissent is criminalized. The state now resorts to covert seizures and ICE-driven brutality, dragging people into remote detention centers under the cover of impunity. What remains is a government unbound by law, willing to disappear anyone who resists. No charges. No trial. Only the cold, disfiguring logic of state terror.

This is authoritarianism laid bare, an eerie fusion of Nuremberg logic and Kafka's nightmares, where punishment has nothing to do with actions but with imagined thoughts, where the state pre-emptively criminalizes dissent before it even exists. This is a grotesque assault on due process and liberty, a perversion of justice that seeks to uproot freedom itself by targeting the mind as the site of political criminality.

No one is immune from the looming terror unleashed by the Trump administration. As Eddie Glaude Jr. has powerfully argued, Americans must confront a brutal truth: the creation and expansion of Immigration and Customs Enforcement (ICE), now the largest federal law enforcement agency is a cornerstone of white supremacy.[27] It is a racist institution, entrenched in an immigration policy designed to uphold the values of white nationalism. In the face of shifting demographics, ICE is tasked with an urgent mission, to make America white again. This is a calculated attempt to turn back the clock on progress, to preserve an imagined past at the cost of justice and humanity.

This is an American-style fascism without apology, unhinged in its violation of rights, justice, and essential democratic freedoms.[28] Such rhetoric transforms dissent into a criminal act before it even occurs, exemplifying the logic of legal and ideological cleansing that underpins fascist politics. It reveals the deeply irrational nature of authoritarian rule, where the state not only controls actions but seeks to control thought itself, justifying state violence and terrorism against those deemed undesirable for their beliefs, speech, or associations. This escalation into ideological terror is the hallmark of fascism, which thrives on the erasure of reason, the criminalization of free thought, and the normalization of state-sanctioned violence.

For the Trump administration to declare openly the power to abduct and imprison individuals not for what they have said or done but for what they might think, secretly believe, or may come to believe, is a mind-numbing manifestation of Orwellian terror. This is a glaring instance of state-sanctioned brutality, nothing less than state terrorism. The power to abduct the innocent is only the first step in a broader choreography of authoritarianism. Once cruelty is normalized as governance, the machinery of terror turns inward, militarizing obedience and sanctifying loyalty to the leader rather than to the law.

Having weaponized fear against the most vulnerable, Trump now extends his purge to the military itself, reshaping it into an instrument of personal rule. Trump's purge of the military, targeting high-ranking commanders and inspector generals, is not mere reshuffling but a calculated attempt to replace constitutional loyalty with personal devotion. It echoes the most dangerous precedents in modern history: Hitler's co-optation of the Wehrmacht, Pinochet's coup in Chile, and the deployment of the military under Videla in Argentina.

This is the scaffolding of militarized authoritarianism, where the armed forces enforce the will of a would-be strongman. If Trump turns the military against dissidents, demonstrators, or student protesters, as he has repeatedly threatened, the expectation is chillingly clear: they will obey.

In this vision, law is no longer tethered to justice, it becomes a weapon of vengeance, exclusion, and raw domination. The silence and craven accommodation to fascism that follow are not peace; they are complicity. And what looms on the horizon is not order but the slow, calculated unfolding of a coup already in motion.

Racial Cleansing and the Scourge of White Supremacy

The architecture of racial cleansing rests on a familiar foundation: white supremacy as policy, not merely prejudice. It is a system that weaponizes fear to maintain hierarchy and normalize disposability. In Trump's America, whiteness itself is mobilized as a political project, an organizing ideology that defines who counts as fully human and who does not. The carceral state, the deportation apparatus, the police, and the border all converge into a single regime of racial management that defines belonging through exclusion and terror.

As Achille Mbembe reminds us, the modern state defines its power through its ability to decide who may live and who must die. In this sense, racial cleansing is the domestic face of necropolitics, the politics of death. From Gaza to Georgia, from ICE detention centers to prison plantations, Trump's regime reproduces this logic of domination, binding racial hierarchy to the machinery of the state. The border becomes both a physical wall and a symbolic boundary, separating those who deserve protection from those deemed expendable.

Racial cleansing, then, is not simply an American pathology; it is part of a global authoritarian script. The same technologies of control, surveillance, and exclusion that mark Black and Brown bodies in the United States echo across borders, in Modi's India, Netanyahu's Israel, and Europe's anti-migrant fortresses. The war against the racialized Other is a war against democracy itself, and it is waged in the name of purity, order, and civilization.

If fascism is the political expression of a death-driven culture, then white supremacy is its moral oxygen. It allows barbarism to masquerade as governance and cruelty as justice. The police chokehold, the deportation flight, the border cage, all are extensions of a single ideology that celebrates domination while annihilating justice. Racial cleansing thrives where memory dies, where the legacy of slavery, colonialism, and genocide are either denied or romanticized as national triumphs.

This is why the struggle against racial cleansing must also be a struggle for historical consciousness. Without remembering the histories of resistance, the abolitionists, the freedom fighters, the civil-rights activists, and the countless unnamed martyrs, democracy becomes an empty ritual. To forget these histories is to surrender the present to the architects of cruelty.

State violence always has a target, and it is painfully clear that those targets are racialized. From the southern border to the voting booth, from campus protests to inner-city neighborhoods, racial cleansing is no longer a hidden strategy; it has become a governing principle. Hundreds of immigrants are detained and deported without due process, often sent to mega-prisons or held indefinitely in ICE facilities where human rights are an afterthought. Black and Brown communities are over-policed, under-protected, and routinely brutalized, caught in the crosshairs of a carceral state that sees them not as citizens but as threats. Police violence has become a normalized form of racial discipline and terrorism, while white supremacist militias are emboldened, armed, and often protected.

Racial cleansing manifests through a cascade of reactionary policies. The right to vote is under siege, restricted through gerrymandering, voter-roll purges, intimidation at polling stations, and laws crafted to disenfranchise communities of color. Diversity, Equity, and Inclusion (DEI) programs are being dismantled under the pretense of eliminating racist policies, when in truth they are targeted precisely because they seek to redress systemic racism. In schools and universities, anti-racist pedagogy is vilified, books by authors of color are banned, and any effort to center marginalized voices is cast as indoctrination. Muslim communities are relentlessly surveilled; their lives scrutinized under policies that disproportionately target them. Latinx neighborhoods are raided. Indigenous sovereignty is ignored. And students who protest these injustices, especially those defending Palestinian rights, are labeled as extremists and enemies of the state.

Conclusion: Educating for Organized Resistance

In an age when fascism no longer hides in the shadows, we must learn to see with clarity the architecture of cleansing that is hollowing out an already fragile democracy, socially, ideologically, legally, and racially. This crisis is not the product of isolated policies or rogue leaders; it is the expression of a total system, a form of neoliberal fascism that thrives on despair. It feeds on a public that has lost faith in its institutions, which distrusts its leaders, who feels abandoned in workplaces stripped of dignity, and that trembles before an uncertain future. To resist, the American public must recover its historical consciousness and cultivate a new civic literacy. It must learn how language deceives, and how collective struggles are won. This means getting at the roots of how power circulates not only through the grand machinery of the state but also through the everyday rhythms of life. Only by making visible what has been hidden, by naming the forces that normalize cruelty, can democracy be reclaimed as a living, collective struggle rather than a fading memory.

People must learn to name the roots of their suffering, exclusions, and the violence inflicted upon them by the state. At the roots of this suffering lies a form of gangster capitalism that corrodes democracy from within. It breeds staggering levels of inequality of wealth and power, constructing a world where class privileges and white Christian nationalism thrive alongside mass misery, insecurity, and despair. As a form of neoliberal fascism, capitalism has evolved into a machinery of cruelty that can sustain itself only through distraction and deceit. No longer able to legitimate itself, it turns to fascist politics that merges state violence and racial cleansing. That is, in order to protect its obscene concentrations of wealth, it manufactures enemies: immigrants, Black people, refugees, the poor, those rendered disposable so that the real sources of exploitation remain hidden. As Richard D. Wolff has brilliantly argued, what emerges is not simply an economic system but a moral catastrophe, a breeding ground for fascism that weaponizes fear and division to preserve the power of the few over the lives of the many.[29]

As the late sociologist Pierre Bourdieu reminds us, authoritarian capitalism, or its updated version of neoliberal fascism, thrives not only through repression but through the death of imagination, the dismantling of critical thought and informed judgment, and the destruction of the very institutions that nurture them. It is essential to challenge the formation of oppressive identities, agencies, and subjectivities, while equally vital is the cultivation of cultural and pedagogical forces capable of undoing them.

Just as we must confront the economic, financial, and institutional structures of neoliberal fascism, both nationally and globally, it is equally crucial to recognize that domination operates on an intellectual and pedagogical level, shaping minds and ideas as much as markets and policies. What is needed now is a politics of clarity and outrage, joined to a movement of collective resistance. At the heart of that struggle is an embrace of education as the decisive terrain where dangerous memories are preserved, where the cleansing politics of authoritarianism is exposed, and where truth becomes an act of civic courage. Education must be reclaimed as a powerful political force, a transformative public good capable of producing critical, informed, and fearless citizens who refuse the violence of historical erasure and stand against the machinery of state-sanctioned forgetting. Without such an educational project, democracy cannot be renewed, defended, or imagined anew.

SECTION THREE

Culture as a War Zone and Site of Struggle

7

Culture as a Pedagogical Battlefield in the Fight Against Tyranny

Rise of the Police State

On June 6, 2025, resistance erupted in the streets of Los Angeles to confront the Trump regime's brutal campaign against immigrants, enforced by ICE agents and the machinery of mass deportation. In a chilling escalation, Trump branded the protesters "insurrectionists" and threatened the use of military force, turning dissent into a crime and protest into a pretext for repression. Stephen Miller, White House deputy chief of staff, called Los Angeles "occupied territory," adding: "We've been saying for years this is a fight to save civilization."[1]

This was not merely the rhetoric of strongman fantasies but the language of fascist ambition, a calculated pretext to invoke the Insurrection Act and erect a police state. Beneath this nightmarish facade lies something far darker: the weaponization of the war on immigrants as a means to orchestrate ethnic cleansing, veiled under the apparatus of law and the grotesque spectacle of state power. Moreover, as Kristi Noem [since fired] and Trump have blatantly outlined, their assault on immigrants extends beyond individual lives; it is a direct attack on America's largest cities, like Los Angeles, Chicago, and New York, which stand as Democratic Party strongholds.[2] When Trump and his allies claim to be liberating these cities from "socialists," they are not merely waging ideological warfare; they are laying the groundwork for a fascist coup rooted in division, fear, and destruction.

What must also be acknowledged is that the police state is not only about overt repression and the brutality of police violence, but also about using every arm of the state, from the Justice Department and FBI to the courts, the IRS, and intelligence agencies like the CIA and NSA, to intimidate and silence dissent, compelling people into submission. This is the calculated theater of authoritarian rule to escalate state violence, instill terror, criminalize dissent, and legitimize white nationalist ideology. By framing defiance as treason, Trump seeks to cloak his own authoritarian crimes while constructing a political climate where any challenge to power is met with brutal retaliation. As Michelle Goldberg noted in *The New York Times*: "This is what autocracy looks like."[3]

The authoritarian dream is rooted in the belief that state violence should serve as the primary tool of governance. This is precisely what unfolded in Los Angeles, where Trump deployed the National Guard and Marines to crush protests against his mass deportation policies. In doing so, he mobilized ICE as a modern-day KKK, a force of masked men invoking the familiar terrors of racial domination and white vigilantism. This form of state terrorism is on full display in Chicago, and increasingly in a number of states. The long-standing carceral state in the United States has now been upgraded to a police state, a masked, anonymous, and unaccountable internal army that terrorizes American cities while masquerading as the defender of order.[4]

Ian F. Blair writes in *The Intercept* that "The police state of our nightmares is nearing its final form." The expansion of police power, "arm in arm with immigration agents, the military, and the rest of the federal agencies," are unfolding in plain sight and framed as part of a war against an internal enemy.[5] We have crossed a moral and political line so stark that even centrist commentators like Rachel Maddow have raised alarms. She notes that what is on full display, as both a spectacle of fear and a culture of violence, is

> masked secret police breaking people's car windows and snatching people off the streets and out of church parking lots and courtroom hallways, taking them away with no charges, no notice, no paperwork, no explanation, not letting them see lawyers, and then moving them secretly to what are effectively black-site prisons where they won't tell you who's there and where no one's allowed in to see what's going on, off the books, out of sight, beyond counsel.[6]

This Gestapo-like reality is not new but its tools of repression signal an even more horrifying integration of technology, propaganda, surveillance, and fascist politics.

It has become a common occurrence to witness ICE conducting military-style raids, breaking into apartments, kicking down doors without a warrant, ignoring due process, using flash bang grenades, pointing a weapon at a resident recording an ICE agent, detaining children in zip ties, injuring journalists, forcefully slamming political leaders to the ground, and using excessive force that should never be tolerated.[7] More and more images are appearing on social media revealing how ICE is terrorizing American citizens. Judd Legum describes one of many horrifying examples of ICE brutality that took place in Chicago.[8] He writes:

> Last week, hundreds of heavily armed federal agents descended on an apartment complex in Chicago, arriving in Black Hawk helicopters and moving trucks. After they arrived at 7500 S. South Shore Drive, agents from Border Patrol, the FBI, and other agencies busted down nearly every door. Residents were pulled from their apartments in the middle of the night, including children, some of them reportedly naked. The Department of Homeland Security (DHS) said the raid was targeting the Tren de Aragua gang, but "gave no evidence to support the assertion." ... 67-year-old Roderick Johnson, a U.S. citizen, "said agents broke through his door and dragged him out in zip ties." After telling agents he was a citizen, Johnson was told he "had to wait until they looked me up." His requests to see a search warrant or speak to a lawyer were ignored. Johnson "was left tied up outside the building for nearly three hours before agents finally let him go."[9]

Media coverage of this act of domestic terrorism was swift and scathing, capturing with menacing precision the images of "jackbooted federal agents busting down doors and dragging children, some naked, out into the dark streets."[10] Yet the MAGA propaganda and disimagination machine wasted no time in perverting horror into spectacle. In a grotesque act of state-sponsored theater, it released a propaganda video that revamped the assault as an action film, complete with the "thrilling spectacle of defeated-looking migrants in handcuffs."[11] Here, terror and cruelty became performance. Violence was aestheticized, fetishized, and sold back to the public as entertainment, a cheap simulacrum of heroism masking the moral rot of a burgeoning dictatorship. What unfolded was a theater of domination, a spectacle of cruelty staged to make violence appear righteous and humiliation a public virtue. It was a ritual of degradation masquerading as law and order, where brutality was turned into a civic performance of obedience and fear.

According to historian Heather Cox Richardson, Trump's so-called "One Big, Beautiful Bill Act" handed ICE an astonishing windfall, more than $170 billion over four years "for immigration and border security."[12] The law tripled ICE's annual budget, granting it more money than all state and local police forces in the United States combined. Such an expansion was not merely bureaucratic; it marked a decisive step toward normalizing domestic militarization under the guise of "security." In Trump's hands, ICE has evolved into a weapon of social control, brutalizing immigrants and citizens alike, while constructing a surveillance state designed to track, punish, and intimidate those deemed disloyal. As Ian F. Blair reports in *The Intercept*, ICE's sprawling surveillance apparatus now extends far beyond the border, embedding itself in local police networks, data-sharing systems, and private databases, an infrastructure of fear hiding in plain sight.[13] He states:

> ICE [has] obtained access to begin the use of Israeli spyware to hack phones and encrypted apps. And a week later, 404 Media reported

> ICE spent $10 million on Clearview AI facial recognition software to support Homeland Security Investigations, supposedly allowing the agency to track people it accuses of "assaulting" officers. This is all on top of HSI's contract with Peter Thiel's Palantir, which, according to a dossier of documents reviewed by *The Guardian*, built a platform called ImmigrationOS that "will service ICE branches beyond HSI" and includes a "searchable super-network" for agents to comb through government and private databases.

This convergence of surveillance, policing, and corporate technology marks the birth of a new authoritarian order, one that merges state terror with the machinery of profit. The increase in lawless violence, abductions, and an expanding threat of surveillance is matched by sweeping directives by the Trump administration that expands the government's definition of domestic terrorism. Under order, NSPM-7, the government is creating "a national strategy to 'investigate, prosecute, and disrupt entities and individuals engaged in acts of political violence and intimidation' that suppress lawful political activity or obstruct the rule of law."[14] At work here is a repressive notion of domestic terrorism that includes "a wide range of political beliefs, identified as anti-American, anti-capitalist and anti-Christianity," all of which are designed to silence critics of Trump's policies by attacking free speech. As the Lemkin Institute makes clear, this is more than a resurrection of McCarthyism; it is a cleansing ideology rooted in genocidal thinking.[15] This is a species of fascism masquerading as redemptive violence, which I address again in Chapter 9.

What cannot be ignored or disputed is that the militarization of civil society is not merely an overreaction or illegal response to a fabricated insurrection; it is the very foundation upon which martial law is established, paving the way for a fully realized fascist state. What unfolded in LA was not an insurrection; it was the people rising in defense of democracy. The true insurrection happened on January 6, with Trump as its chief architect. Yet once again, state violence is used not to protect democracy, but to crush it.

What we are witnessing is a spectacle of domination. The deployment of troops, the vigilante targeting of Democratic lawmakers, the planned grotesquerie of Trump's military parade, and Trump's order for ICE to target cities led by Democrats are all scenes of the same authoritarian snuff film.[16] Together, they fuse militarism and national identity, designed to normalize cruelty, fetishize strength, and retooled obedience as patriotism. As Susan Sontag warned, fascism cloaks violence in aesthetics, making submission not only palatable but seductive.[17] This is the pornography of power, where culture and repression merge in a theater of fear, scripted to extinguish political imagination and render dissent illegible. Spectacle replaces substance, and emotion replaces analysis. Politics becomes a performance of domination staged for public consumption.

In this moment of escalating violence, Trump's use of force is more than a show of control; it is a pedagogy of submission meant to etch repression into public consciousness. This is fascist aesthetics reimagined for a media-saturated age, where power must not only be wielded but displayed. Domination is choreographed and televised, turned into a civic lesson. The spectacle becomes a tutorial in obedience, transforming images of state violence into instruments of mass indoctrination. Culture obliterates reality, replacing memory with myth, dissent with loyalty, and resistance with silence. The convergence of Trump's militarized crackdowns with his self-aggrandizing parades of force reveals a machinery of destruction no longer hidden but flaunted, a grotesque exhibition engineered to numb the senses and turn state terror into a national ritual.

The Terrain of Culture Is Central in the Struggle Against Authoritarianism

In the current political moment, we would do well to remember Milan Kundera's words from *The Book of Laughter and Forgetting*: "The first step in liquidating a people is to erase its memory. Destroy its books, its culture, its history. Then have someone author new books, manufacture a new culture, invent a new history. Before long, the nation will begin to forget what it is and what it was."[18]

Kundera's words cut to the heart of our current crisis. Dominant culture is not peripheral to politics; it is its primary battleground, its arsenal, theater, and pedagogy. In this context, culture becomes the means through which tyranny educates. Under Trump, culture is not merely an accessory to power, it is both the weapon and the war zone.

Democracy is not shattered only by the blunt force of military coups; it can be eroded from within, undermined by the ghosts of past tyrannies reanimated through symbols, digital technologies, and the ever-churning machinery of social media. Today, power speaks in the seductive language of images, images laced with bigotry, seeded with cruelty, and amplified by algorithms engineered for outrage. Culture has become the site of erasure as much as expression. It functions pedagogically through what Ariella Aïsha Azoulay names "imperial technologies," colonized imaginaries, and what I have called "disimagination machines."[19] These right-wing narcotizing apparatuses detach the public from the conditions that steal their rights, agency, and power. They are designed to strip the colonized not only of their futures but of their histories, their very presence in the world.

Michael Tomasky is right to argue that right-wing media now wields more influence than the mainstream press, not only because of its scale but because of the unified voice of grievance and resentment it projects.[20]

This voice relentlessly vilifies Democrats and liberals as treasonous elitists who despise the people, while painting Republicans and conservatives as God-fearing patriots defending the nation. In this closed pedagogical loop, enemies are invented daily and fear becomes the grammar of belonging. They claim to be the last bastion against "those others" who do not conform to their narrow, exclusionary vision of what it means to be an American, a vision that casts out Black, Brown, immigrant, queer, and dissident citizens. This is not political rhetoric; it is a pedagogy of hatred that weaponizes identity, reshapes moral perception, and stokes division at every turn.

In this age of resurgent fascism, we see its effects everywhere: in the normalization of cruelty, in the legitimation of genocidal assaults such as Israel's war on Gaza, and in the scorched-earth campaign against historical memory and civic belonging carried out by the Trump regime. Culture, once a domain of meaning, evidence, and imagination, has been turned too often into an instrument of control, a machinery that teaches submission rather than critical agency.

As Catherine Caruso points out in *Harvard News*, "AI-powered autonomous weapons represent a new era in warfare and pose a concrete threat to scientific progress and basic research."[21] Yet the danger extends far beyond the battlefield. Artificial intelligence now shapes policy, curates knowledge, and narrows ethical debate, legitimizing what can only be described as a culture of war. It reconfigures not only how we fight but how we think, molding public consciousness around surveillance, efficiency, and control rather than empathy, solidarity, or justice.

For instance, the rise of artificial intelligence is accelerating a cultural transformation that is as dangerous as it is seductive. When OpenAI recently restricted access to politically sensitive reasoning, it wasn't a glitch, it was a warning.[22] AI is not just organizing knowledge; it is curating memory, defining what can be said, and erasing what must be forgotten. In the wrong hands, and increasingly in the hands of authoritarian regimes and corporate overlords, AI becomes a weapon of ideological control and surveillance. Brett Wilkins reports that "commercial AI models are directly being used" by Israel in Gaza for mass surveillance and the targeting of "critics, dissidents, and opponents."[23] Israel's use of AI models like Lavender is determining who is deemed a citizen and who is deemed a target. It is AI who is deciding who gets bombed. Culture, in this context, is engineered, automated, and sanitized. Israel use of AI tools like Lavender and Habsora to identify bombing targets in Gaza has led to a dramatic increase in violence against civilians and a dangerous erosion of accountability in warfare.[24] This convergence of corporate AI, state violence, and militarized surveillance represents a new frontier of authoritarian pedagogy, one that teaches fear, obedience, and erasure.

Capitalism Is Not Merely an Economic System

Too many on the Left have long overlooked a fundamental truth: the real battle against gangster capitalism and its updated fascist forms is not fought only in parliaments, markets, or on billboards, it is fought in culture. The struggle for democracy begins with the struggle over meaning. The Left's failure to recognize culture as a primary terrain of power has left it vulnerable to right-wing forces that understand how deeply the emotional, symbolic, and pedagogical dimensions of culture shape political life.

Historically, some strands of Marxist and progressive thought have dismissed culture as secondary or irrelevant, a critique that scholar Judith Butler powerfully challenged in their 1997 essay, arguing that the Left's cultural focus was wrongly seen as abandoning the materialist core of Marxist politics, often accused of being "factionalizing, identitarian, and [narrowly] particularistic."[25]

Such dismissals fail to grasp that culture is the connective tissue of power. Downplaying the role of culture is not just a tactical misstep, it is a profound theoretical error. As Antonio Gramsci warned, all politics is pedagogical, and every exercise of "hegemony" is an education. Culture is not a byproduct of politics but its precondition. In a capitalist society, the power of education does more than repress critical thought; it recruits. It creates subjects, molds emotions, and defines what people accept as natural, desirable, and possible.

As Theodor Adorno argued, capitalism is not merely an economic system but a totalizing cultural force that shapes desire through what he called the "culture industry." It reduces human experience to commodified clichés, numbing imagination through endless repetition and distraction.[26] Adorno warned that the greatest threat to democracy lay not only in the state but in the cultural machinery of film, radio, and television, which "operates in dictatorial fashion even when no dictatorship is in place." As Alex Ross notes, Adorno insisted that this apparatus "enforces conformity, quiets dissent, and mutes thought."[27]

For the Frankfurt School, the power of capitalist domination resided as much in ideology as in economics, in what C. Wright Mills later called "the cultural apparatus."[28] Raymond Williams expanded this insight, arguing that culture is both ordinary and political, embedded in the everyday practices through which people live and make meaning.[29] Like Václav Havel, he believed that the political does not precede the cultural, it follows it. Culture provides the grammar through which politics becomes intelligible.[30]

In this view, politics follows culture because culture is the terrain on which power is made visible, identities are forged, and the boundaries of loyalty are drawn. Stuart Hall deepened this understanding, showing how culture is the site where ideology takes root and where identities are formed, contested, and secured.[31] As Bruce Robbins observes, Hall recognized that everyday life could not be separated from politics as a matter of lived experience, and that culture could not be removed from "the political and economic structures that constrained it."[32] This insight is especially evident in Hall's critique of neoliberalism, which he framed not merely as an economic system but as a comprehensive pedagogical project, a way of teaching people how to live, think, and feel under capitalism.[33] For Hall, capitalism is not imposed solely from above; it is lived, felt, and reproduced from below, woven into the intimate structures of daily life. Its most insidious triumph lies in convincing people that there is no alternative. Culture in this sense is a battlefield—a space through which today fascism is normalized through tools such s aesthetics, media, and artificial intelligence. It is a pedagogical regime that teaches people how to relate to themselves, others, and the wider society.

Here Hall lays bare neoliberalism's most insidious violence: it does not merely govern economies, it colonizes the very terrain of subjectivity, turning the market into the ultimate arbiter of human worth. In this hollowed moral universe, the language of empathy withers, replaced by the cold grammar of calculation; community dissolves into competition, and citizenship is emptied of civic responsibility, reduced to the narrow rituals of consumer choice. What emerges is a cultural machinery that glorifies ruthless individualism, casts solidarity as weakness, and erases the historical memory necessary for critical judgment and collective action.

Under the Trump regime, this assault intensifies as culture itself becomes a primary site of domination. It is here that knowledge is manufactured or silenced, that moral meanings are weaponized, that imagination is disciplined and fear normalized. History is not simply forgotten but actively censored, rewritten to serve the demands of power, while identities are engineered within a politics of exclusion, disposability, and spectacle. In such a landscape, culture no longer nurtures the conditions for democratic life, it becomes an instrument for its undoing, a pedagogy of domination that teaches people not how to think, but how to submit.

Thomas Piketty expands Hall's insight in Capital and Ideology, showing how capitalism perpetuates inequality by fabricating the very narratives that justify it.[34] Piketty offers a comprehensive examination of the historical dynamics that shape inequality, highlighting how entrenched capitalist systems not only perpetuate vast disparities of wealth but also fabricate ideological structures that justify them. His analysis reveals that economic exploitation endures because it is naturalized through education, culture, and law, each shaping how inequality is rationalized as merit, destiny, or divine order. Piketty's contribution underscores that ideology is not an afterthought to wealth, it is its architecture. Piketty's contribution enriches Hall's insights by showing that capitalism's grip on both the material and ideological spheres is not an economic inevitability but a political project that can, and must, be contested. For Piketty, capitalism is a pedagogical regime that functions through a set of unspoken values that are deeply anti-democratic and central to a politics of cultural engineering that suppresses critical thought, memory, and imagining alternative futures.

One of the more astute recent commentators on the role of culture in the rise of the far-right and fascism is Richard Seymour, whose perspective intersects with Hall's.[35] Both thinkers recognize neoliberalism as a cultural and pedagogical force as much as it is an economic structure. While Hall emphasizes how capitalism permeates the most intimate spheres of life, reshaping identities and relationships, Seymour delves into the psychological and cultural consequences of neoliberalism's dominance. Seymour highlights how dismantled solidarity and weaponized individualism produce a society marked by alienation and disintegration.

Seymour underscores the pivotal role of culture in fueling the far-right's rise and deepening political violence. Drawing from Gramsci, he explores how culture and circumstance, rather than just economic interests, shape social attitudes. He argues that neoliberalism has not only made competition the governing logic of society but incubated a "paranoid system" where the absence of collective solidarity breeds resentment, envy, and rage. In such an environment, the far-right finds fertile ground, exploiting isolation and anxiety. Individuals, stripped of belonging, are pushed into a vicious cycle of competition and distrust.

As Daniel Trilling notes, this is a world where public goods are derided, solidarity is treated as weakness, and welfare recipients are regarded as "freeloaders."[36] It is a recipe for anxiety, rage, and despair, the emotional bedrock upon which the far-right thrives. Seymour's analysis makes clear that neoliberalism is not sustained by prosperity but by pedagogy: it teaches people to see others as threats, to confuse cruelty with strength, and to find identity in resentment.

This is why the struggle against capitalism cannot be reduced to the redistribution of wealth, it must be a struggle over meaning, subjectivity, and everyday life. Both Hall and Seymour remind us that capitalism is lived as culture before it is endured as economy. The battle for democracy, then, is not waged only in legislatures or markets but in classrooms, media, and the micro-politics of emotion and perception.

Culture is where capitalism hides, and where it can be exposed.

Confronting the Dominant Culture of Violence

We are, in this Trumpian historical moment, suffocating under a dominant culture that functions as a powerful disimagination machine, shaping desires, identities, and common sense through a vast network of pedagogical sites, from social media and news platforms to advertising, entertainment, and the relentless spectacle of politics. This is a culture that does not merely distract, it depoliticizes, teaching people to mistake cruelty for strength and ignorance for freedom.

Education is no longer confined to schools; it has become the decisive cultural arena where consciousness is produced and contested. Stuart Hall understood this with prophetic clarity. For him, culture is never outside politics, it is its terrain, especially in the politics of identification. Culture teaches people how to locate themselves in the world, who to love, and who to hate.

Later in his life, Hall warned that the Left had failed to grasp the educative dimension of politics, the need to transform not only policies but the very frameworks through which people interpret reality and their place within it. In a 2012 interview with *The Guardian*'s Zoe Williams, Hall put it bluntly: "The Left is in trouble. It's not got any ideas, it's not got any independent analysis of its own, and therefore it's got no vision. It just takes the temperature: 'Whoa, that's no good, let's move to the right.' It has no sense of politics being educative, of politics changing the way people see things."[37]

For Hall, without this pedagogical imperative, the Left forfeits its ability to generate hope, build alliances, and forge new political subjectivities. Politics without pedagogy becomes management without vision. In the shadow of rising state terrorism, bodies are broken, abducted, and freedoms extinguished. Silence spreads like a fog, blanketing the cries of the young, the starving children of Gaza, their lives obliterated by bombs and buried by indifference. Entire families are erased while the world looks away.[38] The horror knows no borders, mirrored at home as immigrant youth in the United States are torn from their families and thrust into a trauma so vast it swallows the future.[39]

Meanwhile, as Peter Baker notes in *The New York Times*, the demagogue-in-chief revels in gifts from dictators, ranging from a luxury flying palace from Qatar to collecting "$320 million in fees from a new cryptocurrency" and shamelessly brokering "overseas real estate deals worth billions of dollars."[40] Trump displays his corruption not as shame but as spectacle, normalizing greed and impunity. Corruption has become a performance art, a ritual of domination enacted for public consumption. What clearer evidence of corruption exists than his "opening an exclusive club in Washington called the Executive Branch [while] charging $500,000 apiece to join,"[41] all the while presiding over a regime that slashes "funding for health care, food and education through some of the largest cuts in US history, while even raising taxes on many low-income families"?[42]

This is a Trump-engineered ethos of ruthlessness, ramped up to grotesque extremes, which amount to a form of state terrorism. Beneath the surface, the agenda is clear: Trump's budget, which he calls "one big, beautiful bill" is a deliberate weapon of mass inequality, crafting windfalls for the financial elite while punishing the most vulnerable. Every dollar cut from health care, housing, or education is an investment in despair. In addition, it also has the "potential to increase the federal deficit by up to $3.8 trillion over the next decade."[43]

This monstrous budget, conceived in the fevered imagination of Trump and his MAGA enablers, stands as a testament to unrestrained cruelty and moral rot. It is a blueprint for a nation stripped of compassion and reason, where wealth cascades upward to the obscenely rich while the machinery of state violence expands in the name of order, punishment, and control. Every line-item reeks of contempt for the vulnerable and exclaims a devotion to power. This is an economy of domination masquerading as governance, built on the wreckage of justice and the withering of the social good.

Fascism today is not only wrapped in lawless decrees and armed repression; it is also cloaked in the seductive language of cruelty, its eugenic fantasies and its terminal exclusions. Elon Musk and Steve Bannon raise Nazi salutes as if rehearsing for the dark future they crave, while Stephen Miller channels Hitler's rhetoric under the guise of patriotism, invoking the myth of "real Americans" untainted by alien blood. Trump resurrects the ghosts of the Confederacy, embracing its monuments, flags, and genocidal logic as sacred relics of white redemption. Trump does more than rehabilitate the leaders of the Confederacy, he regards their rebellion as heroic.[44]

In their hands, fascism is not hidden, it is performed, televised, monetized, and normalized. What we are witnessing is the death of democracy and the withering of civic conscience.[45] A collective numbness has set in, a culture of forgetting and cruelty where silence becomes complicity and indifference replaces outrage and apathy triumphs over care. In such a moral desert, empathy is subversive and memory becomes a form of resistance.

This culture is nourished by a virulent anti-intellectualism, a civic illiteracy that reduces thought to opinion and knowledge to noise. It thrives on the instantaneity of social media, a culture of immediacy that banishes reflection and turns critical thought into a shameful act. Institutions once devoted to reflection and dissent such as universities, public media, libraries, are now branded as breeding grounds of treachery rather than guardians of democracy.

We are not only facing the death of imagination, but an assault on any institution that sustains what Hannah Arendt once called "thinking without a banister."[46] At the heart of this decay lies a cultural ethos cultivated by capitalism for decades: to live is to consume, selfishness is freedom, personal responsibility eclipses the social, and solidarity is weakness. Culture has become both the weapon and the wound, the arena where domination and desire entwine.

Today, culture is a battlefield amplified by digital technologies and the spectacle of everyday cruelty. These platforms do not merely reflect domination, they magnify it, shaping the contours of public consciousness. As social atomization deepens, we are left with what Jonathan Crary calls "vacant forms of attentiveness," a distracted public severed from history, empathy, and solidarity.[47]

Corporate-controlled media now hold immense pedagogical power, reconfiguring the relationship between knowledge, power, and everyday life. They produce a populace trained to feel intensely but think rarely. The result is a tsunami of distraction that fragments society and renders the public incapable of sustained attention or collective resistance. In this climate, the ideological mobilization of memory, agency, and desire becomes inseparable from the pedagogy of neoliberal power, laying the groundwork for a new authoritarianism.

Essential to this emerging fascism lies a culture where memory is inaccessible, critical thinking is criminalized, and dissent is branded treason. The Trump regime has weaponized terror, abduction, and corruption to destroy the very conditions for democratic agency.

Yet culture is not merely absorbed into domination, it has become the front line of resistance. The Right understands this well, turning schools, universities, and the press into ideological battlegrounds. Trump's attacks on higher education, oppositional media, and dissident politicians reveal his fear of institutions that teach accountability instead of obedience, refusal instead of resignation.[48]

At the same time, the capitulation of major universities, including Brown, Columbia, Cornell, Northwestern, the University of Pennsylvania, and the University of Virginia, reveals a deepening crisis of moral courage at the heart of elite institutions. Columbia's surrender to Trump-era surveillance and its repression of pro-Palestinian voices is not an isolated case but part of a broader pattern of institutional retreat. As Chris Hedges observes, these "capitulations and crackdowns on pro-Palestine activism" have resulted in the suspension, expulsion, and dismissal of students and faculty who dare to protest the genocidal assault on Gaza.[49] What is at stake here is more than academic freedom, it is the transformation of the university from a critical public sphere into an apparatus of compliance, one that polices dissent rather than nurtures it, and in doing so aligns itself with the very forces of authoritarianism it should be challenging.

In this climate of fear, education stands as the last fragile bridge between despair and the possibility of a different future. Critical education is not an accessory to politics but its lifeblood, the force that links hope to justice and turns private discontent into collective resistance. Without an educational project rooted in critical thought, historical memory, and moral courage, the left risks surrendering both its imagination and its capacity to defend democracy itself. Critical education is where resistance is born, where dangerous memories are kept alive, and where the struggle for a real, radical democracy takes shape. To deny the centrality of education is to concede the battle over consciousness, the battleground on which authoritarianism wins before it ever fires a shot.

Building a Culture of Solidarity

Cultural politics has always been a cornerstone of radical thought, from Gramsci and Hall to Robin D. G. Kelley, the Frankfurt School, the Situationists, and the Black Lives Matter movement. In the face of today's resurgent fascisms, that tradition must be rekindled, not as nostalgia, but as necessity. The task before us is to reclaim culture as a force of imagination and solidarity in an age of ecological collapse, digital surveillance, and the creeping normalization of cruelty.

As former Uruguayan President José Mujica argued in *Jacobin*, "Capitalism is not just property relations, it is a set of cultural values that the Left must confront with a culture of solidarity." Mujica insisted that revolution cannot succeed without transforming consciousness, without dismantling the values of greed and accumulation that sustain capitalist domination. He warned that social change cannot be reduced to economic reform alone, because "capitalism is a culture," a way of seeing, feeling, and desiring that must itself be understood, analyzed, and resisted.[50]

Mujica's reflection on the limits of revolutionary strategy underscores the central argument of this chapter: that any genuine transformation must begin in culture, in the struggle over meaning, identity, and belonging. Without a profound shift in cultural consciousness, systemic change remains unattainable. Fascism, as Trump's America shows, cannot be countered by policy alone; it must be met with a moral and cultural revolution rooted in solidarity, empathy, and historical memory.

Mujica's warning is prophetic. "My generation," he reflected, "mistook seizing the means of production for transforming society itself." (We forgot that capitalism endures not merely through coercion but through habit, the everyday rhythms and desires that bind people to domination.) His insight reveals a basic challenge of our current crisis: we cannot defeat fascism without a cultural revolution grounded in community, care, and humility.

If we are to resist the death cult of fascism, if we are to reclaim democracy not as a slogan but as a living ethic, we must begin with culture. Not the commodified culture of spectacle and consumption, but culture in its deepest sense: the shared web of meanings, values, and relationships that make us human. We need a cultural revolution rooted in solidarity, compassion, and limits, a refusal of the arrogance and excess that define capitalist modernity.

To be revolutionary today means more than calling for redistributing wealth; it means redefining what it means to live well, to live with dignity, security, and hope. It requires teaching one another how to resist greed, how to break the narcotic of cruelty, and how to build communities of interdependence rather than domination. Mujica's simple but radical observation, "Poor is the one who needs a lot," becomes a moral compass for a society that confuses excess with freedom.[51]

Culture, as an educational force, does more than mirror society; it challenges dominant ideologies, unsettles hierarchies, and nourishes the moral imagination necessary for collective resistance. But awareness alone is not enough. Consciousness must become praxis. Knowledge must ignite action; critique must move toward transformation. Critical consciousness must be joined with organized movements that confront the machinery of inequality, dispossession, and ecological ruin. Without this fusion of understanding and struggle, culture risks becoming reflection without consequence, critique without courage.

The challenge before the Left, then, is to build an anti-capitalist culture that merges literacy, historical consciousness, and visionary imagination. We must name and resist the long legacy of colonialism and its fantasies of extermination and displacement, the very fantasies Trump revives in his grotesque embrace of Israel's genocidal assault on Gaza, the ethnic cleansing of Palestinians from their indigenous lands, and his imperial dreams of annexing territories like Canada, Panama, and Greenland.[52]

Trump's neocolonial dream is cultural imperialism draped in empire, a death wish disguised as destiny. His delirious vision of conquest and "civilization" exposes the rigor mortis of a moral order rotted by greed and domination. Intoxicated with power, his worldview fuses capitalism's drive for accumulation with fascism's lust for purity and control. This is cultural politics in the service of death, where domination parades as destiny and destruction masquerades as renewal.

There is no future without a cultural shift away from gangster capitalism and toward collective renewal. Without it, the Left risks becoming a ghost of itself, mouthing slogans while the planet burns. The horrors of the past are back, but so too can be our memory, imagination, and courage to begin again.

We must resist not as mourners but as creators of a new radical democratic culture, one that remembers the children, listens to the silences, and refuses to let the future be stolen. Resistance, in this sense, is not simply opposition; it is creation, the remaking of life itself against the machinery of death.

The fight against fascism demands a new language, one that bridges material and cultural struggles, linking pedagogy to liberation and culture to justice. As Judith Butler reminds us, any meaningful resistance must address not only the "passions authoritarianism exploits" but also the fears it produces, the fear of migrants, of Palestinians, of gender, of the Other itself.[53] She asks, "Who is this 'migrant' so dangerous they must be deported, this 'Palestinian' whose death secures the social order, this notion of 'gender' that so threatens family and society?"[54]

Butler's vision rejects all rights-stripping and eliminationist politics, insisting that once a single vulnerable group is deemed disposable, fascist logic has already triumphed. Her call for a world built on equality and interdependence may appear naive, yet it is the only foundation upon which democracy can be reborn.

Pedagogy, then, is not peripheral to this struggle, it is the struggle. Education, culture, and everyday life form the triad where fascism is normalized or resisted. This is where consciousness is shaped, and where radical hope begins. As the late political philosopher Sheldon Wolin warned, "The central challenge of our time is nurturing a discordant democracy," one that depends on awakening "the civic consciousness of the nation."[55] That awakening begins in culture, where critique becomes conscience, and imagination becomes resistance.

8

The Spectacle of Terror: Living in the Warfare State

The Trump administration's race toward fascism is unfolding at breakneck speed and on multiple fronts.[1] At the heart of this transformation lies the emergence of the United States as a warfare state that reunites the interests of the military–industrial–academic complex with the toxic ideologies of white nationalism and white supremacy.[2] What makes this moment especially dangerous is that warfare no longer refers solely to foreign conquest; it has become a central organizing principle of governance at home. The state itself has been weaponized, turning inward against its own population, normalizing domestic terrorism as a tool of rule. The state no longer merely governs, it terrorizes.

The scourge of militarization, rooted in the terror apparatus constructed by Bush and Cheney after 9/11, has intensified into a defining feature of both domestic and foreign policy.[3] The long legacy of armed intervention abroad by the US now appears on the streets of Chicago, Washington, DC as well as in universities, courthouses, and even sports fields. As Melissa Gira Grant notes, "federal agents are the new proud boys."[4] Perpetual war has become the new language of politics, its violence now waged against Americans, legitimated as a normal condition of politics. This militarized politics finds its most insidious expression in the policing of everyday life, where the apparatus of war turns inward against the vulnerable, producing new forms of domestic terror and civic dispossession.

The Systemic Assault on Democracy

This is a full-spectrum assault on democracy. Every act of ruthlessness, every racist law, every violent metaphor chips away at the social contract. A culture of authoritarianism is now used to demean those considered other, both citizens and non-citizens, critics and immigrants, naturalized citizens and those seeking such status. They are labeled as unworthy of citizenship, now defined by the Trump regime as a privilege rather than a right. A media ecosystem built on clickbait has normalized moral anesthesia and turned brutality and oppression into public spectacle.

In this fog, language itself is emptied of meaning. Truth and falsehood blur. As Freire warned, the tools of the oppressor are often adopted by the oppressed.[5] For instance, people adopt the language of hate, market values, a regressive anti-intellectualism, loathing of unions, a virulent misogyny and a distrust of the welfare state. We now see that the logic of fascism has seeped into the culture, eroding civic sensibility, destroying moral imagination, and rendering resistance almost unspeakable.

The Normalization of Tyranny

Trump's authoritarian fantasies do not alienate his base, they galvanize it. What was once unthinkable is now policy. What was once fringe has become mainstream. Savagery is not something to be deplored and avoided at all costs; it is a central feature of power, wielded with theatrical and spectacularized brutality. Under the current acting ICE Director, Todd Lyons, this punitive logic has intensified: Lyons oversees a $4.4 billion Enforcement and Removal Operations apparatus staffed by over 8,600 agents across 200 domestic locations,[6] using militarized tactics, surprise raids, and aggressive targeting of immigrant communities to sustain a regime of fear. ICE's presence is at the heart of Trump's hyper-police state, and its funding has been greatly expanded under Trump's new budget bill, creating what journalist Will Bunch calls Trump's "own gulag archipelago of detention camps across a United States that's becoming increasingly hard to recognize."[7]

Meanwhile, figures like Tom Homan, who led ICE under Trump's first term, laid the groundwork with Gestapo-style operations, midnight raids, family separations, and public declarations that undocumented immigrants "should be afraid."[8] As the "border tzar" under Trump, Homan has initiated deportation policies that are even more aggressively violent and cruel than those that took place in Trump's first term as president. As Bunch notes, take the case of "the 64-year-old New Orleans woman, Donna Kashanian, who fled a tumultuous Iran 47 years ago, volunteered to rebuild her battered Louisiana community after Hurricane Katrina, never missed a check-in with U.S. immigration officials, and was snatched by ICE agents in unmarked vehicles while she was out working in her garden and sent to a notorious detention center."[9] These Gestapo-like abductions have seized children on their way to school, at sports events, even while entering immigration offices with their parents, transforming everyday acts into haunting echoes of authoritarian terror. These horror stories now take place daily in cities extending from Los Angeles to Providence, Rhode Island.

Far-right white nationalists such as Stephen Miller, Tom Homan, and Todd Lyons do not treat cruelty as a regrettable side effect; for them, cruelty is the currency of power. Suffering becomes a spectacle, and violence a ritual of statecraft. Tyranny is not inching forward in silence; it is advancing at full speed, cheered on by those who treat fear as a governing principle and pain as public policy. At stake here is the practice of fascist dehumanization and exploitation. More specifically, as historian Timothy Snyder observes, Trump has laid the groundwork for a sprawling network of punitive detention sites across the United States, "which could easily turn into concentration camps producing slave labor."[10]

What is happening in the United States is not a passing storm. It is the death throes of a system that has long glorified violence, commodified everything, and fed on division. Trump's language is not a performance; it is preparation. His words build the scaffolding of a society stripped of empathy, justice, and democracy. This convergence of militarized policing, bureaucratic viciousness, and white nationalist ideology crystallizes in a new formation of state terror directed inward.

This is domestic terrorism, the transformation of inflammatory, fear-mongering, and dehumanizing rhetoric into acts of state violence. It is a form of necropolitics tied to the rise of a corpse-like order, creating what Achille Mbembe calls "death worlds," zones of existence where populations are stripped of vitality and reduced to the status of the living dead.[11] Trump's regime of domestic terrorism, especially his war on immigrants and naturalized citizens is driven by a death married to the dictates of capital accumulation, racial hierarchy, and the open embrace of white supremacist symbols. Under Trump's authoritarian capitalism and politics of vengeance, there is no room for anyone in the US except for white supremacists and supine loyalists.

There is no pretense of democracy here, only the workings of gangster capitalism masquerading as the future. When a government deploys violence and coercion to intimidate its own population, driven by nativism, racism and political extremism, it meets the definition of domestic terrorism. Its policies and language are designed to cultivate fear, intimidate, and amass power in the hands of the wealthy. Dehumanizing speech does not merely insult; it punishes and prepares the ground for detention centers, expulsions, and the culture of hate that turns citizens against one another. Words like "invaders" and "criminals" are weaponized against immigrants to mark them as objects of fear. Policies of family separation, mass deportation, and indefinite detention are constructed not only to punish but to terrorize. Confronted with this dehumanizing rhetoric and violence-soaked policies, Trump, chillingly and without irony, declares, "A lot of people are saying maybe we'd like a dictator."[12]

Trump's authoritarian obsession with violence and punishment is evident in his relentless drive to criminalize dissent and weaponize the state against what he calls "enemies of the people."[13] He has demanded draconian penalties, including prison time, for those who burn the American flag, an act of protest protected under the constitution. Stephen Prager argues in *Common Dreams* that Trump has issued an executive order that puts in place portals and legal mechanisms that may permit "'random fascist vigilantes' to help him crack down on protests across the country, according to one prominent civil rights lawyer."[14] In addition, he has called for the reinstatement of the death penalty for murder cases in the nation's capital, deploying the ultimate form of state violence as both spectacle and warning.[15] These are not isolated authoritarian postures but acts of domestic terrorism, where punishment, repression, and vengeance merge into a single political aesthetic of fear.

Trump's spectacularization of war and violence could not be clearer than in his executive order renaming the Department of Defense the Department of War, a gesture of authoritarian rebranding meant to signal brute strength and scorn for restraint. *The New York Times* notes this as part of his effort to project dominance while rejecting what he and Defense Secretary Pete Hegseth deride as "wokeness," a term they claim undermined the military's morale under former President Biden. In doing so, Trump invokes America's past wars not to reflect on their costs but to lament that they "have not been celebrated enough."[16]

Hegseth embodies the most grotesque expressions of Trump's delusional masculinity, a swaggering cult of dominance, racism, and misogyny masquerading as patriotism. He derides top military leaders for having beards or being out of shape, echoing fascism's obsession with the "perfect male body" as a symbol of moral virtue. In *The War on Warriors*, he advances a primitive creed that physical toughness, push-ups, and brute endurance win wars, reducing military excellence to the level of a gym contest. He ridicules Black soldiers as pampered and weak, unworthy of what he calls "warrior culture," and condemns diversity in the ranks as a symptom of "woke decay." His claim, cited in Fintan O'Toole that "a Black or female soldier who gets promoted primarily because of the color of their skin or the genitalia between their legs, gets people killed" could have been written by a member of the Ku Klux Klan.[17] Hegseth's world is one where whiteness defines worth, American men had pure blood, heartlessness defines courage, and violence masquerades as virtue, a fascist fantasy dressed up as moral renewal.

Hegseth speaks as if he were a relic of the Crusades resurrected for the present. He does not merely endorse war, he sanctifies it. In his rhetoric, military aggression against Iran is elevated to a divine mandate, a form of holy violence cloaked in theological certainty. As Julia Carrie Wong observes in *The Guardian*, he repeatedly invokes "God's almighty providence," insisting with unwavering conviction that God stands on the side of American military power.[18]

This is not casual language. It is the vocabulary of absolutism, where doubt is banished and violence becomes righteous. His dehumanization of

Iranians as "barbaric savages," coupled with calls for Americans to pray for victory "in the name of Jesus Christ," reveals a worldview in which war is stripped of moral ambiguity and defined as a sacred duty. Hegseth emerges as an ideological extremist, a fervent religious zealot who cloaks violence in the language of divine purpose. His rhetoric drifts into a kind of death-haunted religiosity, where war is not merely justified but sanctified. As Frank Bruni observes, he has made clear that "every missile the United States fires, every bomb it drops, every Iranian it kills, is for Jesus."[19]

In this framing, religion does not restrain brutality or call it to account; it consecrates it, transforming instruments of destruction into expressions of holy will.

Hegseth is not an anomaly. He is symptomatic. He embodies a broader historical convergence in which economic greed, political authoritarianism, religious fundamentalism, and militaristic fervor fuse into a single ideological formation. In that fusion, democracy gives way to dogma, critical thought yields to blind allegiance, and violence is no longer an instrument of last resort but a celebrated expression of national and divine destiny. This is the cultural logic through which fascist social orders take root, not at the margins, but at the very center of power. In Trump's political theater, spectacle and militarized religious fanaticism collapse into one, producing a culture in which violence is aestheticized for public consumption and legitimated as a sacred duty. Trump's fixation on force and impunity reveals an addiction to a culture of war and fear, an intoxicating fusion of political theater, state propaganda, and spectacle. Endlessly circulated through government-produced videos, this machinery of representation transforms violence into civic ritual and reprehensible theatrics: ICE pepper spraying protesters, parading immigrants in shackles as they about to be deported,[20] and DHS social media posts showing "primarily Black and Brown people in posts celebrating ICE agents' arrests and detention."[21] It is important to connect Trump's use of ICE to impart fear to Americans as part of a similar project in which he has told the military that their loyalty is to him rather than to the constitution and that the payoff for them is "what fascist leaders have always offered their followers: a peculiar amalgam of the thrill of transgression and the submissive surrender to absolute obedience."[22]

What we are witnessing in the United States is not simply the corrosion of democratic norms but the rise of an aggressive fascist politics that weaponizes the threat of punishment to enforce Trump's whims and vanities. As Ruth Ben-Ghiat warns, Trump aims to bend the nation's war-making apparatus to his own will, refashioning the military into a blunt instrument of personal authority.[23] He openly boasts of deploying armed troops into Democratic-run cities he despises, treating the armed forces not as a public institution but as his private enforcers. Journalist and historian Garrett Graff captures the gravity of this authoritarian turn, noting that "America has finally tipped over into fascism."[24] While Graff does not explicitly invoke the term *domestic terrorism*, his depiction leaves little doubt that a politics of state terror has taken root under Trump's regime. He writes:

> America has become a country where armed officers of the state shout "Papers please!" on the street at men and women heading home from work, a vision we associate with the Gestapo in Nazi Germany or the KGB in Soviet Russia, and where masked men wrestle to the ground and abduct people without due process into unmarked vehicles, disappearing them into an opaque system where their family members beg for information.

It is crucial to recognize that Trump's assault on federal agencies, long regarded as apolitical, as well as on institutions devoted to the public good, is central to his project of consolidating power in his own hands. Every attack is a step toward dismantling the very notion of governance in the public interest, replacing it with loyalty to a single man. His decision to deploy more than 2,000 troops in Washington, DC was not merely an act of security but a theatrical display of authoritarian might. Meanwhile, his personal army of ICE agents, thugs empowered to abduct people from shopping centers, workplaces, and city streets, has grown into one of the largest law enforcement institutions in the United States, used primarily as a domestic militia serving not the public but the president. What binds together these diverse expressions of authoritarian policy is the relentless drive to concentrate power in the presidency, hollowing out every check, every safeguard, every institution that might stand in the way. As Jonathan Freedland reminds us, "Control is the goal, amassing power in the hands of the president and removing or neutering any institution or person that could stand in his way. That is the guiding logic that explains Trump's every action, large and small, including his wars on the media, the courts, the universities and the civil servants of the federal government."[25]

Anti-Communism Fanaticism and the Ghost of Roy Cohn

It is precisely out of this obsession with control, punishment, militarism, and terror that Trump revives another of fascism's oldest weapons: the anti-communist smear. It has been recycled as a script of fear that once destroyed lives and now returns as a rallying cry for authoritarian rule. Underlying this politics of fear, dissenters are denounced, and branded as traitors. In the McCarthy era it was used to silence dissent, dismantle unions, and destroy lives, think especially of "the Hollywood Ten."[26] Trump's version resurrects this tradition, fusing Cold War hysteria with digital-age malice.

Under Trump, anti-communist slurs are wielded not as arguments but as weapons; these are labels designed to mark whole movements, cities, and communities as enemies of the state. This tactic transparently brands critics as subversives, and seeks to transform disagreement into treason, dissent into danger. An alarming illustration came during a rant by white nationalist Stephen Miller. Speaking at Washington, DC's Union Station on August 20, 2025, alongside Vice President J. D. Vance and Defense Secretary Pete Hegseth, Miller answered protesters shouting at the infamous trio by declaring:

> They're the ones who have been advocating for the one percent. They're criminals, killers, rapists, and drug dealers. And I'm glad they're here today because me, Pete, and the vice president [are] going to leave here and inspired by them, we're going to add thousands more resources to this city to get the criminals and the gang members out. We're going to disable those networks, and we're going to prove that the city can serve law-abiding citizens. We are not going to let the Communists destroy a great American city, let alone the nation's capital ... So, we're going to ignore these stupid white hippies, who all need to go home and take a nap because they're all over 90 years old, and get back to protecting the American people and the citizens of Washington, DC.[27]

Here the word "Communists" does not name an ideology, it operates as an epithet, a scarlet letter of treason designed to criminalize protest and erase dissent itself. As Thom Hartmann reminds us, fascism rarely arrives with tanks rolling down the avenues; it seeps into everyday life through language that glorifies violence, legitimizes brutality, and sanctifies authoritarian power.[28] By branding critics as "Communists" and ridiculing protesters as "criminals" and "stupid hippies," Miller exposes how hate-saturated speech fuses with state repression to cultivate a culture where violence appears natural and even necessary.[29]

Miller surely knows the lineage he invokes. Anti-communist rhetoric, once the preferred tool of Senator Joe McCarthy and Richard Nixon, functioned as a weapon to justify brutality against so-called "domestic enemies." It crushed labor movements, silenced civil rights activists, and produced the atmosphere of fear that defined Cold War America. The irony is unmistakable: Miller resurrects the anti-communist hysteria of Roy Cohn, Trump's mentor and enabler during the darkest days of McCarthyism, channeling a script of fear and denunciation that once destroyed lives and now returns as a blueprint for authoritarian rule.

History leaves little doubt that the anti-communist vocabulary revived by Trump, MAGA, and their sycophants is not rhetorical excess but a deliberate strategy; that is, a time-tested script for silencing opposition and legitimating state violence. It is the ideological scaffolding of fascism updated for the twenty-first century: a politics of accusation that trades in fear, racial panic, and moral cleansing, all in the service of unchecked power.

Stephen Miller and the Making of the Fascist Subject

Stephen Miller, Trump's White House Deputy Chief of Staff, is a well-documented white nationalist and one of the most influential architects behind Trump's racist policies.[30] He has long aligned himself with extremist media ecosystems and the dark networks of xenophobia that define Trump's base. His outspoken opposition to DACA and his calls to end Temporary Protected Status for predominantly nonwhite populations further expose his deeply entrenched racism. His attacks on international students, higher education, and immigrants reveal a politics of vengeance that wields the power of the state against anyone who defies his vision of white Christian citizenship. His bigotry is so notorious that even his own family members have publicly denounced him.[31]

A central player in this regime of state terrorism, systemic racism, mass arrests, deportations, and the criminalization of dissent, Miller has been behind Trump's most repressive policies. During Trump's first term, he authored the Muslim ban, the family separation policy, and "routinely collaborated with anti-immigration hate groups like the Federation for American Immigration Reform (FAIR) and the Center for Immigration Studies (CIS)," both of which have deep ties to white nationalist ideologies, and a eugenicist worldview.[32] In Trump's second term, Miller has become even more extreme, pushing for mass deportations, the abolition of birthright citizenship, and the revocation of naturalized citizenship for those who fall outside his white supremacist definition of "the American."[33]

Infamous for his rabid attacks on immigrants, Miller has long been the ideological architect of Trump's fascism.[34] Miller's toxic nationalism, rooted in white supremacy and a seething contempt for anyone who defies his vision of an "America only for (white) Americans," has become both a blueprint and a permission slip for a new generation of far-right zealots. His rhetoric offers moral cover and ideological legitimacy to the emerging MAGA youth who turn his dogma into open fascism. Unsurprisingly, he has publicly endorsed Trump's dictatorial ambitions, declaring "that only one party should be allowed to exercise power in the US."[35] His grotesque claim that "The Democrat party is not a political party; it is a domestic extremist organization" reveals his fascist politics.[36]

Miller's racism and nativism fuel three central pillars of his authoritarian project. First, he insists that all immigrants are criminals, figures to be expelled or incarcerated. Second, he treats immigration enforcement as the foundation for a militarized police state, one that erodes justice, truth, and civic freedom. Third, he has become one of the leading architects of the war on public and higher education, branding them cancerous, communist, woke culture that is "destroying the country."[37] This language, echoing Trump's lexicon, is code for dismantling the critical, inclusive, and democratic possibilities of education: the chance for diverse students to learn, to question, and to act as informed agents of a democratic society.

For Miller, schools are not places to cultivate civic imagination but arenas for indoctrination, where children must be trained to love America uncritically and to fear "communist ideology." The details of this pedagogical crusade are chillingly familiar: banning books, whitewashing history into a racist mythology, abolishing critical pedagogy, and hollowing out the capacity for informed, critical and ethical thinking. What emerges is a pedagogy of repression, one that seeks to erase historical memory, extinguish democratic values, and turn education into a factory of indoctrination.

Miller's ranting speech on "Children will be taught to love America" could have been lifted whole from the fascist culture of the 1930s. It seethes with ideological fanaticism, dehumanizing rage, ecstatic ignorance, and paranoic rigidity, laced together by a torrent of lies and moral corruption. The feverish spirit of myth and hate that drives it is not merely reminiscent of fascism; it is its reincarnation. What we are witnessing is not political rhetoric but the language of purification, abduction, disappearance, and contempt that once paved the road to the Nazi state, reborn for the digital age.

What makes Miller's tirade so terrifying is not only its embrace of political purity on steroids, but its virulent hatred of education itself, of thought, reflection, and moral agency. He despises any institution or idea capable of producing critical consciousness, civic courage, or compassion grounded in responsibility for others. His words drip with fear, fear of knowledge, fear of imagination, fear of democracy itself. He is the unholy fusion of George Wallace's racial fury and Joseph Goebbels's propaganda zeal, a figure in whom fanaticism and hatred converge, resurrecting the ghost of white supremacy in its purest, most vindictive form.

This is barbarism made flesh, a grotesque performance of malice masquerading as conviction, ignorance weaponized into ideology. What should alarm us most is how this rhetoric, once unthinkable, now circulates openly, validated and amplified at the highest levels of power. In such a poisoned atmosphere, silence is no longer neutral; it becomes complicity. The corrosion of democratic culture does not come through sudden coups but through the slow normalization of mercilessness, the hollowing out of truth, and the death of conscience disguised as patriotism. The terror Miller embodies is not confined to one man or one ideology; it has become the grammar of a political movement, the updated language of American fascism. He is the living symptom of a society where cruelty has become conviction, and domination masquerades as destiny. In Miller, we see Orwell's prophecy made flesh, "If you want a picture of the future, imagine a boot stamping on a human face, forever." That image is no longer metaphor; it is the script of our time, rehearsed daily in policies of exclusion, violence, and erasure.

The Rise of the Punishing State and the Attack on Citizenship

What begins in language soon hardens into policy, as words of hatred find their echo in the architecture of the state. This is not an isolated campaign. The broader discourse of racism, white nationalism, and state repression is now flaunted by Trump and his cadre of shock troops across mainstream media, not with shame but with fanatical glee, and rarely interrogated as the lifeblood of fascist ideology. It is this aura of legitimacy, this normalization of repression, which gives state violence its sheen of inevitability.

One stark example makes this clear. Christopher Rufo, one of the most influential propagandists of the MAGA movement, recently declared in a Substack post that agencies like ICE should "dispatch unmarked vans to follow key agitators and snatch them from the streets while the media are not looking."[38] Here, the essence of fascism is revealed, not through grand decrees but through cold bureaucratic maneuvers. Trump and his allies understand that forced disappearances and masked federal agents operating without identification or accountability are no accidents. They are the signature practices of authoritarian rule. Trump's domestic terrorism and war on immigrants are not only masks for creating a police state, they are also profit engines for private prison companies that thrive on the regime's feverish attempts to incarcerate thousands of immigrants, dissenters, and anyone opposed to his dictatorial ambitions.[39]

The erosion of due process, equal justice, and the very meaning of citizenship marks the most devastating frontier of the new warfare state. As John Ganz argues, the essence of Trump's authoritarian movement lies in its assault on the very concept of American citizenship, stretching from birtherism and the "stolen election" lie to efforts to revoke birthright citizenship and expand denaturalization.[40] In Trump's world, citizenship no longer exists as an inalienable right; it is stripped of its universality and altered as a privilege. In his hands, it becomes both gift and cudgel, "a transferable and revocable commodity," wielded to divide, discipline, and destroy.[41]

This is the state's cold choreography of fear, where terror, abduction, and disappearance form the grammar of governance and the language through which power speaks. Citizenship becomes a weapon of control used to deport, to banish, to resurrect the ancient horror of statelessness, expelling individuals not only from the nation but from humanity itself. Ganz is right: Trump's assault on citizenship is not merely reactionary; it bears the unmistakable signature of fascism, the totalitarian logic that decides who counts as human and who may be erased.

This politics of exclusion does not stand alone; it marches in step with a broader militarization of national life, where belonging itself is defined through obedience, violence, and the cult of strength. Trump's attack on citizenship cannot be separated from his project to militarize every facet of American life. As Greg Grandin notes in *The New York Times*, this is "a fight over the meaning of America," revealing both the white racism that drives MAGA nationalism and the regime's claim to decide "who gets to call themselves American in Mr. Trump's America."[42] Grandin adds:

> Mr. Trump and operatives like Mr. Miller are waging a war not only on migrants but also on the concept of citizenship. According to one report, Immigration and Customs Enforcement expelled as many as 66 citizens during Mr. Trump's first term, and now he has issued an executive order ending birthright citizenship. His government is exiling children who were born in the United States, including a 4-year-old boy with late-stage cancer. The Justice Department says it is "prioritizing denaturalization," establishing a framework to revoke citizenship from naturalized citizens the White House deems undesirable.[43]

To dismantle citizenship is to enact a project of racial cleansing, to purge the body politic in the name of racial purity, casting targeted groups outside the boundaries of belonging. In this violent calculus, people are not merely excluded; they are rendered disposable, stripped of memory, voice, and the right to exist. Deportation, detention, and denaturalization are not bureaucratic measures but weapons of political violence. This is domestic terrorism in its purest form, the transformation of incendiary rhetoric into instruments of state violence. Ganz is on target: Trump's attack on citizenship carries the unmistakable signature of fascism, the logic of totalitarianism reborn. The totalitarian machinery of erasure is now turned against the present, transformed into spectacle, a perverse performance made for instant consumption, where meanness and suffering supply the rush that functions as fascism's pleasure quotient.[44]

Rachel Maddow lays bare the full scope of this authoritarian transformation.[45] She argues that the United States has already crossed the threshold into a form of consolidated autocracy, one that turns immigrants into perpetual scapegoats while threatening even its own citizens with the loss of belonging and basic rights. Whole swaths of US territory have been reclassified as military zones, with armed, active-duty troops now exercising arrest powers. Massive detention centers and prison camps are being built on military bases and in cities and towns across the United States. Universities, the press, and courts are militarized, coerced, or dismantled. Spaces once dedicated to justice, knowledge, and care have been turned into instruments of fear. As Mark Peterson points out in *The New Yorker*, spaces, such as court hallways, are now captive as sites of intimidation, fear, and disappearances.[46] The rhetoric of a captive state is no longer metaphor, it is the lived reality of fascism in real time.

The Spectacle as Opiate and Cover

The spectacle operates as both narcotic and pedagogy. By dramatizing state violence as entertainment, through militarized parades, campaign rallies, and sensationalist media coverage, the Trump regime trains the public to view authoritarian repression not as horror, but as theater. The spectacle functions as civic anaesthesia and civic illiteracy; it numbs historical memory, erodes critical thought, and recodes brutality as patriotism.

But the spectacle is more than a culture of distraction, it is camouflage for systemic violence.[47] Behind the pyrotechnics lie black-site detention centers, militarized cities, and surveillance networks that record, monitor, and manipulate daily life. The corporate media, obsessed with immediacy and false balance, has become complicit in this performance. Its saturation coverage of Trump's every provocation transforms authoritarianism into a show, reducing terror to stenographic scribblings by the mainstream media and violence to spectacle. The deeper and more horrible truth is buried: the United States is living under the consolidation of an authoritarian warfare state.

Under Trump, the media's hunger for shock and drama turns repression into mass entertainment, flooding the public sphere with images of conquest, erasure, and savagery, even as executive power tightens its grip. Guy Debord's vision of *The Society of the Spectacle* returns with a vengeance, reborn in the toxic glow of screens, where video games and state-crafted videos fuse violence with entertainment and nationalist myth, and hashtags circulate cruelty as civic pride, aestheticizing domination and normalizing war as both pleasure and policy. What too many commentators dismiss as "Trump's stunts" are not digressions, they are rituals of pedagogy, lessons in domination that whisper: ruthlessness is virtue, repression is order, vengeance is justice, and fear is the price of belonging.

Consider the arming of the National Guard in Washington, DC, staged as patriotic pageantry rather than as a militarization of civic life. The raid on the home of John Bolton, once a close adviser, later a critic, was choreographed as a national morality play in which betrayal is punished publicly. As mentioned previously, Trump's retaliatory campaigns against adversaries like New York Attorney General Letitia James, Adam Schiff, and other so-called "enemies of the state" transform into grotesque spectacles of retribution, political theater driven by an unyielding demand for loyalty. These acts unfold as a public, performative display of power, relentlessly signaling that dissent will not only be silenced but criminalized. The bombing of Iran's nuclear facilities is framed as a display of strength, not reckless escalation, while ICE raids and masked agents abducting immigrants become propagandistic fodder for national security dramas. These scenes, endlessly replayed across media, merge terror with pedagogy, cruelty with consent, both as performance and an unmistakable threat. But beneath this spectacle lies a deeper truth: a wannabe dictator using state power against, not for, the people and the principles of democracy. Today, state violence targets ICE victims, students, protesters, dissidents, and anyone on Trump's retribution list, but in the end, no one will be safe from his fascist regime.

These orchestrated displays go beyond Trump's personal vendettas and national theatrics; they have become the blueprint for a new political aesthetic that turns repression into performance and violence into visual currency. This celebration of barbarism and state violence is not confined to Trump's enemies but extends through slick promotional ventures used by his political allies. Real and AI-generated propaganda transform state terrorism into a spectacularized form of entertainment. As mentioned in Chapter 6, then Secretary of Homeland Security Kristi Noem embodied this violent, sadistic aesthetic, using human suffering for political gain. In one ghastly example, she filmed a promotional video at El Salvador's Terrorism Confinement Center (CECOT), surrounded by shirtless, caged prisoners, flaunting a $50,000 Rolex.[48] This grotesque spectacle was part of a series of what Naomi Klein and Astra Taylor call "sadism-chic photo ops," where Noem appeared atop a horse at the US–Mexico border or wielding a machine gun while arresting immigrants in Arizona.[49]

Through these staged images, Noem crafted a fusion of militarized power and dehumanizing spectacle, turning callousness into a celebrated emblem of authority. Her performance transformed a brutalizing system of abduction and incarceration into an aesthetic of power and punishment, a stage set for political ambition. Noem's spectacle also revealed how authoritarian pageantry circulates transnationally, with El Salvador's prison state becoming a visual template for US politicians eager to display toughness, exporting the grammar of fascist performance across borders.

In this spectacularized culture, politics no longer governs, it performs. It feeds on the aesthetics of malice, transfiguring lawlessness into order and domination into theater. This is what Wilhelm Reich, in *The Mass Psychology of Fascism,* called the libidinal core of fascist power: a perverse economy of desire in which obedience and aggression, submission and pleasure, intertwine. The spectacle of power is not merely meant to terrify; it is meant to gratify. Power is now cojoined with "the libidinal aestheticization of Nazis," marked by an erotic attraction to engineered spectacles characterized by "obedience and surveillance."[50] Fascism's libidinal investments and erotic attractions invite citizens to participate in cruelty, to find emotional release in the punishment of others, to mistake domination for freedom.

Theodor Adorno's analysis of the authoritarian personality takes on renewed force in this context. He understood that fascism cultivates not only obedience but a psychic economy in which subjugation feels like empowerment. The authoritarian subject desires domination even as it destroys them, mistaking the master's whip for the promise of protection. This is the pedagogy of spectacularized obscenity: it teaches citizens to consume cruelty as entertainment, to eroticize domination, to transform complicity into pleasure, and pleasure into loyalty.

What emerges is an authoritarian economy of desire in which cruelty is transformed into theater. Images of militarized parades, mug shots of political enemies, or caged immigrants circulate across media platforms like advertisements for repression, producing both fear and illicit pleasure. The spectacle trains citizens to consume cruelty as entertainment, to eroticize domination, and to accept vengeance as the highest civic virtue. Watching becomes complicity; complicity becomes a source of satisfaction; satisfaction becomes a form of loyalty.

In the Trump era, this fusion of spectacle and terror extends far beyond US borders. Nowhere is this more visible than in Israel's genocidal assault on Gaza, where mass death is broadcast in real time as both propaganda and pedagogy. Entire neighborhoods are leveled under the gaze of drone cameras, while governments and media justify annihilation in the language of "defense." Gaza becomes both laboratory and mirror, an arena of domination where militarized cruelty is perfected and exported as political lesson. What Trump performs domestically, Israel enacts globally: the normalization of annihilation as necessity, the erasure of moral constraint as policy.

Under these conditions, moral witnessing collapses, the burden of conscience on a global level is undermined, solidarity withers, and the public's moral imagination dies a slow death. Cultural and educational institutions, once tasked with sustaining memory, justice, and care, are militarized or gutted. The rise of the military–prison–carceral state becomes not a scandal but a form of entertainment, fusing torture, pornography, and distraction into the dominant language of politics.

The spectacle numbs thought, erases memory, invents false villains, and produces a civic illiteracy that leaves the public disarmed before fear and manipulation. What disappears in this haze is the recognition that the United States is undergoing not a temporary aberration, but the consolidation of a new fascism, one that fuses militarized violence, pedagogical terrorism, and state-sanctioned domestic cruelty to construct a fascist subject fit for the twenty-first century. Fascism today does not need a coup; it thrives in the glare of the camera, in the tweet, the clip, the meme. It teaches through images, commands through emotion, and governs through spectacle. It is a pedagogical regime, an apparatus of cultural engineering that decides who counts as a citizen, whose lives matter, and whose may be discarded.

Domestic Terrorism as a Pedagogical Regime

Under the Trump administration, culture is not simply a mirror of political power; it is the terrain upon which authoritarianism takes root, fashions its subjects, and reproduces itself. Trump's addiction to violence, his expansion of the carceral state, and his glorification of brute force are undeniable. Yet the most enduring battlefield of his domestic terrorism is not the street, it is consciousness itself.[51] Here, citizens are trained to forget, taught to interpret lies as truth, and disciplined into obedience through the machinery of fear and distraction.

This is the essence of pedagogical terror: a project that seeks not only to control bodies but to colonize minds, reducing the imagination to rubble. Through its disimagination machines, the media empires, digital platforms, and culture industries that saturate daily life, the Trump regime has turned cultural engineering into a weapon. It decides what is remembered and what is erased, which histories are celebrated and which are forbidden. The goal is not simply to control politics but to seize the human capacity to think otherwise.

In this war on thought, education becomes the first fatality. The attack on schools, universities, and the arts is not incidental, it is the foundation of fascism's pedagogy. The word "woke," once a call for an awareness of social injustices and a commitment to actively address them, is now transformed into a code to fear and eliminate any instance of racial justice, a term to be denigrated and eliminated.

The Trump administration has long insisted that higher education is overrun with "communist professors" and "woke educators" supposedly turning students toward "useless majors" and producing young people who "hate our country and like to go to riots."[52] Such absurdities are not mere rhetoric; they are weapons. Under this manufactured panic, the administration wields federal funding as a blunt instrument of control, freezing, bargaining, and redirecting millions of dollars to punish universities, discipline dissent, and turn higher education into an ideological battleground. Such assaults are not isolated; they form part of a coherent authoritarian strategy: to weaponize culture and memory in order to manufacture a passive, obedient, and amnesiac citizenry.

Militarizing Society and the Machinery of State Terror

These attacks on education, culture, and critical thought are not simply about dismantling DEI programs or suppressing critical race theory. They are part of a much larger project, the militarization of everyday life, where authoritarian power and pedagogical control merge to reshape both institutions and consciousness. Under Trump, repression operates through a double colonization: one aimed at the body through coercion and surveillance, the other at the mind through propaganda, fear, and enforced ignorance.

ICE terror, secret abductions by masked paramilitary forces, the criminalization of dissent on university campuses, and the surveillance of public spaces all form part of a single machinery of control. At stake is not just the militarization of policing, but the militarization of culture itself. Trump's rhetoric of crime, corruption, and invasion does not describe reality, it manufactures it. The endless repetition of these terms functions as a political ritual, transforming entire populations into imagined enemies.

The language of internal warfare with its repeated rants about Marxists, communists, fascists, and others Trump brands as "sick" and "evil," are not mere demagogic insults but part of a fascist script of alleged internal enemies. Its purpose is not merely to dehumanize; it is to justify violence as virtue. Trump's call to "liberate" Democratic cities from "socialists" is not a metaphor. It is an order of occupation, a declaration of domestic war in which multicultural urban centers are cast as zones of contamination. Federalized National Guard units are deployed, masked ICE agents unleashed, and protesters brutalized, all in the name of restoring order—a euphemism for domestic terrorism.

This is not law enforcement, on the contrary, it is martial law in slow motion. Such language and spectacle mark the return of a familiar terror: Bull Connor's dogs in Birmingham, Alabama, the National Guard's bullets at Kent State, Ohio, Pinochet's tanks in Santiago. The continuity is unmistakable: state violence turned inward to crush dissent, to secure white supremacy, and to replace democracy with rule by fear.

The militarized state feeds private profit. Every raid, detention, and surveillance contract enriches corporations whose business model depends on suffering, aimed largely at immigrants and people of color. The prison-industrial complex, private security firms, surveillance industries, and weapons manufacturers form an unholy trinity linking gangster capitalism to an updated fascist politics. In this fusion, the tools of war abroad become the instruments of governance at home, the warfare state has come home in America.

As Kristi Noem, former Secretary of Homeland Security declared, federal troops must occupy Democratic cities to "liberate them from the socialists."[53] Her rhetoric exposes what Jackson Lears has described as "a regime drunk on exceptionalist fantasies and committed to conquering populations it deems inferior."[54] This is the logic of empire turned inward, a nation devouring its own democracy under the false claim of eliminating crime. The United States has become both the battlefield and the colony, governed by the same logic of domination that it once exported abroad.

Militarization, then, is not simply a policy, it is a pedagogical regime of terror. It teaches the public to equate security with submission, fear with safety, and violence with virtue. It transforms citizens into spectators of their own subjugation, encouraging them to find reassurance in the very forces that repress them. A massive police presence in the cities becomes a civic ritual; the drone strikes on boats in the Caribbean become a masculine gesture of national pride. In this theater of control, the aesthetic of domination replaces the ethics of justice.

The result is a culture in which power no longer needs to hide its violence; it celebrates it. The tools of surveillance and coercion are not merely instruments of control; they are symbols of belonging, emblems of a perverse citizenship grounded in obedience and fear. This is the pedagogy of fascism in its contemporary form: a system that governs through laws and guns in conjunction with the internalization of hierarchy, cruelty, and silence.

What we are witnessing is not simply the militarization of the state but the militarization of the social imagination, an erasure of memory, a deadening of consciousness and awareness. That is, a deep restructuring of how people see, feel, and relate to one another. The lesson to be learned here is that resistance to this machinery of state terror operates on the cultural and pedagogical levels. Domination endures not only through force or economic structures but through persuasion, belief, and the shaping of consciousness itself. Culture and popular imagination are thus crucial sites where people must unlearn the lessons of colonization and propaganda and reclaim the capacities for empathy, solidarity, critical thinking, and collective defiance. The struggle for democracy begins where authoritarianism first takes hold: in the realm of culture, consciousness, and pedagogy, where matters of agency and ethics are hardened or awakened, and where the possibility of freedom is either extinguished or reborn. The struggle for democracy must begin where authoritarianism has taken root: in the realm of culture, consciousness, and pedagogy itself.

Militarizing Public Space: The Fascist Aesthetic Reborn

Domination endures not only through force or economic structures but through persuasion, belief, and the shaping of consciousness itself. In this context, culture and popular imagination are pedagogical spaces where people must unlearn the lessons of colonization and propaganda and reclaim the capacities for empathy, critical judgment, and collective defiance. The struggle for democracy begins where authoritarianism first takes hold: in the realm of culture, consciousness, and pedagogy, where agency and compassion are hardened or awakened, and where the possibility of freedom is either extinguished or reborn.

Public consciousness is under siege like no other time in American history. Official videos, campaign advertisements, and social media clips merge the pornography of fear with the seductive grammar of style. Authority is posed, polished, and aestheticized. Repression wears designer sunglasses. The visual language of militarism, order, discipline, strength, becomes indistinguishable from the iconography of fashion and celebrity. The fascist aesthetic has returned, not in jackboots and banners, but in camera angles, lighting effects, and the rhythmic editing of violence. It is fascism's twenty-first century makeover: sleek, algorithmic, and market tested.

This is not propaganda in the old sense of the word. It is a pedagogy of desire refashioned for a culture of immediacy, the new age of social media. The militarized image doesn't simply show power, its reach is pedagogical; it teaches people to crave it, bask in its swindle of fulfilment, culture of lies, and false notions of order and security, always wrapped in the production of fear. Images of soldiers kneeling on protesters' necks, ICE raids framed as action scenes, and drone footage of "enemy" cities glowing in night vision are all lessons in submission. They tell us that to be safe we must surrender, that obedience is the highest civic virtue. As with all fascist pedagogy, these images naturalize hierarchy, embrace lawlessness, and transform repression into reassurance.

A primitive tribalism of toxic masculinity now merges with the digital tools of empire. The result is a politics that fetishizes violence as beauty and obedience as strength. As Ariella Aïsha Azoulay observes, American politics has been militarized even as the military has been politicized, a deadly feedback loop in which every act of force becomes an aesthetic statement and a testimony to obedience.[55] The choreography of drones, the spectacle of police marches, the omnipresence of armed officers at protests and rallies, these are not neutral gestures of control. They are rituals designed to educate the public in the logic of fear.

At the heart of this authoritarian aesthetic lies the fusion of punishment and erasure. The spectacle of punishment teaches submission, while the act of erasure destroys memory by colonizing it. Together they create a pedagogical loop that conditions people to accept domination as normal and to forget the histories that make resistance possible. ICE raids, police violence, and algorithmic surveillance are not only mechanisms of coercion; they are lessons in helplessness. They instruct the public that democracy is untenable, rights are conditional, and dissent is dangerous.

Erasure complements this pedagogy of fear by cleansing the crimes of power from historical memory and cultural consciousness. At work in the Trump regime are apparatuses of depoliticization that murder dreams, cancel out a future, and promote the dissolution of informed judgment and civic courage. Under such circumstances, democratic public spheres collapse, and inconvenient truths disappear from the social imagination.

Together, punishment and erasure create a culture of pedagogical terrorism in which repression is naturalized, memory is policed, and forgetting is policy; authoritarian rule not only controls bodies and institutions but, once again, also remakes culture itself as lever of domination. Dissent becomes unthinkable, empathy subversive, and critical thought an act of rebellion. The result is a culture of pedagogical terrorism, in which citizens are trained to internalize fear and reproduce it in their daily lives.

Colonizing Memory and the Militarization of Consciousness

It is worth repeating, fascism does not simply occupy institutions; it occupies memory. It decides what can be remembered and what must be forgotten, what counts as truth and what is condemned to silence. The most insidious aspect of the warfare state is that it does not simply control institutions, it colonizes thought by weaponizing knowledge as a form of power. It legitimates war as a permanent condition, teaches cruelty and fear as civic virtues, and portrays care for others as a weakness.

Adorno's work on *The Authoritarian Personality* illuminates this process: authoritarian regimes cultivate not just obedience but a psychological disposition that equates domination with strength and compassion with treason. What Ergin Yildizoğlu aptly calls fascism's pedagogical regime rests on the militarization of thought itself. It is a machinery of teaching and unlearning, of repetition and repression, designed to empty language of meaning and replace dialogue with command.[56]

Fascism teaches submission as virtue and ignorance as protection. It teaches people to see complexity as chaos, to crave authority as comfort, and to mistake conformity for belonging. Its pedagogy is one of domination: it scripts emotions, dictates values, and implants narratives that define who must be hated, who must be forgotten, and who must remain invisible. This is the pedagogical core of fascism: it teaches people not only what to think but how to feel, elevating emotion over reason.

Language itself becomes an arsenal. Words like "freedom," "security," and "patriotism" are emptied of meaning and reloaded as weapons to attack the very ideals they once embodied. Memory, once a reservoir of resistance and hope, is repurposed as a tool of control. The fascist project depends on this linguistic inversion, where war becomes peace, ignorance strength, and silence loyalty.

Fascism erases the past by silencing historical memory, narrows the horizons of imagination, and drains public life of critical vitality. It produces subjects who are loyal not to truth but to power, obedient not to conscience but to command. This is the ultimate aim of pedagogical terrorism: not only to militarize the state, knowledge, and values, but to also militarize the mind. By narrowing what can be said, remembered, or imagined, it criminalizes dissent and turns language itself into an arsenal of cruelty. Fascism appeals to free speech to defend racist, homophobic, and misogynist discourse while limiting what can be said to challenge its toxic beliefs, practices, and policies.

If fascism is not only a form of gangster capitalism but also a culture, then resistance must extend beyond the economic and ideological to the pedagogical, the sphere where conscience is formed and imagination awakened. Education must become the moral pulse of politics, and culture a language through which people can see themselves anew, recognize their shared humanity, and join in the collective labor of resistance and the building of a democratic socialist society. Against fascism's pedagogy of erasure, we must build a pedagogy of liberation, one that expands political imagination, restores human dignity, and rekindles collective memory as the foundation for mass struggle and the creation of a radical democracy.

Conclusion: Resisting the Warfare State

The people of the United States are now living under a warfare state that fuses domestic terrorism with pedagogical terrorism. Its purpose is not only to dominate bodies but to colonize minds, erase memory, and manufacture a culture of passivity, obedience, and brutality. Resistance, then, cannot be reduced to exposing corruption, police violence, or opposing policy, however important; it must reclaim culture, language, and memory as the lifeblood of critique and democratic possibility. Only through this reclamation can we grasp how the darkest impulses of the past have been resurrected in the present, and how new media platforms and disimagination machines work tirelessly to normalize fear, ignorance, state violence, domestic terrorism, and the making of militarized subjects.

With respect to the making of militarized subjects, ignorance is not simply the absence of knowledge, it is a form of violence. It is woven into the fabric of everyday life by disimagination machines that train us not only to consume pain but to take pleasure in it, to elevate cruelty into entertainment. Trump has sanctioned and expanded this spectacularized culture of abandonment, legitimating a politics where justice is disposable and civic institutions are stripped to a lifeless shell. He is the distilled emblem of gangster capitalism—a postmodern Frankenstein monster, theatrical and self-absorbed, who embodies decades of greed, savagery, and cruelty reaching their poisonous endpoint in American authoritarianism.

Gangster capitalism marks the slow death of the civic imagination. Under Trump, the state no longer governs through consent but through fear, producing a populace conditioned to mistake domination for safety and surveillance for freedom. This spectacle of fascist politics is the main event. As T. J. Clark observes, Trump instinctively understands the spectacle's power to "scent out the reaction of a virtual audience."[57] Naomi Klein and Astra Taylor remind us that the Trumpian spectacle, with its apocalyptic narratives, signals an ideology that has abandoned not only democracy but the very livability of our shared world.[58] What emerges is a war culture, an authoritarian pedagogy in which cruelty is naturalized, memory is obliterated, and fear becomes the grammar of everyday life.

Against this militarized pedagogy of dispossession, every element of spectacularized fascism must be exposed: its cruelty illuminated, its lies unmasked, and its machinery of terror dismantled. Education should become an axe that breaks through the manufactured "common sense" of authoritarianism, a language that speaks to the deepest needs of the public, rekindles memory, and makes visible both suffering and the capacity to resist. If fascism teaches fear and obedience, then democracy must embrace the power of critique, hope, solidarity, and mass resistance.

The warfare state does not simply repress; it educates. It teaches indifference as civic duty, erases the line between soldier and citizen, and renders public institutions extensions of military power. In this grim pedagogy, the lesson is clear: power is truth, violence is virtue, and submission is freedom. What disappears in this process is not only democracy but the very capacity to imagine its renewal.

Yet resistance begins precisely where imagination refuses to die. To confront the warfare state, we must reclaim education as the practice of freedom, not indoctrination. Pedagogy must become an act of rebellion, a refusal to forget, a defiance against the normalizing power of organized cruelty, and a labor of remembrance that links the past to the demands of justice in the present.

As Freire argued, especially in *Pedagogy of Freedom*, every moment of education is a political choice: we either humanize or dehumanize, liberate or domesticate. Against the pedagogy of violence, we must create a pedagogy of hope, one that transforms outrage into action and memory into resistance. Hope here is a social endeavor, it is not naïveté but moral courage: the belief that history can still be reclaimed, that words can still tell the truth, and that education can still shape a world not yet lost to fascist despair.

Democracy cannot survive without an educated public, one capable of seeing through the machinery of deceit and standing together against the architecture of fear. Resistance must therefore be collective, rooted in solidarity, nourished by critical thought, and sustained by the moral imagination. It must reach across classrooms, unions, media, and the arts, wherever memory and vision can still breathe, to reclaim public life from the clutches of authoritarianism.

To resist the warfare state means teaching generations not to accept the boot on the human face as inevitable, but to remove it, and to remember that the act of remembrance is itself a form of rebellion, the precondition of a mass movement of intense struggle. The future depends on whether we can transform the pedagogy of fear into a pedagogy of freedom, the culture of war into a culture of solidarity. As long as we can remember, teach, and think otherwise, the warfare state will never have the final word.

The task before us is not only to defend the remnants of democratic institutions but to cultivate a cultural and educational imagination capable of shattering the grip of authoritarianism. To resist is to reclaim the future: to forge a pedagogy of liberation that restores dignity to memory, possibility to politics, and justice to the social fabric. Only then can we dismantle the machinery of terror and reclaim the possibility of a radical democracy as a living, breathing project of freedom, equality, and justice.

9

Resisting the Poisonous Language of Fascism

Language in the Age of Fascist Politics

In an age when authoritarianism corrupts meaning itself, language no longer merely communicates, it disciplines, deceives, and divides. As Toni Morrison has noted, "language is not only an instrument through which power is exercised," it also shapes agency and functions as an act with consequences.[1] These consequences ripple through the very fabric of our existence. For every word we speak carries the weight of meaning and truth, and with them, the fate of our collective future. Each syllable, phrase, and sentence becomes a contested site where truth and power collide, where silence breeds complicity, and where justice hangs in the balance. Throughout history, from Mikhail Bakhtin and Ludwig Wittgenstein to Michel Foucault and Jacques Derrida, critical theorists have made clear that the role of language is central to matters of politics, culture, agency, and action. As Eric Kin notes, "Words shape perception, perception shapes reality. Strip a people of the words they need to name their pain, and you disarm them. You blind them. You atomize their resistance."[2]

In response, what is urgently required is a new vocabulary capable of naming the fascist tide and the militarized language now engulfing the United States. This is not a question of style or rhetorical finesse; it is a question of survival. The words we need will not come from the legacy press, still tethered to the very institutions it should expose, nor from the right-wing propaganda machine of Fox News, the Sinclair Networks, or Elon Musk's X, where fascist ideals are not merely defended but exalted as patriotism.

Toni Morrison's warning in her Nobel Lecture resounds with renewed force: the language of tyrants, saturated with violence, deception, and moral rot, is "a dead language." For her "a dead language is not simply one that is no longer spoken or written," it is an unyielding language "content to admire its own paralysis."[3] It is a repressive language infused with power, censored and censoring. Ruthless in its policing duties and dehumanizing language, it has no desire or purpose other than maintaining the free range of its own narcotic narcissism, its own exclusivity and dominance. "Though moribund, it is not without effect" for it actively thwarts the intellect, stalls conscience, and "suppresses human potential."[4] Unreceptive to interrogation, it cannot form or tolerate innovative ideas, shape other thoughts, tell another story, or fill baffling silences.

This is the language of official power whose purpose is to sanction ignorance and preserve it. Beneath its glittering spectacle and vulgar performance lies a language, as Morrison notes, that is "dumb, predatory, sentimental." It offers mass spectacles, a moral sleepwalking state of mind, and a psychotic infatuation for those who seek refuge in unchecked power. It forges a community built on greed, corruption, religious cults, and hate, steeped in a scandal of hollow fulfillment. It is a language stripped to its brutal essence, animated by a relentless drive to construct an architecture of violence. It surfaces in Trump's discourse of occupation, in the steady militarization of American politics,[5] and in his deployment of an army of trolls to turn hatred into digital spectacle of swagger and engineered suffering.[6] More troubling still is the genocidal register of his rhetoric toward Iran. In a post on Truth Social, Trump declared that "a whole civilization will die tonight, never to be brought back again." As the Lemkin Institute observes, such language does not target a regime or military apparatus but an entire people, their identity, their history, their culture. It is precisely this totalizing logic that marks one of the clearest public articulations of genocidal intent in the post-Genocide Convention era.[7]

Even the liberal mainstream now echoes this language of evasion, dressing cruelty in the rhetoric of civility.[8] Language, once a powerful instrument against enforced silence and institutional atrocity, now too often serves power, undermining reason, normalizing violence, and replacing justice with vengeance.

In Trump's oligarchic culture of authoritarianism, language becomes a spectacle of power, a theater of fear, crafted, televised, and performed as a civic lesson in mass obedience. It is a language that embraces censorship, fears imagination, and rages against independent thought. It thrives on institutional brutality and chaos, deploying a rhetoric of hate that silences dissent and erodes democratic values. As Leon Wieseltier observes, this authoritarian style is amplified by "the technological instruments of manipulation and demagoguery designed to promote a uniformity that autocratic (and theocratic) regimes desire. They harbor a top-down fantasy of perfect consensus."[9]

Drawing a unsettling parallel between Trump's regime of censorship and the linguistic engineering of Nazi ideology, Wieseltier points to the concept of *Gleichschaltung*, which he defines as "synchronization, regimentation, integration, coordination, the unification of disparate elements in government and society under a single ideological description, so that all diversity and dissonance is banished and smoothed out into a seamless and coercive general will that reflects the ideals of the regime."[10] In Nazi Germany, Gleichschaltung operated under the practice of coordination so all aspects of German life came under Nazi control. Culture and the institutions that supported it were reduced to propaganda machines. Moreover, language, in this view, is no longer a medium for critical reflection or civic dialogue but a weapon of ideological conformity.

To reclaim language from the grip of authoritarian distortion, as Jared Marcel Pollen reminds us in a different context, is to reclaim "the preservation of dignity, the overcoming of ignorance and degradation, and ultimately ... survival."[11] Resisting linguistic violence means rejecting the false reality imposed by despotic power and reclaiming the emancipatory potential of language itself. To remain silent is to surrender to what William Davies calls "an age of anti-politics," a time when fear silences conviction and taking "a substantive political position [is] seen as a risk."[12] It is precisely this paralyzing fear that the Trump regime cultivates, turning language into a weapon of conformity rather than a medium of freedom and truth.

If language is the vessel of consciousness, then we must forge a new one, fierce, unflinching, and unafraid to rupture the fabric of falsehood that sustains domination, disposability, and terror. The late novelist Ngũgĩ wa Thiong'o was right: "language was a site of colonial control," inducting people into "colonies of the mind."[13] Ngũgĩ's reflection on the power of language offers a profound understanding of its role in shaping histories of domination and resistance:

> Language has always been a battlefield of ideas. It is a war zone in the struggle between enslavement and empowerment, between the dominated and the dominating, the colonized and the colonizing. The history of language ... is often a story of possession and dispossession, territorial struggle, and the establishment or imposition of a culture. Language has been as much the tool of conquest and resistance as the sword. Indeed, some of the fiercest battles have been fought and continue to be fought in this zone.[14]

Building on Ngũgĩ's insight, we must recognize that this linguistic struggle now defines the broader political landscape, where democracy itself is under siege. The institutions that once nurtured the social imagination and civic dialogue are being dismantled, replaced by a toxic language of hate and exclusion. This is the grammar of fascism reborn: a vocabulary of punishment that transforms politics into spectacle and conscience into casualty.

As growing numbers of people rebel against this dystopian order, neoliberal ideology fuses with the forces of fascist politics to contain and distort their rage, to turn legitimate grievances against ruling elites and the cruelties of capitalism into instruments of fear, distraction, and division.

What emerges is a machinery of misdirection that transforms public discontent into private despair.[15] The current crisis, of agency, representation, values, and language itself, demands more than resistance; it calls for a new vocabulary of critique and possibility, one capable of dismantling the cultural and ideological architecture through which neoliberal capitalism renews its own savagery. For under Trump, the cynical language of neoliberalism has been weaponized, feeding directly into a politics of disposability that deems entire populations expendable.

What must be addressed is how neoliberalism has been able to enlist in such a compelling way the consent of so many Americans. That is, how has the educational force of the culture worked pedagogically to produce neoliberal ideology, values, and consent, how the popular imagination both deploys power and is influenced by power. Lawrence Grossberg has argued rightly that the popular imaginary is far too important as part of a larger political and educational struggle not to be taken seriously. He writes:

> The struggle to win hegemony has to be anchored in people's everyday consciousness and popular cultures. Those seeking power have to struggle with and within the contradictory realms of common sense and popular culture, with the languages and logics that people use to calculate what is right and what is wrong, what can be done and what cannot, what should be done and what has to be done. The popular is where social imagination is defined and changed, where people construct personal identities, identifications, priorities, and possibilities, where people form moral and political agendas for themselves and their societies, and where they decide whether and in what (or whom) to invest the power to speak for them. It is where people construct their hopes for the future in the light of their sense of the present. It is where they decide what matters, what is worth caring about, and to what they are committed.[16]

State Terror and Trump's Politics of Disposability

As Trump's regime consolidates power, it fuses law, order, and violence into a single, terrifying doctrine, the cornerstone of a politics built on social abandonment and the corruption of conscience.[17] Cruelty is not incidental; it is the grammar of his rule. The forced disappearances, the branding of immigrants as "rapists," the disdain for due process, and a domestic-terrorism memo that defines dissent as "anti-American, anti-capitalist, and anti-Christian" make unmistakably clear that Trump's violent language is not metaphor, it is a blueprint for repression.[18] Words stripped of justice, dripping with cruelty, have become the architecture of his policy. In Trump's hands, words become weapons, metaphors become mandates. What begins as a politics of resentment ends as a machinery of terror, where hatred, threats, and dehumanization are transformed into the organizing principles of the state.[19]

This is not careless talk; it is the deliberate fusion of speech and policy, rhetoric and repression. Trump's threats to arrest and deport critics such as Zohran Mamdani reveal his willingness to weaponize the state for political vengeance.[20] His discourse does not persuade, it incites. It transforms cruelty into civic virtue and repression into spectacle. Trump is not alone. Many of his MAGA followers echo his hateful discourse.

For instance, conservative pundit Ann Coulter wrote, in response to a speech by Melanie Yazzie, a Native artist and professor, about decolonization: "We didn't kill enough Indians."[21] This is not merely harsh rhetoric; it is the open dress rehearsal for state violence, the public staging of a genocidal imagination that has long animated authoritarian rule. What is unfolding here is a declaration of war on the very conditions that make democratic life possible. When language is weaponized, when meaning is gutted and truth is pulverized, tyranny marches in with impunity, intent on silencing whole populations and normalizing the unthinkable.[22] Language is the canary in the coal mine, warning us that democracy dies without an informed citizenry.

Trump's linguistic warfare travels globally, finding echoes in Israel's genocidal assault on Gaza, where euphemism replaces atrocity. Writing in *CounterPunch*, Jamal Kanj dissects this manipulation of language, focusing on Israel's so-called "Humanitarian City," a walled compound designed to hold 600,000 displaced Palestinians from northern Gaza. He writes:

> The Israeli new concentration camp, envisioned to confine over a quarter of Gaza's population, dwarfs many of the Nazi camps of World War II. Calling a concentration camp a humanitarian city is part of Israel's linguistic warfare. In this context, Israel has perfected the weaponization of language. Israel doesn't starve Palestinians; it imposes "calorie restrictions." It does not establish ghettos; it constructs "safe zones." It does not ethnically cleanse; it gives an option for "voluntary" emigration. And now, it does not commit mass displacement, it proposes a "humanitarian city."[23]

Such euphemisms do more than mask brutality, they normalize it. They echo and reinforce a global culture in which class and racial warfare, both at home and abroad, are accepted and even celebrated. This is the international language of disposability; the lexicon of what Achille Mbembe calls necropolitics, the power to decide who may live and who must die.[24]

Trump's unwavering support for Israel's genocidal war, spearheaded by the criminal leadership of Netanyahu and Ben-Gvir, binds him morally and politically to the slaughter of thousands of children in Gaza. Netanyahu's efforts to silence criticism of Israel by labeling it antisemitic are not only disingenuous but morally grotesque.[25] It is an inversion of ethics: those who condemn genocide are branded as bigots, while those who enable it claim the mantle of virtue.

The irony is undeniable. Trump himself has a long, well-documented history of antisemitism, reflected in his defense of the white supremacists at Charlottesville who chanted, "Jews will not replace us,"[26] and his dinner at Mar-a-Lago with Kanye West and Holocaust denier Nick Fuentes.[27] This is not moral confusion; it is moral corruption.

It is difficult to miss the bitter irony of the MAGA right casting itself as the guardian against antisemitism. As John Ganz observes, the real energy of antisemitism has always pulsed within the ranks of the far right, woven into its history and rhetoric.[28] From conservative icons like William F. Buckley and Pat Buchanan to today's reactionaries such as Nick Fuentes and Tucker Carlson, the lineage is unmistakable. Its latest incarnation surfaces in the vile antisemitic exchanges of the Young Republicans' leaked group chat, a stark reminder that beneath the right's feigned outrage lies a long and rancid tradition of hatred now parading as moral virtue.

Genocide cannot be concealed behind hollow platitudes or weaponized accusations of antisemitism, especially when the massacres in Gaza unfold in plain sight, visible to the entire world. Many Jewish intellectuals, prominent international organizations, and states have condemned Israel's actions, acknowledging them as genocide. Among them is Omer Bartov, a leading Israeli American historian and expert in genocide studies, who wrote in *The New York Times* that, in light of Israel's relentless violations of international law, his "inescapable conclusion has become that Israel is committing genocide against the Palestinian people."[29] He further states, "This is not just my conclusion. A growing number of experts in genocide studies and international law have concluded that Israel's actions in Gaza can only be defined as genocide."[30] Bartov is joined in this assessment by Francesca Albanese, the UN Special Rapporteur for the West Bank and Gaza, Amnesty International, and even South Africa, which has filed a case of genocide against Israel at the International Court of Justice.

The horrors unfolding in Gaza are a stark testament to the violence of unchecked power, the grim reality of which demands our collective moral reckoning. The power of the Israeli state, the United States, and Germany, in particular, to evoke antisemitism against any criticism of genocide, racism, ethnic cleansing, dehumanization, and a politics of disposability is well established. The danger at work here goes far beyond suppressing dissent. As David Theo Goldberg observes, accusations of antisemitism intensify precisely when Israel escalates its violence in Gaza. What emerges is not a good-faith defense against hatred, but a politically and media-driven moral panic designed to discredit and silence critics of state power.[31]

The historian Omer Bartov sharpens the warning: when Israel and the United States conflate criticism of a genocidal war with antisemitism, they do more than deflect accountability, they erode the very foundations of genocide studies itself, undermining the imperative to name, prevent, punish, and remember such crimes.[32]

As David Theo Goldberg makes clear, "targeting of Israel's critics as antisemitic appear to ramp up exactly when Israel's government ... carries out its violent plans in Gaza. Charges of "antisemitism" against critics now represent a textbook case of a politically- and media-inspired moral panic largely designed to dismiss all criticisms of the Israeli government."[33] Omer Bartov goes further stating that Israel and the US attempt to smear criticism of Israel's genocidal war against Palestinians as antisemitic "threatens to erode the foundation of genocide studies: the ongoing need to define, prevent, punish and reconstruct the history of genocide."[34]

To challenge the actions of the Israeli state and hold it accountable for its crimes is not an expression of antisemitism, but a defense of human rights and dignity, rooted in the ethical imperative to oppose all forms of oppression, regardless of the perpetrator. It is worth repeating. The charge of antisemitism serves to suppress history, slander dissent, and prevent public debate and so has become a form of intellectual thuggery for authoritarians like Netanyahu and Trump.

The politics of denial, weaponized through the charge of antisemitism, has long served as a smokescreen to deflect any critique of Israel's policies, particularly when draped in the moral authority of the Holocaust. This maneuver, which equates criticism of Israeli state violence with an assault on Jewish memory itself, is now facing growing resistance. Pankaj Mishra, writing in the *London Review of Books*, argues that the memory of the Shoah has been transformed into a political mythology, one that absolves Israel of moral responsibility and shields it from ethical scrutiny.[35] He traces a long lineage of dissent, from Primo Levi and James Baldwin to Tony Judt and Nelson Mandela, all of whom condemned Israel's use of the Holocaust as a moral alibi for its institutionalized machinery of state repression.[36]

Israeli American historian Raz Segal, speaking on *Democracy Now!*, powerfully exposes how this shield has been used to denigrate Palestinians as Nazis, vilify Holocaust scholars who dissent and insist on the moral infallibility of the Jewish state. Under the guise of Holocaust remembrance, he argues, a dangerous logic takes hold: Israel, as the putative state of Holocaust survivors, is rendered beyond reproach, immune to the very charges, war crimes, ethnic cleansing, even genocide, that its own founding violence made possible. As Segal explains:

> I mean, in the field of Holocaust studies, Holocaust studies has always been based [on] just the study of the Holocaust itself. Then we have also genocide studies and what we call Holocaust and genocide studies. But Holocaust studies was also always based on the idea that the Holocaust is unique. And this also meant that Israel, the state of Holocaust survivors,

or the state that portrays itself as a state of Holocaust survivors, the Jewish state, is also unique. And this is really the basis of Nakba denial, right?, the idea that Israel cannot perpetrate any crime under international law, let alone genocide. So, this was very central also in Holocaust studies always, this kind of protection for Israel from criticism and really the perpetuation of Nakba denial, the denial, right?, of the ongoing Nakba, as well, the continued assault on Palestinians.[37]

Language, the Crisis of Conscience, and the Death of Empathy

Gangster capitalism lays the foundation for Trump's racist and fascist politics. The United States has descended into a state of political, economic, cultural, and social psychosis, where cruel, neoliberal, democracy-hating policies have prevailed since the 1970s.[38] Underlying this authoritarian shift lies a systemic war on workers, youth, Black peoples, and immigrants, increasingly marked by mass violence and a punishing state both at home and abroad. The US empire is now internally dominated by a callous, greedy billionaire class that has dismantled any remnants of democracy, while embracing the fascistic ideology of white Christian nationalism and white supremacy.[39] American fascism marches not only beneath the flag, but also under the shadow of the Christian cross.[40]

At the center of this moral decay stands the billionaire class, a ruling elite that has turned calculated brutality into its civic religion. The moral compass of America has shifted from the cult of unrestrained individualism, celebrated in Ayn Rand's *Atlas Shrugged*, to the worship of greed and violence embodied by Gordon Gekko's credo "greed is good" and Patrick Bateman's psychotic excesses in *American Psycho*. What began as a philosophy of selfish ambition has curdled into a theology of domination, where cruelty becomes virtue and profit the highest form of grace.[41]

This descent into barbarity reaches its apex in theocratic hatred masquerading as moral renewal. In pulpits across the country, reactionary preachers sanctify violence as virtue. One sinister and dark example comes from Justin Zhong of Sure Foundation Baptist Church in Indianapolis, who called for the deaths of LGBTQ+ individuals during a sermon, citing biblical justification and branding them "domestic terrorists."[42] It gets worse. During a Men's Preaching Night at Sure Foundation Baptist Church, Zhong's associate, Stephen Falco, suggested that LGBTQ+ people should "blow [themselves] in the back of the head," and that Christians should "pray for their deaths."[43] Another member, Wade Rawley, advocated for violence, stating LGBTQ+ individuals should be "beaten and stomped in the mud" before being shot in the head.

Welcome to Trump's America, where empathy is derided as weakness and the market becomes the measure of all human worth. Elon Musk, Trump's erratic ally, expresses this ethos most nakedly: "The fundamental weakness of western civilization is empathy."[44] In a single sentence, he gives voice to the moral bankruptcy of neoliberal fascism. As Julia Carrie Wong observes in *The Guardian*, the stakes extend far beyond casting empathy as a "parasitic plague."[45] Empathy's true power lies in its ability to disrupt the conditions that make dehumanization possible. Rather than enabling violence, it challenges the narrowing of moral boundaries and insists on expanding the "definition of who should be included in a democratic state."[46]

The neoliberal ruling class despises empathy because it exposes the rot essential to their project: a world of privatized cruelty and corporate power disguised as freedom. Empathy destabilizes their fantasy of self-sufficiency by insisting that freedom without solidarity is merely privilege. In their dystopian vision, public institutions vanish, private mercenaries replace the social contract, and democracy gives way to an algorithmic feudalism run by the ultra-rich.

In this nightmare vision, private mercenaries replace public institutions, AI stands in for human care, and cryptocurrencies serve as the bloodline of a new feudal order.[47] Democracy, with its insistence on equality, public goods, and collective responsibility, poses the most profound danger to this emerging regime of neoliberal fascism.

Naomi Klein and Astra Taylor perfectly capture the fundamental barbarism and moral collapse fundamental to neoliberal fascism:

> The fact that their profits are predicated on planetary devastation helps explain why do-gooder discourse among the powerful is giving way to open expressions of disdain for the idea that we owe each other anything by right of our shared humanity. Silicon Valley is done with altruism, effective or otherwise. Meta's Mark Zuckerberg pines for a culture that celebrates "aggression." Alex Karp, Thiel's business partner at the surveillance firm Palantir Technologies, rebukes the "losing" "self-flagellation" of those who question American superiority and the benefits of autonomous weapons systems (and, by association, the lucrative military contracts that have made Karp's vast fortune).[48]

This is the gospel of neoliberal fascism: a world where greed replaces grace, domination supplants decency, and technology becomes the theology of control. Empathy dies so that profit may live.

Naming the Deep Roots of the Police State

Ruth Ben-Ghiat has warned that "America has been set on a trajectory to become a police state," pointing to the passage of the Brutal and Bellicose Bill (BBB), which handed ICE a budget larger than the militaries of Brazil, Israel, and Italy combined.[49] Yet the roots of this state violence run far deeper. They stretch back through the bipartisan war on terror, mass incarceration, and racialized policing that normalized cruelty as governance long before Trump.

The foundation was laid under Bush and Cheney, whose "war on terror" birthed Guantánamo, Abu Ghraib, black sites, mass surveillance, and extraordinary rendition.[50] What Trump has done is strip these earlier authoritarian practices of pretense, transforming them into open governing principles. The state of exception has become the rule.

The police state did not begin with Trump, it reached maturity through him.[51] Today we see its terrifying evolution: racial cleansing disguised as immigration policy, hatred normalized as political speech, dissent criminalized, birthright citizenship threatened, and everyday life militarized. This is not politics as usual; it is fascism rebranded for the twenty-first century.

Trump's fascist politics grow even more dangerous when we recognize that his language of colonization and domination has helped transform American society into what Ngũgĩ wa Thiong'o chillingly describes as a "war zone."[52] This war zone extends from city streets to digital networks, from classrooms to courthouses. It now spans the internet, podcasts, social media, and educational platforms, breeding grounds for fascist symbols, reactionary fantasies, and the algorithmic resurrection of colonial logics.

In this battlefield of meaning, the language of colonization does more than obscure truth, it erodes critical thinking, silences historical memory, and disarms the possibility of agency. What remains is a nation scarred by suffering, haunted by loneliness, bound by fear, and anesthetized by the numbing rituals of a punishing state.

As noted earlier, America's transformation into a war zone finds its most visible expression in the rise of Trump's omnipresent police apparatus. This authoritarian machinery reveals itself through the mechanisms of state-sponsored terror.[53] ICE now functions as an occupying army rather than a law-enforcement agency, conducting raids, abductions, and mass detentions that echo the logic of counterinsurgency rather than civil administration. The rapid expansion of detention centers increasingly resembles a network of forced-labor compounds.[54]

As Fintan O'Toole warns, Trump's deployment of troops onto the streets of Los Angeles is not merely symbolic, it is "a training exercise for the army, a form of reorientation."[55] In this reorientation, soldiers are no longer defenders of the Constitution but are being retrained as instruments of authoritarian power, bound not by democratic ideals but by obedience to a singular will. In this instance, the militarizing of American politics cannot be separated from the weaponization of the American military, an ongoing project for Trump. According to O'Toole:

> Donald Trump's desire to militarize American politics and politicize the American military is unfinished business. Militarizing American politics means defining all those who do not conform to his version of normality as mortal enemies to be confronted as though they were hostile foreign nations. Politicizing the military means dismantling its self-image as an institution that transcends partisan divisions, is broadly representative of the US population, and owes its primary loyalty not to the president but to the Constitution. These aims are intertwined, but the first cannot be consummated until the second has been accomplished. Trump failed to do this in his first term, but he is determined not to be thwarted again.[56]

Nevertheless, liberals, the mainstream media, much of the academic establishment, and the public continue to shrink from naming the fascist threat. They recoil from calling the Trump regime what it is: a neoliberal-fascist state engaged in domestic terrorism. In doing so, they remain blind to the reality that economic inequality, global militarism, and the genocidal logics of empire are not peripheral, they are central to America's crisis.

Why is it so difficult to admit that we are living in an age of American fascism? Why do the crimes of the powerful pass without scrutiny while the victims are blamed or erased? These questions cut to essence of moral failure: the refusal to link everyday repression to the long continuum of empire, racial capitalism, and settler colonialism that made the police state possible in the first place.

The Collapse of Moral Imagination

What the United States faces is not only a political crisis, partly in the collapse of conscience and civic courage, it is also a profound moral collapse.[57] The Trump regime's war on immigrants, the poor, and the marginalized is at once a war on thought, on historical memory, and on the courage to dissent. This is a war against conscience itself, a deliberate campaign to extinguish the moral and intellectual capacities that sustain democracy.

It is a war not merely against individuals but against the very idea of a just future. Trump's politics of cruelty seeks to make compassion appear naive, to render critical thought subversive, and to turn moral indifference into the new civic virtue. This is a genocidal war for stupidity, for the death of reflection, for the annihilation of any robust sense of justice.

Viktor Klemperer, in his seminal work *The Language of the Third Reich*, offered a crucial warning that resonates with alarming accuracy today: "With great insistence and a high degree of precision right down to the last detail, Hitler's *Mein Kampf* teaches not only that the masses are stupid, but that they need to be kept that way, intimidated into not thinking."[58] Klemperer revealed that Nazi politics did not arise in a void; it was cultivated in a culture where language became the breeding ground of fear, lies, and conformity. He understood that civic illiteracy, propaganda, and manufactured ignorance were not mere tools of fascism, they were its preconditions.

Trump's language recalls the genocidal campaigns against Indigenous peoples, the enslavement of Africans, and the systematic exclusion of those deemed disposable. It is a necrotic lexicon resurrected in service of tyranny, a vocabulary of extermination disguised as renewal. It gives birth to politicians with blood in their mouths, who weaponize nostalgia and bigotry, cloaking brutality in the false promises of patriotism and "law and order." The moral collapse of the nation is inseparable from the collapse of language itself. When words lose meaning, atrocities become thinkable. When state violence is aestheticized, it becomes contagious. Trump's fascism thrives on this moral inversion: it makes violence appear virtuous, ignorance heroic, and compassion suspect.

Language as War and the Return of Americanized Fascism

Trump's language is not mere rhetoric; it is a call to arms. Trump's words do not simply shelter fascists; they summon them. They silence dissent, normalize torture, and echo the logic of death camps, internment camps, and mass incarceration. His discourse, laden with hatred and lies, is designed to turn neighbors into enemies, civic life into war, and politics into a death cult and zone of terminal exclusion. Undocumented immigrants, or those seeking to register for green cards or citizenship, are torn from their families and children, cast into prisons such as Alligator Alcatraz, a grotesque manifestation of the punishing state. As Melissa Gira Grant writes in *The New Republic*, this "American concentration camp" was "built to cage thousands of people rounded up by ICE," constructed on Indigenous Miccosukee land without consultation, an act of colonial violence layered upon colonial violence.[59] Here, fascism fuses the past and present, reviving the colonial logics of conquest in the name of national security.

This is the face of modern cruelty draped in the American flag. Language becomes the weapon through which violence is orchestrated, refined, and made ordinary. Culture is no longer peripheral to politics; it is the central medium through which authoritarianism seduces, disciplines, and legitimates itself. The fascist lexicon turns civic life into a theater of fear and public cruelty into political performance.

In Trump's America, the language of domination becomes policy, and policy becomes spectacle. Dehumanizing metaphors, "vermin," "invaders," "animals," prepare the public imagination for the machinery of deportation, detention, and death. These linguistic assaults create what Hannah Arendt once called the "banality of evil," where atrocity becomes thinkable because it has been linguistically normalized.

Trump's regime of propaganda and punishment collapses the distance between speech and violence. To speak in fascist language is to act in fascist ways; words here are not expressions but weapons. Laura Loomer's grotesque remark that the "wild animals surrounding Trump's new immigration center will have at least 65 million meals" is not a rhetorical flourish, it is a death wish wrapped in irony.[60] Her language enacts genocidal violence by turning suffering into entertainment, murder into metaphor.

Change.org, along with others such as *Pod Save America* co-host Tommy Vietor noted that her comment "is not only racist, (but also) a direct emotional attack and veiled threat against Hispanic communities. This kind of speech dehumanizes people of color and normalizes genocidal language."[61] Her racist remark not only reveals the profound contempt for human life within Trump's inner circle but also highlights how cruelty and violence are strategically used as both a policy tool and a public spectacle. Loomer's remark is a symptom of the fascist logic animating this administration, where death itself becomes a political message. Her blood-soaked discourse is symptomatic of the criminogenic politics fundamental to the working of the Trump regime.

Such discourse belongs to the lineage of extermination. Loomer's invocation of death recalls the Nazi designation of *Vernichtungslager*, extermination camps, where, as Primo Levi observed, "imprisonment and execution were inseparable."[62] In this repetition of history, language again becomes the accomplice of atrocity. The United States' internment of Japanese Americans during World War II, often sanitized in public memory, functioned through a similar grammar of suspicion and disposability.

Judith Butler reminds us that some lives are rendered invisible, lives deemed "ungrievable," stripped of the right to be mourned.[63] In fascist regimes, this erasure of empathy is not an accident but a project: a pedagogy of cruelty that teaches who deserves protection and who can be discarded. In Trump's America, cruelty has become pedagogy, and pedagogy a form of political terror.

For Trump, J. D. Vance, and their enablers, fascism is not a ghost to exorcise but a banner to wave. The spirit of the Confederacy, the corpse of white supremacy, and the symbols of militarized nationalism have been resurrected and sanctified. Neo-Nazis march openly; Confederate flags adorn public parades; and Trump renames US warships and bases after Confederate generals as acts of racial provocation and political theater.[64]

In a direct nod to its embrace of white supremacy, the Trump administration is restoring and reinstalling the statue of a Confederate official, Albert

Pike, who not only "sided with the Confederacy during the civil war and fought to protect slavery as an institution," but was also allegedly a member of the Ku Klux Klan.[65] As Peter Wade points out in *Rolling Stone*, in a desperate attempt to deflect attention "about his relationship with the deceased sex trafficker," Jeffrey Epstein, Donald Trump boldly proclaims his full-throated nativism, calling on sports teams to restore their racist legacies.[66] In one instance, he demands, with great fanfare and zero shame, that the Washington Commanders football team reinstate their racist "Redskins" name, which is not about sports, it is about reviving a language of domination, legitimizing insult as identity. This obsession with symbolic violence mirrors his broader project: to normalize the obscene, to aestheticize cruelty, to make the unthinkable acceptable.

Nowhere is this more evident than in the mainstream media's failure to address the racial and ideological foundations of Trump's agenda. His attacks on Haitian immigrants, the travel ban on seven African countries,[67] the shutting down of refugee programs, and his open-door policy for white Afrikaners from South Africa are not merely racist;[68] they are explicitly white nationalist.

The same ideology drives attacks on women's reproductive rights, revealing the deep racial and gender anxieties of a movement obsessed with white demographic decline. These are not isolated skirmishes; they are interconnected strategies of domination.

These converging assaults, white nationalism, white supremacy, patriarchal control, and militarized life, manifest most vividly in the war on reproductive freedom. White nationalists encourage white women to reproduce, to halt demographic change, while punishing women of color, LGBTQ+ people, and the poor. It is a violent calculus, animated by fantasies of purity and control.

The American public, numbed by spectacle, has become captive to this theater of authoritarianism. Powerful disimagination machines, mainstream media, right-wing propaganda platforms, and tech billionaires, have saturated public consciousness with conspiracy theories, historical amnesia, and spectacularized images of immigrants and others being deported to prisons, foreign gulags, and modern-day black holes.[69] These are not merely entertainment outlets; they are pedagogical weapons of mass distraction, cultivating civic illiteracy and moral paralysis.

Under their influence, the United States has entered what might be called a moral coma, a state of paralysis where citizens can no longer distinguish truth from deceit or justice from cruelty. This is not apathy; it is learned helplessness, the result of decades of neoliberal conditioning and fascist spectacle.

The rise of these reactionary pedagogical machines is not accidental. They are the cultural arm of gangster capitalism, enriching the few by brutalizing the many. Their profit depends on civic ignorance and the algorithmic monetization of rage. In this economy of cruelty, violence becomes the ultimate currency, traded daily across platforms of distraction and despair.

Reclaiming the Language of Resistance

In a decent society, language is the lifeblood of democracy, a vessel of solidarity, truth, and hope. But in Trump's America, language has become a weapon: dehumanizing, excluding, and dominating. His vision is not a warning; it is a blueprint. Words now function as instruments of governance, shaping consciousness while enforcing obedience. We must resist, or we risk losing everything. The stakes are nothing less than the survival of democracy, the retrieval of truth and the refusal to live in a world where cruelty is policy and silence equates to collaboration.

What is needed now is not only a rupture in language but a rupture in consciousness, one that joins critical illumination of the present with a premonitory vision of what lies ahead if fascist dynamics remain unchecked. As Walter Benjamin insisted, we must cultivate a form of profane illumination, a language that disrupts the spectacle of lies and names the crisis in all its violent clarity.[70]

At the same time, as A. K. Thompson argues, we must grasp the future implicit in the present.[71] His notion of premonitions urges us to read the events unfolding around us as warnings, as signs of catastrophe should we fail to confront and reverse the political and cultural paths we are on. It demands that we see the connections that bind our suffering, rejecting the fragmented reality that neoliberalism forces upon us.

The time for complacency has passed.[72] What is required is a new vocabulary of critique and possibility, one that names power, unmasks violence, and rekindles moral imagination. A language capable not only of indicting the present but of envisioning a future rooted in justice, memory, and collective struggle.

As Antonio Gramsci remarked in *Prison Notebooks,* "The crisis consists precisely in the fact that the old is dying and the new cannot be born; in this interregnum, a great variety of morbid symptoms appear."[73] Those symptoms are here: propaganda as pedagogy, cruelty as entertainment, lies as civic currency. Yet amid decay is possibility, the chance to reinvent the social imagination and to make language once again a site of solidarity rather than subjection.

This is the challenge and the opportunity for those who believe in the transformative power of culture, language, and education: to address not only the nature of the crisis but its deeper roots in politics, memory, and moral agency. When fascist politics no longer hide in the shadows but stride openly through our institutions, the defense of language becomes the defense of life itself. The fight for a just and democratic future demands not only outrage but an unwavering commitment to truth, critical consciousness, and collective resistance, before the interregnum hardens into tyranny.

SECTION FOUR

Youth, Resistance, and the Struggle for a Radical Democracy

10

Every Child is our Child—Gaza, Lidice, and the Collapse of Global Conscience

The bronze sculpture by Marie Uchytilová, *Memorial to the Children Victims of the War*,[1] depicting the eighty-two children of Lidice murdered at Chełmno in 1942, serves as a haunting reminder of the barbarity that defined the Nazi-led Lidice massacre.[2] In reprisal for the assassination of Reinhard Heydrich, the Nazis razed the village of Lidice, executed its men, and deported its women and children to death camps. The murder of these innocent children, whose faces are forever memorialized in Uchytilová's sculpture, resonates deeply today, as we witness the suffering of children in Gaza, where the cycle of violence continues unabated. The massacres of these children, then and now, serve as stark symbols of the ongoing tragedy of war and genocide, linking past and present in an unbroken chain of human suffering. As many scholars and organizations have noted,[3] genocide is no longer merely a historical and moral referent, it is unfolding in real time in Gaza, where over "70,000 Gazans have been killed," with "estimates as high as 186,000, according to a study in *The Lancet*."[4]

In Gaza, the atrocities visited upon children are unspeakable, a violence that staggers the imagination. Omer Bartov, a distinguished scholar of Holocaust and Genocide studies, reports in *The New York Times* that more than 19,000 children have been slaughtered in Gaza, including 870 infants not yet one year old.[5] He further reveals that Gaza now has the highest rate of child amputations per capita in the world. Writing in *Jacobin*, Branko Marcetic argues that Israel's genocide in Gaza is one of history's worst crimes ever.[6] The suffering of Gaza's children defies comprehension, a generation annihilated in plain sight.

These accounts are not isolated anomalies; they are symptoms of a system of calculated dehumanization. The suffering inflicted on children, used as shields, shot as sport, tortured in silence, lays bare a regime of cruelty that recalls the worst crimes of the modern era.[7] It evokes memories not just of military conquest, but of moral collapse, of state terror rationalized and normalized through lies, unchecked power, and the rot of military terrorism. What has unfolded in Gaza should haunt the global conscience no less than the legacies of Auschwitz, Hiroshima, Pinochet's Chile, or Argentina's Dirty War. These are not echoes of the past; they are the sounds of a present drenched in impunity and silence.

But the genocide in Gaza, like the slaughter at Lidice, cannot be hidden. It stands as an undeniable, grotesque monument to the unchecked power of the state and the monstrous machinery of war and dispossession. This tragedy is different from past atrocities in one disturbing respect: the suffering of Gaza's women and children, the use of starvation as a weapon,[8] the unrelenting bombardment, and the spectacle of mass murder are laid bare for all to see.[9] As Norman Solomon has consistently argued, the grotesque violence is not concealed; it is flaunted, glorified in the guttural language of demagogues, and amplified by the shameful silence of the mainstream media.[10] In addition, as a testament to the grotesque violence of neoliberalism, entire villages are being bulldozed[11] in the interest of appealing to private investors who can turn Gaza, in the words of President Trump, into a "riviera of the Middle East."[12]

Behind the language of extermination and ethnic cleansing lies a deeper, almost unspeakable horror: the totality of the relentless bombing of Gaza, the pulverizing of its neighborhoods, the erasure of homes, schools, mosques, churches, includes any space that might offer Palestinians a moment's respite from the machinery of genocide. Gaza has been turned into a graveyard of hope, its history erased, and its ruins echoing with the silence of a world that watches, excuses, or cheers.[13]

What intensifies this atrocity is that it is not merely the work of a rogue state committing war crimes, but a policy sanctioned, indeed, often celebrated by a large segment of the Israeli public.[14] The scope and magnitude of Israel's genocidal campaign strain the limits of comprehension. It reveals not only the scale of Palestinian suffering, but also the appalling moral collapse of the so-called liberal international order, which cloaks complicity in the language of diplomacy, legality, cowardice, and restraint. Pankaj Mishra, in *The World After Gaza,* rightly argues that what is unfolding in Gaza must be understood as part of a long and brutal continuum, rooted in the history of Western imperialism, sustained by embedded racism, and shaped by persistent colonial legacies.[15]

As Ishaan Tharoor reports in *The Washington Post*, the veil is lifting. The brutality is no longer obscured by the fog of euphemism or the worn-out alibi of "self-defense."[16] Nor can it be hidden behind the grotesque denial by Israeli Prime Minister Benjamin Netanyahu, who claims, against all evidence, that there is no starvation in Gaza.[17] This is not only a lie; it is also a brazen act of propaganda, a shocking declaration from a leader implicated in crimes against humanity. In that denial lies not ignorance but the cold calculus of a war criminal. Gideon Levy writing in *Haaretz* claims that Netanyahu's denying the forced starvation imposed on Palestinians in Gaza is "no less vile than denying the Holocaust."[18]

What is being done to the Palestinian people, especially the imposed famine, is not merely a war crime but a test of the world's moral imagination. Heba Almaqadma, a 24-year-old Palestinian journalist, translator, and writer living in Gaza City, writing in *Drop Site News*, bears witness to the unbearable: people dying simply "trying to obtain food for themselves and their families."[19] Her testimony exposes how empathy has been displaced by spectacle, how the suffering of Palestinians, especially women and children, has been reduced to background noise in a media landscape addicted to distraction. In this moral void, urgency withers and the echoes of past atrocities fade, revealing a world where liberal democracies normalize cruelty through indifference and silence.[20] Their lofty rhetoric of human rights and dignity lies in ruins, exposed as theater, hypocrisy laid bare for all the world to see. The scale of Israel's unrelenting genocidal assault, intensified by the deafening silence and moral evasions of Western governments, shatters any remaining illusion of neutrality or restraint. It is an assault not only on Gaza but on the conscience of the world. As Ishaan Tharoor reports:

> More than 60,000 people have been killed, according to local health authorities, and famine is "playing out" among the surviving population, per U.N. monitors, as it is experiencing "widespread starvation, malnutrition, and disease." That is driving a rise in hunger-related deaths after months of Israeli blockade and restrictions on humanitarian assistance. The two Israeli rights groups said both Israel's conduct during the war and the rhetoric of numerous Israeli political and military leaders demonstrated "deliberate attempt by Israeli decision-makers to target the whole population of Gaza rather than strictly combatants and to destroy life for the Palestinian people." Those Israeli leaders have called for, among other things, the denial of food and water to Gaza's civilians and the ethnic cleansing of the territory.[21]

Israel's assault on Gaza increasingly resembles a neoliberalized version of the Final Solution, not in historical equivalence, but in its genocidal logic. Far-right Israeli politicians before the "ceasefire" advanced a plan to annex Gaza and "turn it into a hi-tech, luxury resort city for Israelis."[22] As William Christou and Quique Kierszenbaum report in *The Guardian*, "'The master plan for settlement in the Gaza Strip' envisions the construction of 850,000 housing units, hi-tech 'smart cities' trading in cryptocurrency, and a metro system spanning the territory."[23] The document, touting Israel's economic gain, declares without irony, "The right of the people of Israel to settle, develop and preserve this land is not just a historical right, it is a national and security obligation."[24] The plan's success hinges on the forced removal of over 2 million Palestinians. This is ethnic cleansing on a mass scale, a war crime, and a crime against humanity.

This vision of Gaza as a playground for the privileged is not confined to the fringes of Israeli politics. It extends into the global corridors of power and capital. Jonathan Cook observes that "a cabal of Israeli investors, one of the world's top business consulting groups and a think-tank headed by former British prime minister Tony Blair had been secretly working on plans to exploit the ruins of Gaza as prime real estate."[25]

According to *The Guardian*, the secret consortium was actively exploring ways to realize Donald Trump's vision of transforming Gaza into a high-end investment hub and luxury destination, an enclave remade for the wealthy once its Indigenous Palestinian population had been forcibly removed.[26] This plan reveals a horrifying logic. It imagines the site of mass suffering as a future profit center, a place where genocide can be disguised as redevelopment, and where the erasure of a people becomes the precondition for financial speculation. This is a colonial script as old as empire itself. In this instance, the rhetoric of "revitalization" and development becomes the mask for conquest. Trump's proposal belongs to this long genealogy of colonial fantasies, visions that promise luxury, stability, and investment while concealing the brutal reality that such futures are built on the ruins of those deemed disposable. In Gaza, as elsewhere in the history of settler colonialism, the language of development does not simply rationalize violence; it transforms atrocity into opportunity, turning genocide into an entrepreneurial horizon.

As I argued in Chapter 9, the attack on empathy is no minor lapse; it is a prelude to barbarism. Stripping away our ability to connect with and feel compassion for the Other creates a moral void, one in which genocidal violence, already unfolding in Gaza and beyond, can proceed unchecked. This violence is met not with resistance, but with silence, indifference, and even justification. This is how cruelty becomes normalized and conscience extinguished. The contempt for empathy is the dark counterpart to the rise of the criminogenic state.[27]

As I write this, a tenuous ceasefire teeters on the brink of collapse. Netanyahu has already declared the ceasefire proposal dead, alternately accusing Hamas of refusing to return the bodies of hostages or offering a rotating list of invented excuses, all while repeating the same hollow justifications for prolonging a war that continues to kill women and children.[28] The future of the ceasefire remains uncertain, given Israel's long-standing determination to expel Palestinians from all of historic Palestine. The political conditions that fuel this violence, displacement, sovereignty, and colonial dispossession, remain largely unaddressed. Without confronting these root causes, any ceasefire risks becoming yet another temporary pause, leaving the underlying injustice unchallenged and the cycle of violence unbroken.

The collapse of ethics is not an abstraction; it is written on the bodies of the women and children whose lives have been shattered by relentless, state-sanctioned violence.[29] It is inscribed in the hands of those who carry out this brutality against a defenseless yet resilient people. This erosion of humanity is laid bare in the terrifying declarations of Israeli politicians. Former Knesset member Moshe Feiglin pushed this genocidal rhetoric to an unthinkable extreme. In a 2025 interview on Israeli Channel 14, he declared: "Every child, every baby in Gaza is an enemy. The enemy is not Hamas ... We need to conquer Gaza and colonize it and not leave a single Gazan child there. There is no other victory."[30]

Feiglin's words lay bare a harrowing truth: this is a calculated and dehumanizing military campaign aimed at erasing not only the most vulnerable, children, but an entire people from existence. As Arwa Mahdawi reports in *The Guardian*, this vision of annihilation has found resonance among Israeli lawmakers and public figures, who have amplified the haunting words of retired Major General Giora Eiland. Writing in an Israeli newspaper on October 12, 2023, he declared that the aim is to turn Gaza "into a place where no human being can exist."[31]

Nowhere is the heartlessness of the Israeli state, and the shameless indifference of most of the world, more evident than in the deliberate starvation of an entire people. Through enforced blockade and bombardment, Israel has transformed hunger itself into an instrument of extermination. Hunger has been conscripted into the arsenal of war, its slow cruelty more devastating than any bomb.

Giorgio Agamben, writing in *Homo Sacer*, invokes the Nazi death camps to define "bare life" as a condition in which individuals are stripped of political and human value, reduced to mere physical survival under the constant threat of death. In light of the current brutality unfolding under massive military assaults and the use of hunger as a weapon, this concept is indispensable for understanding how entire populations are forced to live on the edge of annihilation, suspended in a state of hunger, destitution, and state-sanctioned violence.

Achille Mbembe expands the notion of "bare life" through, once again, his concept of necropolitics, a mode of governance driven by what he calls the "power of death."[32] He argues that necropolitics points to the various ways in which, in our contemporary world, weapons are deployed in the interest of maximally destroying persons and creating "death-worlds," zones where populations are not merely oppressed but condemned to a social existence akin to the living dead, marked by disposability, suffering, and lawlessness. In such a regime, the "other" is cast outside the protections of legal or moral consideration, rendered a target of state-sanctioned annihilation. In the shadow of Israel's ruthless military campaign and politics of extermination, this notion becomes chillingly prescient. Here, life is not simply devalued; it is made expendable. For Mbembe, necropolitics points to a condition in which those deemed "other" are now defined as existing outside the law itself.

This is not only the fate imposed on Palestinians in Gaza, the West Bank, and within the Green line; it is mirrored in the United States under Trump, whose politics of cruelty normalized the arrest, incarceration, and deportation of undocumented immigrants with a virulence that defies legality but is cloaked in law. Across the globe, politics has entered a death-driven orbit, a necropolitical turn shaped by rising authoritarianism, militarization, widening inequality, carceral regimes, systemic racism, and the spiritual force of white Christian nationalism.

As the works of both Agamben and Mbembe make clear, the atrocities unfolding in Gaza are not simply a "humanitarian crisis," they represent a seismic rupture in our moral universe, a profound decay of moral imagination. As we watch, in real time, the bodies of children shattered by bombs, pierced by snipers, and crushed beneath rubble, we are witnessing the disintegration of the very ethical foundations that bind humanity itself. Israeli airstrikes, often with US made bombs and missiles, indiscriminately target, schools and medical sites full of displaced men, women, and children, who have no safe place to go.[33] The major powers continue to arm Israel, in spite of an alleged ceasefire, while academic institutions remain silent and corporate-controlled media either ignore or vilify those who dare to speak out against Israeli genocide. We are observing what could be described as the Hiroshima of our time, an event that signifies not only the destruction of lives but the erosion of our collective conscience.

Dr. Yasser Khan, a witness to the horrors unfolding in Gaza, shared his testimony alongside Mehdi Hasan and Naomi Klein.[34] His words give a voice to the unimaginable suffering that children endure in this modern-day slaughter. He recalls treating a 14-year-old girl who had been struck by shrapnel in both eyes, her eyeballs shattered and leaving her blind. Her plight is compounded by the fact that she is now orphaned, her family killed by Israeli strikes. With no infrastructure, no access to food, water, or electricity, and constant bombardment, these children are left to die alone, without care or hope.

Dr. Khan's account is more than a mere testimony; it is an urgent call for action. His words, raw, visceral, and filled with anguish, urge us to confront the inescapable truth: we are complicit in this suffering if we continue to look away. The pain and terror faced by these children is not just their burden; it is a tragedy that belongs to us all. Every child, everywhere, is our child. The call for understanding is not enough. We must act.

Like the children of Lidice, the children of Gaza stand as haunting witnesses to what happens when the world's conscience collapses. The ghosts of genocidal violence are not distant echoes lingering only in the forgotten corners of history; they are present, shaping the policies that continue to devastate innocent lives. To ignore these lessons is to abandon our moral compass, to deny our shared humanity, and to let history repeat itself.

We stand at a crossroads. The violence and brutality we are witnessing today demand more than passive observation; they demand collective moral action. The tragedy that has unfolded in Gaza is not an isolated incident; it is part of a broader pattern of state violence and genocide. It is a global issue, one that transcends borders and affects us all. It is time to acknowledge the atrocities being committed and to act with the urgency that the situation demands. The time to dismantle the machinery of death and state terrorism is now.

Once again, the words of Heba Almaqadma cut through the global silence surrounding Gaza with a clarity that cannot be ignored. While much of the world turns away, there is no silence in Gaza, only "the sounds of children collapsing from malnutrition, parents crying in frustration, communities trying to survive without food, fuel, or medicine."[35] As Almaqadma reminds us, no political rationale can erase "the hollow look in a child's eyes" or the "slow and cruel death of a people being starved in full view of the world."[36] What is needed is not pity, she insists, but pressure, on those who block aid, on those who remain silent, and on those who possess the power to act but choose complicity instead. In a world saturated with images of suffering and yet paralyzed by indifference, she leaves us with a haunting question: How many more children must die before the world declares that Gaza deserves to live?

This is where our collective responsibility begins, not as a choice, but as a moral imperative. As Howard Zinn reminds us, every child is our child.[37] This is not a slogan but a profound ethical claim, one that demands boundless solidarity, an unwavering love, and a shared hope fierce enough to defy the machinery of cruelty. It is a call to action, an urgent demand for justice that must break through the silence and complicity that allow genocidal violence to unfold. What is happening in Gaza, and to a lesser degree in Iran, is not an aberration; it is the brutal culmination of the forces this book has traced, a culture of cruelty that normalizes suffering, a politics of racialized "othering" that strips entire populations of their humanity, a spectacle of violence that turns death into a source of national pleasure, and a neoliberal ethos that renders whole communities disposable. These logics, born of empire, white supremacy, and market fundamentalism, form the moral architecture that enables childcide and cloaks it in the language of necessity, invoking "security" and "civilization" while normalizing the disposability of entire populations and the economic and political interests that sustain such violence. To confront this genocide is to address the broader crisis of democracy itself, to recognize that the fight for the future is bound inseparably to the lives of the youngest and most vulnerable among us. Only then can hope become the collective, militant force needed to resist gangster militarism and to build a world where every child is seen as ours.

11

Tears of Blood: Eugenics, Disposability, and the War on Children

Violence, soaked in blood and stripped of shame, has become the defining language of governance in the age of Trump and the global resurgence of authoritarianism. Across the globe, democracy is in retreat, and with it, the very notion of moral and social responsibility.[1] In its place, we find a brutal political grammar scripted by modern-day barbarians, disciples of greed, corruption, racial purity, ultra-nationalism, and permanent war. Compassion is mocked as weakness. The social state is vilified and hollowed out, derided in the language of an unhinged anti-communism.[2] Out of this right-wing playbook emerge policies that produce mass suffering, engineered by the powerful and shielded by the myths of meritocracy and social Darwinism, policies deemed not only acceptable but inevitable.

Among the MAGA elite, democracy is no longer a cherished ideal but a target of scorn and contempt. Echoing Hungary's Viktor Orbán, rejected by voters in the 2026 election, democracy was replaced with illiberal democracy, with its call to eliminate racial mixing and unleash a torrent of repression against free speech, universities, the press, and organized dissent.[3] In this case, fascist politics and strategies have become the new governing norm. Embracing the playbook of ruthless dictators such as Putin and Orbán, Trump expands presidential power, wages war on the rule of law and dismantles democratic institutions, especially those that nurture critical thought,[4] all the while feigning uncertainty about whether the Constitution even applies to him.[5]

Trump's financial backers and ideological allies, like Thiel, bluntly declare that freedom and democracy are no longer compatible.[6] Trump's sycophantic enablers Elon Musk and Steve Bannon pay hollow tribute to democracy by offering their followers Nazi salutes.[7] As Judith Butler astutely observes, too many in positions of power, politicians, powerful lawyers, academic administrators, and the financial elite, surrender to fear, greed, or corruption, allowing cowardice to silence their conscience.[8] In doing so, they "proclaim the inevitable end of democracy at the hands of authoritarianism, effectively giving up the struggle in advance."[9] Without irony, Thiel, Musk, Bannon, Hegseth, Miller, and others proclaim themselves champions of freedom, but the only freedom endorsed by this group is that of white Christian nationalists and billionaire oligarchs, a notion of freedom rooted in racialized authoritarian impulses. These are authoritarians drunk on power in the service of violence and domination. What they despise is any embrace of power as both a moral force and a force for radical democratic change.[10]

We are not adrift in a moment of historical ambiguity, nor suspended in a mere transition between epochs, as some would have us believe.[11] The notion of uncertainty has been shattered by an era fueled by the passionate mobilization of fascism. This intoxicating force has seduced millions with its lies and emotionally charged racism, redirecting their economic anxieties into a maelstrom of hate and the false swindle of fulfillment. Fascism from below fuses with fascism from above, sustained by a reservoir of rage skillfully redirected away from power. The once-clouded vision of what America has become is now as clear as day. The ghosts of the past have returned, cloaked in bloodlust, armed with a language of dehumanization. They are driven by the vision of a new unified Reich, one populated by totalitarian subjects unburdened by truth, morality, critical thought, or democratic agency.

The long descent from liberal democracy into the abyss of neoliberalism, or more brutally, gangster capitalism, has reached its terminal point.[12] A perfidious system once cloaked in the language of freedom and markets now reveals its true face: a predatory order that exalts cruelty, worships profit and sanctifies a pseudoscience and eugenics. At its helm stands an unholy alliance with fascism, where racial cleansing, lawless power, and the erasure of dissent have become governing principles.

As Ben Rhodes observes, fascism today moves across borders with a "rotating cast of villains," bound together by shared hatreds. The connective tissue linking figures like Putin, Orbán—removed through the ballot box in 2026—and Trump lies in their common enemies: "immigrants, Muslims, LGBTQ+ communities, globalists, liberal elites, cancel culture, and George Soros."[13] Each conjures a mythic national identity, the "real" Russian, Hungarian, or American, that must be purified of contamination. What emerges is a transnational politics of resentment, a reactionary fraternity committed to defending the fiction of cultural purity against the realities of pluralism and democracy.

Hard vs. Soft Eugenics in the Age of Updated Fascism

To understand the devastating impact of the current political and social climate on marginalized communities, it is essential to distinguish between two forms of eugenics that have shaped the modern era: hard eugenics and soft eugenics. Hard eugenics, with its violent, lawless application, is historically linked to overt violence, policies of sterilization, genocide, and forced elimination of those deemed "undesirable." The brutal methods that defined this version of eugenics still echo in history, reminding us of the violence that can be enacted in the name of racial purity and nationalistic ideals.

In contrast, soft eugenics operates through more covert, systemic means. It does not require physical violence or open lawlessness but instead utilizes policies embedded in the legal and economic structures of society. Soft eugenics is the weaponization of policy and law to create conditions of exclusion and suffering, targeting vulnerable populations with austerity measures, limited access to education and healthcare, and the stripping away of rights. In many ways, it is the quieter, more insidious form of state violence, one that does not physically eliminate the "undesirable" but ensures their long-term marginalization and, in some cases, their slow destruction. This distinction is crucial as we turn to the policies of the Trump administration, where both hard and soft forms of eugenics converge to shape a new machinery of governance, one that normalizes disposability and entrenches racial hierarchies. These doctrines of cleansing are enacted in the daily erosion of healthcare, the criminalization of dissent, and the calculated abandonment of the most vulnerable. Nowhere is this logic more visible than in the war on children, where working-class youth are sacrificed to the brutal arithmetic of austerity, privatization, and neoliberal neglect. What better proof of his cruelty than Trump's effort to enlist the Supreme Court in blocking a federal judge's order to release desperately needed food assistance for 42 million Americans, many of them children, during the government lockdown? This is not fiscal prudence; it is moral depravity, a policy of starvation that exposes a regime willing to weaponize hunger itself against the poor and the young. This is one facet of domestic terrorism rarely connected to Trump's war on Americans.

Yet this eugenicist project does not end with children. It deepens and expands through immigration policy, where the same cruel calculus is used to preserve a white supremacist vision of the nation. Here, belonging is not only regulated by law but also reengineered by ideology. Immigrants of color are cast as contaminants, while white refugees are welcomed as preservers of a racial ideal. In this context, eugenics reappears not as pseudoscience, but as legitimated policy, a political weapon wielded to reshape the nation's genetic future under the guise of national security and demographic control.

While cruelty has deep roots in the history of the United States, it has now become inextricably linked to an ever-accelerating culture of dehumanization and violence.[14] This culture both fuels the rise of fascist politics and menaces individuals through the weaponization of fear, alongside policies of extreme deprivation and immiseration. These forces strip individuals and entire communities of their power, rendering them not only powerless but also depoliticized.

What sets this moment apart from the past is the language that sustains it, a language that reproduces racial, social, and financial hierarchies steeped in the toxic discourse of social Darwinism. It aligns with the neoliberal eugenicist creed of "survival of the fittest," where personal responsibility is heralded as the sole determinant of success, if not of existence itself.

Moreover, the cruelty embedded in this rhetoric, as exemplified in the GOP's budget bill, does more than line the pockets of the wealthy with enormous tax breaks. It exacts a savage toll on the poor, with benefit cuts so severe that they will cost lives. Paul Krugman rightly refers to this assault on social benefits as an "attack of the sadistic zombies," but his description only scratches the surface.[15] What we are witnessing, especially with the draconian cuts to Medicare and Medicaid, is a form of institutionalized sadism endemic to gangster capitalism.

How can one be indifferent to defunding nursing homes, eliminating health insurance for millions, or denying children the nutritional support they need to survive? This is schadenfreude that draws its power from the same well as the death and misery imposed by the SS in the concentration camps, the IDF commanders ordering strikes on civilian-laden refugee camps, and the indifference of those who tossed dissenting students from planes during the Pinochet regime. This is cruelty without limits, a cruelty turbocharged by the neoliberal resurgence of the "survival of the fittest" ethos, echoing the darkest chapters of human history. It is what I once called zombie politics in the age of casino capitalism, where human lives are nothing more than disposable commodities in the ruthless, unforgiving colonial game of empire.[16]

This era of unchecked cruelty marks the resurgence of eugenics. Hard eugenics in its most violent versions has an extensive history in the United States and is linked to the forced sterilization of Black women, and forms of immoral medical practices and experiments applied to slaves, and later in the century to Black men. One particularly horrendous example of medical apartheid took place in what is known as the Tuskegee Study, in which 600 Black men with syphilis were left untreated in order to see how the disease progressed.[17]

Soft eugenics has also resurfaced in the United States, becoming a central motif for both the Trump administration and far-right ideologues, fueled by the resurgence of white nationalism. Rooted in the belief of racial superiority, American soft eugenics demands that white power and control be safeguarded at any cost by the ruling elite and relies on policies of deprivation to shorten or weed out those who do not measure up to what constitutes a white nationalist ethos and mode of superiority.[18]

The deeply entrenched notion of white supremacy is historically intertwined with the insidious logic of soft eugenics, a concept that underpins policies often rooted in dehumanization and social Darwinism. This dangerous ideology is embodied in the rhetoric of figures like Robert F. Kennedy Jr., who, as Secretary of Health and Human Services, has promoted the idea that resistance to diseases such as measles is part of a natural survival process. In this worldview, the vulnerable are left to fend for themselves, with no support or protection. This view is a central organizing idea behind many of Trump's policies. Kennedy's stance reflects a brutal neoliberal survival-of-the-fittest mentality, suggesting that instead of shielding the most vulnerable with vaccines, they should simply be allowed to "adapt" or "fight" the disease, thus stripping away any sense of compassion or responsibility for those most in need of protection.

This rhetoric is a alarming reflection of a larger, dehumanizing vision that discards the weak in favor of a false and cruel meritocracy. This same ideology also informs Kennedy's view of autistic children whom he stigmatizes as a drain on the social state when he states that "These are children who will never pay taxes, they will never hold a job, they will never play baseball or write a poem, they will never go on a date. Many of them will never go to the bathroom unaided."[19] Jakob Simmank, quoting Volker Roelcke, Professor of Medical History at the University of Giessen, rightly states, "This is social Darwinism."[20] Roelcke further explains that statements like "You will never pay taxes" reflect what he describes as "a dog-whistle rhetoric that is typically social Darwinist."[21]

This reflects the morally bankrupt view that those unable to survive without medical intervention should be abandoned to their fate. Kennedy is not alone in this belief; he joins others in the Trump administration who weaponize the rhetoric of "personal responsibility" to blame the weak for their suffering, an updated form of eugenic thinking that casts illness, disability, poverty, and vulnerability as personal failures rather than the products of systemic cruelty.

Even when this eugenic logic is not explicitly racial, it invariably reinforces racialized hierarchies, since the people most harmed by gutted health programs, punitive budget cuts, and market-driven medicine are disproportionately poor, Black, immigrant, Indigenous, and otherwise marginalized. In this way, their appeals to "individual choice" become a sanitized justification for abandoning entire populations to premature death under the guise of freedom.

Kennedy legitimates the unthinkable. He traffics in pseudoscience, demonizing something as ordinary as Tylenol, while teaching the public to see the vulnerable as predators to be cast out. In this inverted moral universe, those who suffer are framed as the threat, even as the real vultures circle openly: billionaires, tech oligarchs, and reactionary officials who dominate our media landscape and hoard the wealth and resources that make collective life possible.

Immigration as Eugenics: Engineering the Nation's Genetic Future

A version of eugenics thinking also fuels the Trump administration's hard line on immigration, tied to the preservation of a white supremacist vision of America's demographic and genetic makeup. Derek Beres is worth quoting at length on this issue. He writes:

> The increasing frenzy around immigration seems fueled by the desire to shape the population's genetic makeup. Elon Musk's cuts to foreign aid are already leading to increased child mortality and HIV and malaria cases in Africa (the Trump administration's other main policy engagement with Africa has been offering white South Africans refugee status). At the heart of all these policies is soft eugenics thinking – the idea that if you take away life-saving healthcare and services from the vulnerable, then you can let nature take its course and only the strong will survive.[22]

As gangster capitalism hovers on the brink of a legitimation crisis, it turns to the dark power of soft eugenics, weaponizing it to scapegoat racialized communities in order "to justify its imperialist projects," dismantle the welfare state, and provide a veneer of legitimacy for its most virulent policies.[23] This is not just political theater; it is a deliberate strategy rooted in a toxic language of cruelty and state-sanctioned violence. As I have mentioned previously, white nationalist and supremacist figures, like Stephen Miller, have pushed this rhetoric to the forefront, exemplified by his claim at a Trump rally that "America is for Americans and Americans only."[24]

How else can we explain Trump's incendiary claim that migrants have invaded the country and are poisoning the blood of Americans?[25] This rhetoric is not just inflammatory; it embodies a white supremacist worldview that is deeply entrenched in the United States and fueled by the delusions of empire. It is a worldview increasingly wedded to the rising tide of fascism, which draws heavily from the toxic premises of eugenics to legitimize a new order of racial and class hierarchies. These hierarchies are accompanied, as always, by a potent mix of historical erasure, dehumanization, and censorship, tools used to cement the power of those at the top while silencing dissent from those below. This logic becomes even more visible in policy decisions: from slashing domestic support programs to weaponizing agencies like USAID by cutting essential aid globally, ensuring that racialized populations remain hungry, destabilized, and too weakened to resist the very forces that oppress them.

This racist white supremacist ideology is not confined to the fringes but is woven into the fabric of domestic policy, particularly in its treatment of Black people. Updated by the dangerous rhetoric of white replacement theory and a crude neoliberal view of survival of the fittest, it targets the very foundations of racial justice. The war on Diversity, Equity, and Inclusion (DEI) is a stark example of this, an ideological assault aimed at erasing Black history and dismantling policies designed to increase historical and sociological literacy and prevent racial discrimination against people of color. The evidence is undeniable: the banning of books about the history of racism, the targeting of the Smithsonian for its "race-centered ideology," and the defunding of what are labeled "anti-American" ideologies, all part of a broader campaign to suppress the voices and histories of marginalized communities, particularly people of color, from public and federal spaces.

The Language of Eugenics and the Politics of Erasure

The death of history, memory, and the politics of remembering is part of a long-established fascist policy of weakening the power of historical consciousness as a source of insight and truth. The journalist David Corn is right in stating that authoritarians cannot tolerate dissent, free thought, and modes of inquiry that make power accountable.[26] In this context, it is not surprising that Trump wants to erase "dark veins of American history, racism, sexism, genocide, and other nasty business, which have been crucial components of the national story." He adds that Trump has appointed himself as "the ultimate arbiter of history, with the right to police thought."[27] In his whitewashed version of history, there is "no dirty laundry, no references to the mass murder of Indigenous people, the suppression of workers, Jim Crow, the incarceration of Japanese Americans, the mistreatment of Chinese laborers, ugly interventions in Latin America and elsewhere, and so on. Only the glories of the United States shall be acknowledged, that is, worshipped." In the logic of eugenics, the disappearance of ideas, history, and cultures is inextricably bound to the disappearance of bodies, as the erasure of memory and meaning prepares the ground for the elimination of entire peoples. On a global level, this eugenicist language takes a more punishing and violent form. It is often used to justify the politics of social abandonment, terminal exclusion, and genocidal violence. One tactic it uses is to label specific groups as subhuman. For example, in analyzing how prominent Israelis use language to dehumanize Palestinians and promote a policy of ethnic cleansing, Yumna Fatima writes:

> Announcing a "complete siege" of Gaza two days after Hamas' attack on Israel, the latter's defence minister, Yoav Gallant, was straightforward about his view of Palestinians. "There will be no electricity, no food, no water, no fuel, everything will be closed. We are fighting against human animals and will act accordingly." Even this is a throwback to earlier comparisons. In a speech to the Knesset in 1983, then IDF chief of staff Raphael Eitan declared: "When we have settled the land, all the Arabs will be able to do about it will be to scurry around like drugged cockroaches in a bottle." When stereotypes of hate, rooted in fear, are taught to society, dehumanization is no surprise.[28]

The rhetoric of dehumanization, as explored in Fatima's analysis, is not an isolated occurrence but part of a broader, disturbing global pattern, where the logic of soft eugenics is weaponized to justify violence and marginalization. This language of dehumanization, employed by Israeli officials to strip Palestinians of their humanity, mirrors the tactics used by the Trump administration, particularly in its dehumanized characterization of immigrants of color. This kind of rhetoric not only incites genocidal violence but also legitimizes policies that dismantle protection for vulnerable populations, both domestically and internationally.

One of the most insidious components of this discourse is the refusal, by many Israeli leaders, to even acknowledge Palestinians as Palestinians. Instead, they are referred to simply as "Arabs," a linguistic erasure that serves two ideological purposes. First, it reinforces the colonial fiction that Palestinians do not exist as an Indigenous people with a distinct history, culture, and claim to the land. Second, it taps into the racist connotations attached to the word "Arab" in the Western political imagination, terrorist, extremist, invader, thereby mobilizing a preexisting reservoir of fear and hostility. In this rhetorical universe, "A good Arab is a dead Arab" becomes thinkable, even actionable, because the category itself has been emptied of humanity. This manufactured anonymity is not merely semantic; it is a tool of consent-building for dispossession and extermination.

Once language strips a people of their humanity, policy follows, transforming dehumanization into a governing principle. The violence of such language is enacted in executive orders stripping Temporary Protected Status from thousands of Venezuelans, Haitians, and Afghans. At the same time, as I mentioned in Chapter 2, international students, largely people of color, are being abducted and jailed for their political views, a stark example of the administration's deliberate attack on marginalized communities. Deportations, the suspension of due process, and the unchecked use of police terrorism are disproportionately aimed at people of color, revealing a deeply entrenched racial bias in the enforcement of state power. As the

Trump administration strips away the rights of immigrants, it engages in a shocking process of disposability, sending those deemed expendable to gulag-like prisons under the control of dictators, embodying a malignant lawlessness that underscores the growing brutality of state power.

What better proof of racialized injustice than the harsh expulsions and stripped rights imposed on immigrants of color, contrasted with the offer of refuge to white South Afrikaner farmers? Trump's defense of this policy rests on the claim that "some Afrikaners ... are victims of 'mass killings' and suffer from violence and discrimination by vengeful Black South Africans."[29] This is a complete lie, and there is no evidence to support this ludicrous claim of "white genocide," one that is endorsed by Elon Musk, among others. On the contrary, this claim is a delusional fiction of white victimization that lies at the heart of the authoritarian mindset. This blatantly duplicitous policy is not just a policy decision, it is an overt expression of white supremacy, where the lives of Black and Brown people are treated as disposable, while white lives are protected and prioritized. The racism embedded in these policies speaks volumes: it is not merely a political stance but an unapologetic embrace of racial hierarchy, one that starkly contrasts the disposability of people of color with the privileged sanctuary of white refugees.

The War on Children and the Politics of Eugenics

As I have stressed throughout this book, the descent into fascism in the United States is no longer hidden. The neo-fascist project now occupies the center of political life. Fantasies of unchecked power, the normalization of lawlessness, the criminalization of protest, and the violent expulsion of those deemed disposable have become policy. The punishing state expands while the institutions meant to uphold justice, equality, and truth are under siege. Fundamental to this radical transition lies a culture of social abandonment and immense cruelty that renders the unthinkable not only imaginable but routine. Central to this cruelty is a resurgent eugenicist ideology that peddles the notion that mixed races represent the scourge of democracy and must be eliminated. Nowhere is this death of morality and militarized thinking more visible, or more horrifying, than in the escalating war on children, both at home and abroad, and the silence that shadows their suffering.

We are witnessing a war on youth, on poor, Black, and Brown youth in the United States, and on the children of Palestine, waged through the brutal calculus of a resurrected social Darwinism. In this merciless worldview, poverty is a moral failing, vulnerability is a crime, and survival is a privilege reserved for the strong and the favored. This is the eugenicist logic that once fueled the death camps of Nazi Germany, now resurfacing in the quiet violence of policy and the loud indifference of empire. In the United States, it takes the form of the Trump administration's ruthless cuts to social programs, the gutting of education and healthcare, and the militarization of everyday life under a punishing state.

Abroad, the war on youth manifests in the language that describes the children of Gaza as collateral damage, their lives deemed disposable in the machinery of permanent war. Under the iron rule of neoliberal cruelty, these young lives are sacrificed to a political economy that trades in suffering and views compassion as weakness. Yet, as I have stressed throughout this book, perhaps most horrifying is the silence that greets this war on children, a silence that does more than betray the innocence of its victims; it signals a dangerous complicity, revealing how the machinery of fascism is not simply returning but is already operating in plain sight, both at home and abroad.

This war on children is not waged solely through bombs and bullets, nor only in the glare of political spectacle; it is executed through the slow violence of policy, the calculated cruelty of abandoned futures, and the erasure of suffering behind bureaucratic language and economic rationalizations. It operates through what can only be called the politics of disposability, where entire generations are written off as collateral damage in the ruthless pursuit of profit, power, and ideological purity. In this machinery of abandonment, policies become weapons, and silence becomes the accomplice that allows such violence to proceed unchecked. To grasp the full scope of this war, we must examine the specific policies and cultural forces that render the suffering of children invisible, normalizing their pain as the inevitable price of a social order sinking ever deeper into the shadows of authoritarianism. The pain and suffering of children in both Palestine and the United States inform each other by connecting a culture of disposability and extermination that no longer view children as a resource or their care as a measure of democracy itself. This is a shared crisis that makes clear what the horror of fascism looks like when state violence is waged against children. In the age of neoliberal fascism, with Trump as its corrupt enabler, violence is no longer banal, it is sustained by the interrelated systemic erosion of truth, moral judgment, and civic courage. Cruelty is no longer disguised as progress, it is now celebrated, as Walter Benjamin once noted, as a document of barbarism.

The Policies of Disposability and the Global Assault on Childhood as a Shared Crisis

The war on children is hidden in plain sight, embedded in the fabric of both domestic and foreign policy, where suffering is legislated and innocence is bartered away for political gain. In the United States, it begins with the systematic dismantling of the social safety net. Under the Trump administration and its MAGA teenage tech-soldiers, billions have been slashed from federal programs essential to poor and marginalized families, Medicaid, housing assistance, and the Supplemental Nutrition Assistance Program (SNAP), leaving countless children vulnerable to hunger, homelessness, and chronic illness. Eloise Goldsmith argues cuts to Medicaid alone "will kill people."[30] Proposed cuts to Head Start, which serves nearly 800,000 low-income children, have already led to program closures and service reductions, though the administration claims to have backed away from the cuts.[31] If enacted, these policies could strip healthcare coverage from over 500,000 children and deny food assistance to more than 2 million others. These are not bureaucratic oversights or unfortunate side effects; they are deliberate policy choices that treat poor children as expendable in the ruthless arithmetic of neoliberal austerity. How else to explain the Trump administration halting research "to help babies with heart defects," especially since as Tyler Kingkade notes "one in 100 babies in the U.S. are born with heart defects, and about a quarter of them need surgery or other procedures in their first year to survive ... [moreover] worldwide, it's estimated that 240,000 babies die within their first 28 days due to congenital birth defects."[32]

These are not policy failures; they are deliberate acts of violence, calculated decisions rooted in the cold arithmetic of a neoliberal death drive, where the lives of poor, Black, and Brown children are weighed against tax cuts for the ultra-wealthy and found expendable. Trump's healthcare policies further reveal the depths of this disposability. Cuts to the Children's Health Insurance Program (CHIP) and mental health services have left millions of children without access to basic care, even as rates of anxiety, depression, and suicide among youth, especially marginalized youth, continue to rise.[33] The punishing state does not merely neglect these children; it polices, disciplines, and abandons them, making their suffering a permanent condition of life under the rule of capital.

Education, once imagined as a vehicle for emancipation, has also been weaponized in this war. Public schools are increasingly defunded, turned into sites of surveillance and punishment rather than learning and hope. The school-to-prison pipeline tightens its grip, with Black and Brown children disproportionately criminalized through zero-tolerance policies and police presence in schools.[34]

Under Trump, US foreign policy abandoned even the pretense of humanitarian concern, cutting all funding to the United Nations Relief and Works Agency (UNRWA), which had long provided essential health, education, and food services to Palestinian children. At the same time, US-backed Israeli military operations have carried out a campaign of scholasticide, the systematic destruction of schools, universities, libraries, and the intellectual lifeworld of Gaza. This is not simply an attack on infrastructure; it is an assault on a people's capacity to imagine and build a future. In this sense, the destruction of education becomes a central pillar of a broader eugenic project: a racialized effort to extinguish a population's communal memory, intellectual inheritance, and horizon of possibility. By targeting the institutions that nurture children, sustain culture, and transmit knowledge, this violence enacts a slow-motion erasure, an attempt to break a people not only physically but generationally, stripping away the very conditions that allow a community to reproduce itself socially, culturally, and politically.[35]

The obliteration of schools is the obliteration of a people's right to exist, and the numbers that follow testify to that intention. More than 200 schools have been deliberately targeted, displacing over 625,000 students and annihilating any semblance of educational continuity. Every university in Gaza has been targeted or destroyed. As of September 2025, *Quds News Network* reports that "At least 19,424 children have been killed in Israeli attacks over 700 days of genocide in Gaza, the equivalent of one child every fifty-two minutes. Among the victims are 1,000 infants under the age of one. As relentless Israeli bombardment, forced displacement, and starvation continue, warnings grow louder: nowhere in the enclave is safe for children."[36]

Here, the brutal logic of eugenics and empire converge. Children are not merely casualties of war, they are obstacles to be erased, victims of ethnic cleansing, their capacity to remember, imagine, or resist intentionally destroyed. Defined as burdens, drains on resources, or symbols of disposable populations unworthy of the white nationalist ideal of citizenship, they are deemed unworthy of compassion, justice, or freedom. This is not just warfare. It is the politics of displacement and ethnic cleansing, a deliberate construction of racial and class hierarchies. This is a blueprint for extermination and the systematic eradication of poor children of color, carried out with chilling precision and justified through a culture of sustained ignorance, historical erasure, censorship, and silence.

The excessive brutality and violence of Trump's war on children has drawn criticism even from the billionaire financial elite. Bill Gates, writing in the *Financial Times*, accused Elon Musk, the world's richest man, of "killing the world's poorest children" by shutting down the US Agency for International Development.[37] Gates claimed that "the abrupt cuts left life-saving food and medicine to expire in warehouses."[38] He noted that such cuts could trigger the resurgence of diseases such as measles, HIV, and polio. Gates specifically condemned Musk's decision to cancel grants for a hospital in Gaza Province, Mozambique, which prevents the transmission of HIV from mothers to their babies, spurred by the unfounded belief that US funds were supporting Hamas in Gaza. "I'd love for him to go in and meet the children who have now been infected with HIV because he cut that money," Gates said. This is cruelty without remorse, signaling not just the death of moral conscience and social responsibility, but the birth of a politics that resurrects the horrors of a genocidal past.[39]

Massive violence against children now crosses borders and its blood-filled death machines operate through the weaponization of policies designed to produce starvation, health emergencies, and mass immiseration. The war on children is not confined to distant battlefields; it reverberates within our own borders, produced through policies that erode the foundations of child welfare. The parallels between the plight of children in Gaza and those in the United States are stark and unsettling. Whether at home or abroad, the logic is the same: to crush the possibility of agency and dignity by stripping young people of the resources, rights, and dreams that nourish hope and dissent. And the silence that surrounds these atrocities is perhaps the most damning indictment of all. It signals not only moral collapse but complicity. It reveals what the turn toward fascism looks like, not just in policy, but in the deadening of conscience.

These domestic policy decisions, much like the external cuts, disproportionately impact children from marginalized communities, effectively rendering them invisible and expendable. The erosion of safety nets and educational opportunities mirrors the physical destruction witnessed in regions destroyed by endless imperialist wars, underscoring a systemic disregard for the well-being of the most vulnerable.

The convergence of these crises exposes a shared eugenic worldview, one that devalues children not accidentally but by design. Whether through budget cuts that abandon poor and minority children in the United States or through scholasticide and starvation in Gaza, the underlying logic is the same: a calculated determination of which populations are permitted to thrive and which can be erased. Challenging these policies is therefore not simply a humanitarian duty; it is a struggle against a modern eugenics that wages war on childhood itself.

The Culture of Silence and Cruelty: Making the Unthinkable Normal

If policy provides the machinery for this war on children, culture supplies its moral anesthetic. In a society gripped by the ruthless logic of neoliberalism, compassion is cast as weakness, and market values invade every corner of public life. Children are no longer seen as bearers of hope or the promise of a more just future; they are defined as financial burdens, security risks, or, in the cold calculus of empire, collateral damage. This cultural landscape thrives on historical amnesia, erasing the lessons of past atrocities even as it repeats them in real time.

The neoliberal order commodifies empathy, reducing care and concern to hollow performances in the marketplace of virtue. Philanthropy replaces justice, and isolated acts of charity stand in for systemic change, allowing structural violence to continue unchallenged. The suffering of children becomes a spectacle consumed in passing, briefly mourned and quickly forgotten in a media environment obsessed with scandal, celebrity, and the endless distractions of manufactured crises.

This is not merely a culture of forgetting but a culture of moral paralysis, where people are trained to look away, to normalize the unbearable, and to accept cruelty as the price of personal comfort and national security. As the children of Gaza are slaughtered and poor children in America wither and die under the weight of poverty, hunger, and despair, the silence surrounding their suffering becomes a shocking form of complicity. It is a dangerous silence, one that not only betrays the most vulnerable but also clears the path for the resurgence of fascism, not always in marching boots and uniforms, but often in business suits, political slogans, and the technocratic language of efficiency and order.

In such a world, the question is no longer whether fascism is on the horizon but how to deal with the fact that it has already arrived, wearing the face of indifference and operating behind the closed doors of legislative chambers, corporate boardrooms, and media empires. Breaking this silence is not simply an ethical imperative, it is an act of political resistance against a future where the machinery of abandonment becomes permanent and irreversible.

Conclusion: Breaking the Silence, Defending the Future

The war on children, whether waged through Israeli-American bombs in Gaza, the US bombing and killing of over 150 school children in Iran, or budget cuts in America's poorest neighborhoods, is the most damning indictment of our political and moral failures. It exposes a social order that has turned its back on the most vulnerable, trading away the futures of young people for the hollow promises of profit, power, and nationalist pride. But this war does more than produce suffering, it signals the rise of a political project that views democracy as an obstacle, historical memory as a threat, and the lives of marginalized children as expendable. The United States is no longer poised on the edge of fascism—we have crossed the threshold into a dark chapter that betrays not only the anguished cries of the dead who once endured its terrors, but also the fading promise that our children would be spared such unspeakable cruelty. To remain silent in the face of such cruelty is to share in its design. Silence is never neutral; it corrodes language, numbs conscience, and prepares the ground for barbarism.

America is no longer approaching fascism, we are living inside its architecture, each brick laid in silence, complicity, and fear. We have turned away from the cries of the dead who once bore witness to its horrors, and from the fragile promise that our children would never see its return. That promise cannot be located in obscene levels of inequality, in the hatred of the Other, in the narcotic haze of consumerism, or in the cheap, seductive violence of scapegoating. As James Baldwin warned, nothing can be changed until it is faced. And as Hannah Arendt taught, the danger lies not only in monstrous acts but in the slow, quiet erosion of thought, memory, and moral imagination. To remember is to resist. It requires staying awake in a world that urges sleep, refusing to look away, to be "wakeful" as Edward Said might say, while daring to imagine the pain inflicted on children. It means allowing empathy to deepen into outrage, and letting that outrage ignite action. To name this moment is not a choice but a moral obligation. And to fight for the living, for their dignity, their future, their right to simply exist, is the only promise worth making, and the only one worth keeping.

Now is the time to break the silence, to speak with moral clarity, and to organize with the fierce urgency that justice demands. We must reclaim the institutions that once carried the promise of a radical democracy, reimagined beyond the grip of capitalism and grounded in solidarity, care, and the public good. We must shield and fight for those deemed disposable, revive the power of civic literacy, and summon the courage to confront the machinery of cruelty and state-sanctioned terror. Fascism cancels the future, but history is watching and the future does not have to imitate the present. And the fate of countless children, at home and across the globe, hangs in the balance of what we choose to do now.

Conclusion: Saving Education, Saving Democracy: Toward a Politics of Liberation

The most tragic form of loss [is] the loss of the capacity to imagine that things could be different.

Ernst Bloch

This war on democracy, long rehearsed in the politics of emerging fascism, has now come fully into view. No longer concealed behind terrorizing wars on immigrants or the racist language of invasion and criminality, it stands exposed as a project of domination that feeds on fear, ignorance, and historical amnesia. As democracy collapses across the globe, a pathological drive to demonize refugees, people of color, and immigrants has become central to the seductive power of a rebranded fascism. As fascism spreads, the boundary between truth and falsehood dissolves, making it ever easier to weaponize culture, normalize cruelty, and legitimize calls for racial cleansing amid the steady militarization of everyday life.

As James Baldwin warned in *The Fire Next Time*, America's refusal to confront its own lies and brutalities would one day "bring down fire," and that fire now burns across the wreckage of civic life, illuminating the depth of our collective moral collapse. That same fire no longer stops at America's borders; it spreads outward, fanning the flames of authoritarianism across the globe, igniting new forms of repression and cruelty wherever democracy falters and memory fades.

Across the globe, from the United States to Italy, India, and Argentina, authoritarian regimes are hollowing out democratic institutions, silencing dissent, and merging culture and violence into a single apparatus of control.[1] The fusion of politics and cruelty has become the lingua franca of the new global order, where spectacle replaces substance and the machinery of surveillance governs both thought and desire. What we are witnessing is not simply the return of fascism but its mutation, a twenty-first-century model powered by digital technologies, neoliberal cruelty, and the manufactured ignorance of mass media. This is nowhere more evident than in the attack on education. Schools and universities, long viewed as spaces for critical thought, a culture of questioning, and civic development (however imperfectly realized), are being transformed into ideological battlegrounds, reduced to mere appendages of corporate and state power, and increasingly subject to state violence. Journalists now describe this not as reform but as war, a campaign of annihilation. In such times, the question is no longer whether education matters, but whether it can survive as a democratic force.

Under the Trump regime, ignorance has been not only cultivated but weaponized, twisted into a force that shrouds lies as truth and redefines education as an act of violence.[2] In the US and across other authoritarian regimes, a culture of lies and historical erasure serves as a mask for tyranny. Trump, with his grotesque parade of over thirty thousand lies during his first term, continues to poison the public mind, still refusing to concede his 2020 loss.[3] Senator Mike Lee of Utah, in a monstrous distortion, somehow blamed Marxists for the murder of a Democratic state legislator in Minnesota and her husband, a crime committed by a Trump supporter. This is no mere falsehood but a sickening expression of a deeper, unspeakable evil.[4]

The right-wing media, spearheaded by Rupert Murdoch's empire, may have lost a legal battle with Dominion Voting Systems over election lies, yet such conspiratorial rhetoric continues to spread unchecked, corroding public reason. The mainstream media is largely silent about Israel's war crimes in Gaza, until they become too obvious to ignore. For the most part, it has also avoided discussing Trump's bombing of Iran as a violation of international law and a reckless act of militarized violence. In the hands of the far right and MAGA mobs, truth has become a dangerous weapon to be destroyed. Critical thinking, once a hallmark of an informed society, is now treated as subversion, exiled from our libraries, schools, and public discourse.

The American public is sinking into a pit of civic illiteracy. This is not simply a crisis of knowledge; it is a catastrophe of reason, politics, and morality, a curse that will only deepen as public complicity fuels the machine of violence, a national surrender to the forces of darkness and destruction. The growing presence of fascism prospers on the deliberate cultivation of ignorance, where lies are paraded as truth, and a public all too willing to surrender to conspiracy theories finds solace in the comfort of unquestioned illiteracy. David Levi Strauss, drawing on Jerome Kohn, describes "the public spirit" as the lifeblood of democracy, a space where citizens debate, dissent, and struggle collectively for the common good.[5] Yet today, the very foundations that make such public spirit possible are being torn apart: the rule of law is sapped of legitimacy, the institutions of justice are weaponized, the press is vilified, education is attacked, and public spaces are ceded to the politics of fear. As these pillars crumble, so too does our capacity to confront truth, defend shared values, and imagine a future rooted in justice.

The death of civic consciousness and the erosion of culture have paved the way for a macabre fusion in which sanitized illusions mask brutal truths, giving rise to a zombie politics ruled by the living dead, soulless figures with blood on their lips. As Chris Hedges observes, America is a decaying regime, its vitality drained, clinging desperately to spectacles like Trump's grotesque military parades that feed the pathologies of a diseased society.[6]

Under the grip of gangster capitalism, culture has become a vehicle for magical thinking, a tool for distracting the masses from the cruel realities of economic stagnation and social inequality. In this warped landscape, commodified and vulgar entertainment reigns supreme, shaping a culture both Disneyfied and zombie-like. Hedges captures this perfectly when he writes: "The Disneyfication of America, the land of eternally happy thoughts and positive attitudes, the land where everything is possible, is peddled to mask the cruelty of economic stagnation and social inequality."[7]

A population conditioned by sexual commodification, mindless entertainment, and graphic violence is taught to blame itself for its own failures. Thoughtlessness has not only been normalized; it has become the precondition for domination. This is the terrifying terrain we now occupy, where the loss of critical consciousness has created fertile ground for the spread of cruelty and control.

At the same time, Trump's drive to construct an authoritarian regime steeped in a culture of fascism is accelerating at breakneck speed. As David Levi Strauss observes, Big Tech oligarchs are steadily buying up the legacy press, a process "signaled by Jeff Bezos's purchase of *The Washington Post* in 2013."[8] The trend has only intensified: tech magnate and Paramount-Skydance CEO David Ellison is closing in on CBS News and "looking to acquire Warner Bros. Discovery, which owns CNN."[9] The social media landscape is no exception. As Levi Strauss warns, "TikTok is about to be sold to a group of Trump allies, including tech baron Larry Ellison, CEO of Oracle."[10]

Algorithms that curate content on TikTok, X, Instagram, YouTube, and Facebook no longer merely reflect social divisions; they engineer them. "We're not divided," Strauss reminds us, "we're being divided."[11] Authoritarianism now works at full throttle, weaponizing culture, education, and pedagogy, shaping not citizens but subjects, disciplining consciousness itself in the image of fascism.

The MAGA cultural warriors have brought their crusade home, embedding it within a broader social and political formation that bears unmistakably fascist features. As Robin D. G. Kelley explains, "MAGA's organic intellectuals" have forged a new far-right bloc that unites billionaires, fossil fuel corporations, cryptocurrency moguls, Silicon Valley elites, Christian nationalists, and white supremacists.[12] Their alliance represents not merely a political movement but a counterrevolution against democracy itself.

Their project is nothing less than the dismantling of democracy's social foundations, gutting the social safety net, dismantling labor unions, weakening affordable health care, and hollowing out public protections, erasing trans people, civil-and-disability rights, academic freedom, and defunding renewable energy. What they seek to construct is a social order cleansed of difference, anchored in exclusion, and exalted by profit. This is the architecture of white nationalism in its contemporary form, a project that marries "mass deportation" to environmental racism, radical deregulation to the destruction of public institutions, and the privatization of education to the consolidation of racial power. Its aim is unmistakable: to refashion America in the image of whiteness while hollowing out the rule of law and turning entire populations into targets of disposability.[13]

The first casualty of authoritarianism is the critical mind. This is not only a political issue but an educational one. Education has never been neutral; it is always political, always entangled with values, power relations, and competing visions of the future. Fascist movements understand this all too well, turning pedagogy itself into a tool of ideological control.

In the age of the neoliberal university, many educational institutions have abandoned these responsibilities.[14] Under the weight of privatization, standardization, and corporate influence, their public purpose has been reduced to a brittle facade. Universities increasingly function not as spaces of inquiry but as credentialing centers and ideological filters, training students for compliance rather than critical engagement. Driven by the instrumental dictates of savage capitalism, the logic of the market has reduced students to consumers, faculty to managed labor serfs, and knowledge to a commodity.

Ranking systems, performance metrics, and austerity budgets have supplanted public investment, intellectual freedom, and pedagogical citizenship. As universities submit to far-right ideological pressure, chase corporate funding, and refuse to define themselves as defenders of democracy, they abandon the mission of cultivating critical, engaged citizens capable of imagining a radically different future, and become laboratories of conformity. Aligned with the forces of predatory capitalism, they erode public conscience, celebrate corporate values, promote unrestrained self-interest, extreme individualism, deregulation, and privatization.

Yet an even more insidious force is at work. In addition to market-driven logic, higher education is being reengineered to serve authoritarian control.[15] In both subtle and overt ways, universities are increasingly transformed into sprawling laboratories of white Christian nationalist indoctrination and into citadels of fear. They have been criminalized by the Trump administration and collectively cast as a vast crime scene in the culture wars. What we witness across the United States is not merely the erosion of democratic education but its replacement with a theocratic, ethnonationalist order rooted in exclusion, historical erasure, and moral authoritarianism.

Curricula are being purged of so-called "divisive concepts," anti-racist scholarship is demonized, and educators who teach about settler colonialism, gender, or Palestinian liberation are censored, surveilled, or summarily dismissed. As mass consciousness surrenders to the dictates of racism, white nationalism, and the militarization of everyday life, history itself is rewritten or obliterated, its moral weight replaced by slogans of purity and obedience. The memory of resistance, the knowledge of what fascism destroys, is slowly disappearing. With that disappearance comes a dangerous amnesia, one that erases not only history but the moral imagination required to prevent its return. In this climate of enforced forgetting, the horrors of mass death and suffering fade into abstraction, something everyone should know, but too few any longer remember.

In *The New Republic*, Indigo Olivier argues that Trump's war on education extends beyond the suppression of campus dissent. It is a deliberate and coordinated campaign to seize the essence of higher learning, remaking it in the image of authoritarian rule built on power, control, and the erasure of critical thought. She writes:

> In recent months, Trump has signed an executive order to dismantle the Department of Education, suspended student loan repayment programs and $400 million in funding to Columbia University, and threatened Harvard University's tax-exempt status after freezing over $2 billion in federal funds. Dozens of universities now face federal investigations as part of Trump's anti-diversity, equity, and inclusion campaign. Perhaps most disturbingly, he has encouraged U.S. Immigration and Customs Enforcement to target international students involved in Gaza solidarity protests for deportation; several are currently being held in a processing facility in Louisiana ... Taken together, these actions have been widely seen as a devastating assault on academic freedom and institutional self-governance that threatens to undermine the character of American higher education itself.[16]

Olivier's account reveals how these actions are not isolated excesses but elements of a coherent authoritarian project. Trump's assault on the autonomy of universities, through financial blackmail, ideological intimidation, and weaponized bureaucracy, represents an attempt to transform higher education from a space of inquiry and dissent into an arm of state propaganda. It marks the institutionalization of a new kind of cultural warfare, one that fuses privatization with persecution, and bureaucratic decree with ideological cleansing.

This project mirrors, with sobering precision, the ideological reengineering of higher education under past fascist regimes. In Nazi Germany, universities were purged of Jewish professors and political dissidents, while academic disciplines were reshaped to propagate racial pseudoscience and legitimate Aryan supremacy. In Mussolini's Italy, intellectuals were coerced into swearing loyalty to the fascist state, and scholarship became a tool of nationalist propaganda, intertwining classical myths with imperial ambition.

As Ruth Ben-Ghiat notes, "Leftists, liberals, and anyone who spoke out against the Fascists were sent to prison or forced into exile."[17] In Franco's Spain, the university was subjected to Catholic authoritarianism, with philosophy, history, and literature marshaled to serve an ultra-conservative and patriarchal order. In Chile, as Ben-Ghiat writes, under the brutal regime of dictator Augusto Pinochet, universities were condemned as "hotbeds of Marxism and targeted ... for 'cleansing'." She notes that "by 1975, 24,000 students, faculty, and staff had been dismissed, thousands imprisoned and tortured, and entire philosophy and social science departments disbanded."[18]

In an article at *The Conversation*, building on these historical echoes, education scholar Iveta Silova adds how swiftly and systematically German universities were transformed under Hitler: "Within a few years, German universities no longer served knowledge; they served power."[19] The Trump administration's efforts to dismantle DEI programs, censor dissenting faculty, and freeze funding to elite institutions like Columbia and Harvard echo this same dangerous legacy. These are part of a calculated attempt to remake higher education into an instrument of ideological control. The pattern is unmistakable: authoritarian leaders understand that universities must either serve the state or be silenced. By attacking critical scholarship and punishing intellectual independence, they seek to destroy the very conditions that make democracy possible.

Under Trump, this war on education has reached a fever pitch, with the attacks on Columbia and Harvard serving as key elements of a broader strategy. By branding campus protesters as "terrorists," labeling faculty as "enemies of America," invoking false allegations of antisemitism against dissenters, and threatening to revoke federal funding, Trump is mobilizing state power to crush intellectual resistance and remake the university in the image of racial purity, blind obedience, and white Christian nationalist mythology.[20]

Yet even amid this reactionary onslaught, resistance cannot be squelched. Across campuses in the US, Canada and around the world, students and educators have refused to be conscripted into authoritarian narratives. From the earlier pro-Palestinian encampments protesting genocide to the nationwide student walkouts opposing book bans and censorship and driving the successful New York City election of Zohran Mamdani, young people are are still attempting to transform educational and public spaces into laboratories of dissent and collective imagination. These acts of defiance recall earlier waves of resistance, from the Free Speech Movement in Berkeley to the student uprisings in 1968 Paris,[21] from the Black campus revolts of the 1970s to the anti-apartheid university occupations of the 1980s, as well as a historical moment when women, refusing to be confined by patriarchal norms, broke through the walls of misogyny to demand autonomy, equality, and liberation.[22]

Resonating with past movements, a number of brave students are reclaiming education as an act of resistance, not a preparation for conformity and ideological indoctrination. They are forming assemblies, teach-ins, and counter-courses, horizontal spaces where knowledge is co-created, solidarity is forged, and the university is reimagined as a site of justice rather than domination. Faculty, too, are pushing back: filing lawsuits, penning public letters, creating sanctuary classrooms, and insisting that pedagogy must serve freedom rather than power. This is why fascists hate higher education and are waging a full-fledged attack on it.[23] A number of universities have refused to accept the Trump regime's latest act of extortion titled "Compact for Academic Excellence in Higher Education."[24]

The so-called Compact would weaponize federal funding to bring universities into line with the authoritarian dictates of the Trump administration. In exchange for financial support, institutions would be coerced into adopting a reactionary ten-point program designed to transform campus life in the image of the far right, stripping diversity from admissions and hiring, imposing rigid and exclusionary definitions of gender, policing academic freedom, and curbing foreign student enrollment. Behind the bureaucratic language of "reform" lies a dark ambition: to transform higher education into an ideological training ground for white nationalism and patriarchal conformity, to turn inquiry into indoctrination and dissent into heresy.

As the Trump administration seeks to transform universities into instruments of obedience and exclusion, the classroom becomes one of the few sanctuaries of thought, imagination, and moral courage, a frontier where the struggle for democracy endures against the encroaching shadows of fascism. In this context, critical pedagogy becomes more than an academic method; it becomes an act of political and ethical defiance, a refusal to surrender the university to authoritarian control and a commitment to making it a space where new forms of collective life can be imagined, nurtured, and fought for.[25]

In cities like Los Angeles, Chicago, and New York, students joined with immigrants, workers, artists, activists, and a handful of courageous politicians to resist Trump's ruthless immigration policies, the criminalization of dissent, and "his unfolding conspiracy to establish a military dictatorship under his personal control."[26]

This convergence of struggles signals a growing recognition that education can no longer be separated from the larger fight for human rights, sanctuary, and democratic life, struggles now imperiled by the steady normalization of authoritarianism. Out of these alliances, a new critical pedagogy of resistance is emerging, rooted in memory and insurgent hope, sustained by the belief that another future remains possible, even in the darkest of times.

Drawing upon the lessons of history and the radical value of critical education, the Foro de Sevilla collective writes, "Auschwitz was much more than a concentration camp, it was a laboratory of dehumanization."[27] Gaza, too, has become such a site, where children, schools, and entire futures are being systematically annihilated. Education, in this context, is not just about knowledge transmission but about moral witnessing and ethical reckoning. It must preserve memory as a living force, capable of shaping civic courage and alerting us to the dangers of silence, complicity, and ideological manipulation. From Auschwitz to Gaza, from Nazi Germany to Trump's America, we see the same dangerous arc: a politics of exclusion that depends on erasure, which turns classrooms into sites of fear rather than freedom.

To meet this moment, educators must embrace a pedagogy inseparable from politics. Critical pedagogy begins not with answers but with probing questions, about history, justice, identity, power, and possibility. It refuses the notion that teaching is a technical act, a homage to empty instrumentalism divorced from context, insisting instead that education is always implicated in the struggle over meaning and memory. As Pierre Bourdieu warned, some of the most powerful forms of domination are symbolic and pedagogical.[28] If authoritarian regimes aim to control not only public institutions but the public imagination, then our task as educators is to illuminate, disrupt, protest, and reimagine. In this struggle, education and culture are not peripheral. They are central to politics, for shaping mass consciousness is the bedrock of any genuine resistance.

Today, that struggle has been hijacked by market fundamentalism and authoritarian rule. Pedagogy has been reduced to training and propaganda; education has been conscripted into the machinery of repression and held hostage by a reactionary group of billionaires.[29] Education is no longer on the side of empowerment for the many; it has been absorbed into the architectures of control, stripped of its democratic mission, and subjected by the Trump administration to mafia-like extortion, indoctrination, and surveillance, while serving as an adjunct of the financial elite.[30] What follows is not merely the collapse of public education, but the emergence of a new social order in which knowledge itself is privatized, commodified, and weaponized against democracy.

Education is a frontline for battles over identities, values, and power. As such, it carries the potential to either suppress or empower, or, as is often the case, to be a complex mix of both. Freire warns that pedagogy becomes a tool of oppression when it reinforces entrenched power structures. Yet he powerfully extends this argument by emphasizing that education is also a site of struggle, where its potential for both domination and liberation is constantly contested. It can awaken consciousness, empower individuals, and resist the forces of injustice. In this sense, education is not merely a social institution, it is a political and ethical terrain where the struggle for freedom, dignity, and transformation is waged.

The relentless attacks on higher education by authoritarians such as Viktor Orbán in Hungary, who was defeated at the polls in the 2026 election, Narendra Modi in India, Recep Tayyip Erdoğan in Turkey, and the Trump regime at home expose a deeper truth: while universities have not always fully realized their potential as incubators of resistance to authoritarianism and its ever-shifting forms of fascist politics, they have always held that potential. This is precisely why they are viewed as a threat. As public institutions, their central mission could be to defend and nurture democracy, however fragile or imperfect, making them a formidable challenge to those who seek to dismantle it.

Needless to say, higher education has spent the last four decades complicit in its transformation from an alleged public good into a class- and race-based filter that reproduces inequality while pretending to reward merit. It sustains the cruel fiction of opportunity for all while grinding down the very ideals it claims to uphold. The promise of higher education as a democratic sphere, a space of critical inquiry and collective responsibility, has been steadily dismantled by decades of neoliberal restructuring, stripping away its democratic function in favor of market-driven imperatives.

As public funding has declined, higher education has become increasingly commodified, subordinated to market logics that treat students as clients, knowledge as a private good, and the university itself as a profit-generating enterprise. Too many administrators have bartered away the democratizing role of education for the false certainties of neoliberalism, transforming universities into temples of calculation, where spreadsheets replace scholarship and human worth is measured in metrics. What was once a sanctuary for thought has been bent and twisted into an audit culture, a managerial nightmare, and a bureaucratic labyrinth ruled by the cold logic of hedge fund billionaires and the market's indifferent gaze.

As social and economic sorting machines, public colleges and universities now ration opportunities through skyrocketing tuition and fees, leaving students burdened by crushing and often lifelong debt. At the same time, faculty labor has been radically devalued, over 70 percent of instructors now work in precarious, contingent positions, stripped of job security and academic freedom. This two-tiered system, privileged elites at the top and dispossessed adjuncts at the bottom, has gutted the democratic mission of the university, replacing it with a managerial culture obsessed with rankings, revenues, and returns on investment.

This neoliberal assault has not only deepened racial and class inequalities; it has redefined the very meaning of higher education. Elite universities now serve as finishing schools for the ruling class, while for-profit colleges prey on the poor and working class, offering false promises and delivering debt without mobility. The university's historic role as a public good, dedicated to critical inquiry, civic responsibility, and social transformation, has been eclipsed by its function as a sorting mechanism that reinforces structural inequality.

In this context, defending higher education against authoritarianism also means confronting the neoliberal policies that have eroded its democratic possibilities from within. Authoritarianism feeds on neoliberalism's failures, its culture of competition, its commodification of everything, and its moral nihilism. If neoliberalism has trained generations to think of education only in terms of private gain, authoritarianism now exploits that cynicism to destroy the very idea of education as a public right.

In an age when both authoritarianism and gangster capitalism conspire to silence dissent and commodify knowledge, reclaiming higher education as a crucible of democracy and critical thought is not simply necessary, it is revolutionary.[31] This means embracing education as a public good and a site of collective responsibility. It requires curricula that foster a culture of inquiry, equip students with the knowledge and skills to hold power accountable, challenge dominant narratives, and cultivate a historical literacy capable of dismantling the myths sustaining fascist ideologies. To defend education is to defend the moral and political imagination itself.

It calls for defending the university not as a corporate entity or a site of theocratic indoctrination but as a democratic commons, a space where a culture of critique and academic freedom can thrive, and where students are empowered to define themselves and break free from the continuum of willful ignorance and callous ineptitude. To reclaim the university as a public good is to insist that education serve democracy rather than the market, truth rather than propaganda, and justice rather than power.

It demands a language that links freedom with social responsibility, agency with solidarity, and critical thought with civic engagement. As Homi Bhabha once said, civic education must disrupt the consensus of common sense. It must fracture the settled order of things to make space for the not-yet-imagined. In an age where language is stripped of meaning and culture is weaponized by the far-right, education must reclaim its capacity to name injustice and summon hope.[32] We need a language of critique and a language of possibility. One that refuses both fatalism and false neutrality.

As the philosopher Cornelius Castoriadis has noted, there is no democracy without an educated public, and no justice without a language capable of critiquing injustice. In dark times, education must not merely transmit knowledge but cultivate the political and moral imagination necessary to resist tyranny and build a future rooted in equality, dignity, and shared responsibility.[33] To make education central to politics is to insist that the fight for democracy begins not only in the streets or at the ballot box but in the classroom, in the slow, transformative work of teaching people to think otherwise, so they might act otherwise.

As Castoriadis reminds us, democracy is not merely the absence of censorship or the formal guarantee of rights, it is the collective power of the people to shape the conditions of their own existence. Its antithesis is unfolding before our eyes under Trump: a regime that wields power not to serve the public good but to impose a form of internal military occupation, destroying the very foundations of democracy and replacing them with fear, surveillance, and authoritarian control. From Nazi Germany to Mussolini's Italy to Trump's America, the pattern is disturbingly familiar: the attack on education always precedes the collapse of democratic life.[34]

Education is not secondary to politics; it is the foundation of any political struggle. As Gramsci taught us, all politics is pedagogical, and in our times, culture itself has become the primary terrain where consent is manufactured and dissent is criminalized. In this age of manufactured stupidity and historical amnesia, authoritarianism doesn't just need lies, it needs forgetfulness; it thrives on eliminating or rewriting dangerous memories. It prospers on the erasure of memory, on civic illiteracy, and on a public numbed into submission.

For the far-right extremists in power, education as the practice of freedom, informed judgment, and critical thinking is dangerous. It threatens the myths, the hierarchies, and the obedience upon which authoritarianism depends. That is why reclaiming education—in schools, in art, in media, in everyday life—is no longer a luxury, but a vital precondition for democratic struggle. As one of the critical institutions in civil society that function as a bulwark of democracy—or what remains of it—public and higher education are a fundamental public good capable of both defending and enabling the search for the truth, democratic values, compassion, and networks of solidarity. Without such education, democracy loses its language, its memory, and its moral compass.

The stakes of resisting fascism and fighting for a radical democracy, both in the United States and across the globe, could not be more urgent. We live in an age when authoritarianism seeks to erase memory, dismantle agency, and extinguish the very conditions that make democratic life possible. In such a moment, education must be reclaimed as an act of radical hope, a practice of remembrance and resistance that insists on thinking, imagining, and acting otherwise.

We must reject the cynical notion that schools are merely instruments of economic, social, and political reproduction, powerless before the forces of capital and coercion. They are, rather, contested spaces where the struggle over meaning, history, and possibility endures. To defend them is not simply to preserve an institution; it is to defend the lifeblood of democracy itself.

What kind of human beings are we cultivating? What dreams do we nurture, what histories do we honor, what futures do we allow to breathe? These are not abstract questions. They cut to the marrow of how we resist and what kind of world we dare to build for our children. We need a language that breaks through despair, a pedagogy that names domination in all its forms but also dares to imagine something radically different. A language that can both wound and heal, that can shatter complacency while nurturing solidarity.

That means rejecting the seductive language of isolated differences and embracing a politics of totality. What is needed is a vision that recognizes how racism, patriarchy, ecological devastation, militarism, and economic dispossession are bound together in a single machinery of gangster capitalist domination. We should refuse the comforts of liberal gradualism and technocratic fixes and instead summon the courage to name capitalism itself as incompatible with democracy. Only by naming the system that breeds cruelty can we imagine a politics that restores life, with human dignity, and with life itself.

Reclaiming education also means recovering the power of historical consciousness—tracing the long genealogy of fascism from the brutalities of racial capitalism in North America to the legacies of colonialism, and to its crystallization in Mussolini's Italy and Hitler's Germany. Only by confronting these intertwined histories can we build the moral and political imagination necessary to resist their return.[35]

As Stuart Hall insisted, culture, and by extension, education, "is a critical site of social action and intervention, where power relations are both established and potentially unsettled."[36] The task before us, then, is not simply to critique the fascist drift of our institutions but to organize, teach, and fight for an emancipatory vision of education, one rooted in historical memory, ethical responsibility, and collective imagination. Against Trump's empire of ugliness and racial hatred, we need a pedagogy of solidarity. Against the forces that would erase the past, malign the present, and cancel the future, we must teach and live as if the future depends on our refusal to forget, our capacity to dream, and our courage to act.

Resistance cannot be episodic; it must become a permanent way of life. Youth must not only protest but organize, link arms with workers, unions, educators, feminists, cultural workers, the unhoused, the racialized, and all those deemed disposable by the existing order. We must occupy not just physical spaces but cultural ones; turn classrooms, social media, poetry, film, and song into sites of political awakening and radical dreaming. Direct action must be met with deep coalition-building. Mutual aid must be paired with revolutionary pedagogy. We need insurgent schools and abolitionist universities committed to dismantling oppressive structures. We need radical art collectives, community libraries, people's theaters, and street universities, spaces where the dispossessed teach each other how to fight and how to hope.

Resistance, to endure, must become culture itself, a living pedagogy and an expression of freedom. In addition, we must dismantle the institutions that make fascism possible. That means confronting the militarization of everyday life, the normalization of surveillance, the criminalization of dissent, and the systemic violence embedded in a political economy that treats vast portions of the population as disposable. We need a vision of democracy that is not a cover for capitalist rule but a rupture with it, a democracy rooted in socialist principles, collective joy, mutual responsibility, and ecological care. Such a vision begins in the classroom, in the streets, and in the imagination of all who refuse to surrender.

This is not a time for despair, but for a militant hope and mass resistance. A time to build, not just new alliances, but new ways of thinking, new languages of resistance, and new institutions of care that will nourish and sustain a radical democracy.[37] It is a time to reject neoliberal fascism's politics of death, a politics that seeks to extinguish life. Instead, we must embrace a politics that dares to imagine the unimaginable, to fight for a future where all are worthy, all are seen, and treated with respect, dignity, and the conditions that make the flourishing of agency and democracy possible. As Ernst Bloch reminds us, "Hope is the possibility of a place where the lost will find their homes."[38] This hope is not passive but active; it is the revolutionary force that fuels our struggle.

Every act of teaching, every refusal to forget, becomes an insurgent gesture against the machinery of disappearance. Memory, when joined with moral imagination, becomes a form of resistance, a way of saying no to the tyranny of erasure and yes to the promise of becoming fully human. Against the politics of cruelty, we must summon a pedagogy of witness; against the culture of amnesia, we must defend the right to remember. The struggle for democracy is, at its core, a struggle over what stories we tell, what futures we dare to imagine, and whose lives we choose to make visible. If fascism seeks to cancel the future, then education, rooted in justice, nourished by hope, and sustained by courage, remains the most radical act of all.

Baldwin's fire, then, is not merely a warning but a command—a call to moral reckoning, to memory, and to action. The fire next time must not be the flames of vengeance, but the blaze of revolutionary clarity, illuminating the path toward justice and equality. It must be the spark that awakens rebellion from the roots, a fire ignited by collective knowledge, courage, and civic responsibility. A flame that pierces through the lies, corruption, and abyss of neoliberal fascism; relentless, unquenchable, and alive with the power to make us see, to make us feel, and to make us act.

In the end, to save education is to save democracy itself. To teach is to act, to remember, and to dream aloud in defiance of despair. The classroom, the street, the page, and the public square are all battlegrounds for the future, spaces where freedom must first be imagined before it can be realized. The task before us is not small: to turn resistance into a way of life, to reclaim hope as a militant democratic force, and to create the conditions for collective struggle against the forces of fascism, disposability, and organized forgetting.

NOTES

Introduction

1 Franco "Bifo" Berardi, *After the Future* (Oakland, CA: AK Press, 2011), 134.

2 Chandra Talpade Mohanty, *Insurgent Vision: Feminism, Justice, Solidarity* (Durham: Duke University Press, 2025), 184, 187.

3 Timothy Snyder, *On Freedom* (New York: Crown, 2025); Jeff Sharlet, *The Undertow: Scenes from a Slow Civil War* (New York: W. W. Norton, 2023); Anne Applebaum, *Twilight of Democracy: The Seductive Lure of Authoritarianism* (New York: Vintage, 2021); Chris Hedges, *America, The Farewell Tour* (New York: Vintage, 2019); Steven Levitsky and Daniel Ziblatt, *How Democracies Die* (New York: Broadway Books, 2018); Henry A. Giroux, *The Terror of the Unforeseen* (Los Angeles: Los Angeles Review of Books, 2019).

4 Federico Finchelstein, *The Wannabe Fascists* (Berkeley: University of California Press, 2024). Finchelstein's definition is worth quoting and noting that the spirit of his definition informs much of this book. He writes: "In historical terms, fascism can be defined as a global ideology with separate national movements and regimes. A counterrevolutionary formation of the extreme right, it was ultranationalist and xenophobic. Fascists were essentially anti-egalitarian and despised liberalism and socialism. The primary aim of fascism was to destroy democracy from within in order to create a modern dictatorship from above. Fascists proposed a totalitarian state in which plurality and civil society would be silenced and there would be few distinctions between the public and the private, or between the state and its citizens. Fascist regimes shut down the independent press and destroyed the rule of law" (6).

5 David Gilbert, "He Wrote a Book About Antifa. Death Threats Are Driving Him Out of the US," *Wired* (October 9, 2025), https://www.wired.com/story/mark-bray-book-antifa-death-threats (accessed March 16, 2026); Edward Helmore, "US anti-fascism expert blocked from flying to Spain at airport," *The Guardian* (October 9, 2025), https://www.theguardian.com/us-news/2025/oct/09/anti-fascism-mark-bray-rutgers-university (accessed March 16, 2026).

6 Emma Whitford, "Michigan Professor's Praise for Pro-Palestinian Protesters Sparks Furor," Inside Higher Education (May 4, 2026). https://www.insidehighered.com/news/faculty/academic-freedom/2026/05/04/professors-praise-pro-palestine-protestors-sparks-furor?utm_source=Inside+Higher+Ed&utm_campaign=5a9cd3470d-DNU_2021_COPY_03&utm_medium=email&utm_term=0_1fcbc04421-5a9cd3470d-236848298&mc_cid=5a9cd3470d&mc_eid=d1b8e1820b

7 Team Zeteo, "These Horrific Numbers Show the Scale of Israel's Genocide in Gaza Two Years On," *Zeteo* (October 8, 2025), https://zeteo.com/p/these-horrific-numbers-show-the-scale (accessed March 16, 2026).

8 Ali Harb, "Canary Mission: How US uses a 'hate group' to target Palestine advocates," *Al Jazeera* (July 11, 2025), https://www.aljazeera.com/news/2025/7/11/canary-mission-how-us-uses-a-hate-group-to-target-palestine-advocates (accessed March 16, 2026).

9 Scott Cummings, "Stopping Autocratic Legalism in America – Before It Is Too Late," *Verfassungsblog* (March 26, 202), https://verfassungsblog.de/stopping-autocratic-legalism-in-america-before-it-is-too-late (accessed March 16, 2026).

10 Sam Levine, "'A capitalistic cowardice': big law firms being threatened by Trump face pressure to speak out," *The Guardian* (March 25, 2025), https://www.theguardian.com/us-news/2025/mar/26/trump-executive-orders-law-firms (accessed March 16, 2026).

11 Lynne Olson, "Neville Chamberlain: A Failed Leader in a Time of Crisis," *New York Times* (June 10, 2019), https://www.nytimes.com/2019/06/10/books/review/tim-bouverie-appeasement.html (accessed March 16, 2026).

12 Jeffrey St. Clair, "The Rendition of Mahmoud Khalil," *CounterPunch* (March 15, 2025), https://www.counterpunch.org/2025/03/15/first-they-came-for-mahmoud-khalil (accessed March 16, 2026).

13 Racial violence has a long legacy in the United State and represents a home grown version of fascism. This has been documented for years by a number of Black writers extending from W. E. B. Du Bois and Cedric J. Robinson to Ruth Gilmore and Angela V. Davis. See Robin D. G. Kelley, "The Responsibility of Intellectuals in the Age of Fascism and Genocide," *Boston Review* (September 2, 2025), https://www.bostonreview.net/forum/the-responsibility-of-intellectuals-in-the-age-of-fascism-and-genocide (accessed March 16, 2026).

14 Haddy Gassama, "Deaths in Detention: ICE Is Rapidly Expanding Detention Camps into Warehouses Despite Record Deaths," ACLU (April 28, 2026), https://www.aclu.org/news/immigrants-rights/deaths-in-detention-ice-is-rapidly-expanding-detention-camps-into-warehouses-despite-record-deaths

15 Henry A. Giroux, "Fascist politics and the dread of white supremacy in the age of disconnections," *Review of Education, Pedagogy, and Cultural Studies* 46, no.1 (2023): 102–17. doi: 10.1080/10714413.2023.2243203.

16 Will Grant, "Venezuelans deported to mega-prison 'trapped in black hole'," *BBC* (March 27, 2025), https://www.bbc.com/news/articles/cm2y5k2zyz5o (accessed March 16, 2026).

17 France 24 France, "US revokes visa for Nigerian Nobel laureate Wole Soyinka," (October 28, 2025), https://www.france24.com/en/live-news/20251028-nigerian-nobel-laureate-wole-soyinka-says-us-visa-revoked-1 (accessed March 16, 2026).

18 Ben Finley and Konstantin Toropin, "A timeline of US attacks off South America and what Congress has had to say," *Associated Press* (November 6, 2025), https://apnews.com/article/trump-boat-strikes-caribbean-military-venezuela-timeline-2dd9d16f4f74d9dfa4aca76d3123678d (accessed March 16, 2026).

19 See Henry A. Giroux, *Pedagogy of Resistance: Against Manufactured Ignorance* (London: Bloomsbury, 2022).

20 Chris Hedges, "Trump's War on Education," *The Chris Hedges Report* (March 11, 2025), https://chrishedges.substack.com/p/trumps-war-on-education/comments (accessed March 16, 2026).

21 Rashid Khalidi, "Does Columbia still merit the name of a university?," *The Guardian* (March 2025), https://www.theguardian.com/commentisfree/2025/mar/25/does-columbia-merit-the-name-of-university (accessed March 16, 2026).

22 Ian Buruma, "The Uses and Abuses of 'Antisemitism'," *The New Yorker* (September 22, 2025), https://www.newyorker.com/magazine/2025/09/29/on-antisemitism-mark-mazower-book-review-world-enemy-no-1-jochen-hellbeck (accessed March 16, 2026).

23 Amos Goldberg, "Holocaust Memory in a Time of Genocide," *Zeteo* (July 30, 2025), https://zeteo.com/p/holocaust-memory-in-a-time-of-genocide (accessed March 16, 2026).

24 Jason Stanley, *Erasing History: How Fascists Rewrite the Past to Control the Future* (New York: Atria/One Signal Publishers, 2024).

25 Jennifer Mascia, "Trump's Big Crime Lies," *The Trace* (September 25, 2025). https://www.thetrace.org/2025/09/trump-crime-lies-immigrants-democrats (accessed March 16, 2026); see also Rosalind Adams, "How Trump is using 'pure lies' about high crime in US cities to justify federal takeovers," *The Guardian* (August 15, 2025), https://www.theguardian.com/us-news/2025/aug/15/trump-dc-national-guard-crime-rates(accessed March 16, 2026).

26 Nick Turse, "On the Precipice of Authoritarian Rule: The Trump Administration's Miliary Occupation of America," *Tom Dispatch* (October 16, 2025), https://tomdispatch.com/on-the-precipice-of-authoritarian-rule (accessed March 16, 2026).

27 Helene Cooper, "'Dangerous Cities,' the Military, Trump and the Founding Fathers," *New York Times* (October 1, 2025), https://www.nytimes.com/2025/10/01/us/politics/trump-military-founding-fathers.html (accessed March 16, 2026).

28 Helene Cooper, "'Dangerous Cities,' the Military, Trump and the Founding Fathers." It is worth mentioning how this was predicted by Aime Cesaire in his *Discourse on Colonialism* (New York: Monthly Review Press, 1950), p. 36. He writes: "And then one fine day the bourgeoisie is awakened by a terrific boomerang effect: the gestapos are busy, the prisons fill up, the torturers standing around the racks invent, refine, discuss. People are surprised; they become indignant. They say: 'How strange! But never mind—it's Nazism, it will pass!' And they wait, and they hope; and they hide the truth from themselves, that it is barbarism, the supreme barbarism, the crowning barbarism that sums up all the daily barbarisms; that it is Nazism, yes, but that before they were its victims, they were its accomplices; that they tolerated that Nazism before it was inflicted on them, that they absolved it, shut their eyes to it, legitimized it, because, until then, it had been applied only to non-European peoples; that they have cultivated that Nazism, that they are responsible for it, and that before engulfing the whole edifice of Western, Christian civilization in its reddened waters, it oozes, seeps, and trickles from every crack."

29 Ed Kilgore, "Trump Regards Millions of Americans as Enemies of the People," *New York Magazine* (October 3, 2025), https://nymag.com/intelligencer/article/trump-regards-millions-as-enemies-in-government-shutdown.html (accessed March 16, 2026).

30 Brendan O'Brien, Andy Sullivan, and Susan Heavey, "Trump calls for jailing Democratic leaders as troops prepare for Chicago deployment," *Reuters* (October 8, 2025), https://www.reuters.com/world/us/trump-calls-chicago-mayor-illinois-governor-be-jailed-2025-10-08 (accessed March 16, 2026).

31 Minnah Arshad, "Letitia James Indicted as Trump Continues Down His Enemies List," *Zeteo* (October 9, 2025). https://zeteo.com/p/letitia-james-indicted-as-trump-continues (accessed March 16, 2026).

32 Judd Legum, "How federal agents are terrorizing American citizens," *Popular Information* (October 6, 2025), https://popular.info/p/how-federal-agents-are-terrorizing (accessed March 16, 2026).

33 Sherrilyn Ifill, "It Is Not Enough to Fight. You Have to Meet the Moment," *Sherrilyn's Newsletter* (March 16, 2025), https://sherrilyn.substack.com/p/it-is-not-enough-to-fight-you-have (accessed March 16, 2026).

34 Robin D. G. Kelley, "Notes on Fighting Trumpism," *Boston Review* (November 12, 2024), https://www.bostonreview.net/articles/notes-on-fighting-trumpism (accessed March 16, 2026).

35 Andrey Smolyakov, "The hate algorithm: How social media fuels radicalization," *The Insider* (June 19, 2025), https://theins.ru/en/society/282269 (accessed March 16, 2026).

36 David Theo Goldberg, *Dread: Facing Futureless Futures* (London: Polity, 2021).

37 Thom Hartmann offers an insightful critique of rallies and movements that are too short-lived because they are leaderless and lack sustaining organizations. See Thom Hartmann, "When the Chant Fades, Who Builds the Future?" *The Thom Hartmann Report* (October 20, 2025), https://hartmannreport.com/p/when-the-chant-fades-who-builds-the (accessed March 16, 2026).

38 Goldberg, *Dread: Facing Futureless Futures*.

39 Chris Hedges, "Trump's Greatest Ally is the Democratic Party," *The Chris Hedges Report* (November 3, 2025), https://chrishedges.substack.com/p/trumps-greatest-ally-is-the-democratic (accessed March 16, 2026).

40 Chris Hedges, "The Politics of Cultural Despair," *The Chris Hedges Report* (November 6, 2024), https://chrishedges.substack.com/p/the-politics-of-cultural despair (accessed March 16, 2026).

41 Jean-Luc Mélenchon, "We Need a New Civic Morality," *Jacobin* (April 2025), https://jacobin.com/2025/04/melenchon-virtue-universalism-humanity-creolization (accessed March 16, 2026).

Chapter 1

1 Henry A. Giroux, *The Burden of Conscience: Educating Beyond the Veil of Silence* (London: Bloomsbury, 2025).

2 Nancy Fraser, *Cannibal Capitalism* (London: Verso, 2023); Heather Gautney, *The New Power Elite* (New York: Oxford University Press, 2023).

3 Thom Hartmann, *The Hidden History of Neoliberalism: How Reaganism Gutted America and How to Restore Its Greatness* (Oakland, CA: Berrett-Koehler Publishers, 2022).

4 Brad Evans, "Humans in Dark Times," *New York Times* (February 23, 2017), https://www.nytimes.com/2017/02/23/opinion/humans-in-dark-times.html (accessed March 16, 2026).

5 David Theo Goldberg, *Dread: Facing Futureless Futures* (London: Polity Press, 2021).

6 Chris Hedges, "The Politics of Cultural Despair," *The Chris Hedges Report* (November 6, 2024), https://chrishedges.substack.com/p/the-politics-of-cultural-despair (accessed March 16, 2026).

7 Pankaj Mishra, "A Gandhian Stand Against the Culture of Cruelty," *The New York Review of Books* (May 22, 2018), https://www.nybooks.com/online/2018/05/22/the-culture-of-cruelty (accessed March 16, 2026).

8 Étienne Balibar, "Outline of a Topography of Cruelty: Citizenship and Civility in the Era of Global Violence," *We, The People of Europe? Reflections on Transnational Citizenship* (Princeton: Princeton University Press, 2004), 130..

9 Mishra, "A Gandhian Stand Against the Culture of Cruelty."

10 Mishra, "A Gandhian Stand."

11 Robert Mackey, "White House plays racist deepfake video of Democratic leaders on loop," *The Guardian* (October 2, 2025), https://www.theguardian.com/us-news/2025/oct/01/trump-racist-deepfake-video-jeffries-schumer (accessed March 16, 2026).

12 James Speyer, "The Most Powerful Crime Syndicate in History," *New York Daily News* (February 8, 2026), https://www.nydailynews.com/2026/02/18/the-most-powerful-crime-syndicate-in-history (accessed April 13, 2026).

13 Henry Maher, "The neoliberal Great Replacement theory: on the racialization of markets and migration," *Distinktion: Journal of Social Theory* (May 6, 2025). doi: 10.1080/1600910X.2025.2499827.

14 Robin D. G. Kelley, "Notes on Fighting Trumpism," *Boston Review* (November 12, 2024), https://www.bostonreview.net/articles/notes-on-fighting-trumpism (accessed March 16, 2026).

15 Jake Johnson, "Sanders Rips Trump for Finding '$40 Billion to Bail Out Argentina' While Cutting Off Food Aid in US," *Common Dreams* (October 27, 2025), https://www.commondreams.org/news/trump-argentina-bailout-snap (accessed March 16, 2026).

16 Adam Serwer, "The Cruelty Is the Point," *The Atlantic* (October 3, 2018), https://www.theatlantic.com/ideas/archive/2018/10/the-cruelty-is-the-point/572104 (accessed March 16, 2026).

17 Henry A. Giroux, *The Burden of Conscience* (London: Bloomsbury, 2025); George Monbiot and Peter Hutchison, *Invisible Doctrine: The Secret History of Neoliberalism* (London: Allen Lane, 2024).

18 Marina Dunbarrump, "Trump v Comey: a timeline of the president and ex-FBI director's feud," *The Guardian* (September 26, 2025), https://www.theguardian.com/us-news/2025/sep/26/donald-trump-james-comey-timeline-feud (accessed March 16, 2026).

19 Susan Sontag, "Fascinating Fascism," *The New York Review of Books*," (February 6, 1975), https://www.nybooks.com/articles/1975/02/06/fascinating-fascism (accessed March 16, 2026).

20 Jonathan Lambert, "Study: 14 million lives could be lost due to Trump aid cuts," *National Public Radio-Goats and Soda* (July 1, 2025), https://www.npr.org/sections/goats-and-soda/2025/07/01/nx-s1-5452513/trump-usaid-foreign-aid-deaths (accessed March 16, 2026).

21 Fintan O'Toole, "From Comedy to Brutality," *The New York Review of Books* (March 13, 2025), https://www.nybooks.com/articles/2025/03/13/from-comedy-to-brutality-fintan-otoole (accessed March 16, 2026).

22 Colin McCullough, "Trump posts video referencing 'unified Reich' if reelected," *CNN* (May 21, 2024), https://www.cnn.com/2024/05/21/politics/trump-unified-reich-video/index.html (accessed March 16, 2026).

23 Étienne Balibar, "Outline of a Topography of Cruelty: Citizenship and Civility in the Era of Global Violence," *We, The People of Europe? Reflections on Transnational Citizenship* (Princeton: Princeton University Press, 2004), 130.

24 Sean Seddon, "What is USAID and why is Trump poised to 'close it down'?," *BBC* (February 7, 2025), https://www.bbc.com/news/articles/clyezjwnx5ko (accessed March 16, 2026).

25 Apoorva Mandavilli, "With Aid Cutoff, Trump Halts Agency's Legacy of 'Acting With Humanity'," *New York Times* (February 8, 2025), https://www.nytimes.com/2025/02/08/health/trump-usaid-health-aid.html (accessed March 16, 2026).

26 Ralph Nader, "Trump/Musk Dictatorship Is Galvanizing the American People's Resistance," *CounterPunch* (February 17, 2025), https://www.counterpunch.org/2025/02/17/trump-musk-dictatorship-is-galvanizing-the-american-peoples-resistance (accessed March 16, 2026).

27 Anne Applebaum, "There's a Term for What Trump and Musk Are Doing," *The Atlantic* (February 13, 2025), https://www.theatlantic.com/ideas/archive/2025/02/doge-civil-servant-purge/681671 (accessed March 16, 2026).

28 Jessica Colarossi, "'It's Unacceptable': BU Mathematician Tracks How Many Deaths May Result from USAID, Medicaid Cuts," *The Brink* (March 20, 2025), https://www.bu.edu/articles/2025/mathematician-tracks-deaths-from-usaid-medicaid-cuts (accessed March 16, 2026).

29 Daniella Medeiros Cavalcanti, Lucas de Oliveira Ferreira de Sales, Andrea Ferreira da Silva, Elisa Landin Basterra, Daiana Pena, Caterina Monti, et al., "Evaluating the impact of two decades of USAID interventions and projecting the effects of defunding on mortality up to 2030: a retrospective impact evaluation and forecasting analysis," *The Lancet* (July 19, 2025), https://www.thelancet.com/journals/lancet/article/PIIS0140-6736(25)01186-9/fulltext (accessed March 16, 2026).

30 Israel News, "The State of Israel," *Haaretz.com* (November 29, 2025), https://us18.campaign-archive.com/?e=6fd29bcfda&u=d3bceadb340d6af4daf1de00d&id=e465573192 (accessed March 16, 2026).

31 Lorenzo Tondo, "Israel has violated ceasefire 47 times and killed 38 Palestinians, says Gaza media office," *The Guardian* (October 8, 2025), https://www.theguardian.com/world/2025/oct/18/israel-has-violated-ceasefire-47-times-and-killed-38-palestinians-says-gaza-media-office (accessed March 16, 2026).

32 Directorate-General for Competition, "Commission designates six gatekeepers under the Digital Markets Act" (September 6, 2023), https://digital-markets-act.ec.europa.eu/commission-designates-six-gatekeepers-under-digital-markets-act-2023-09-06_en (accessed March 16, 2026).

33 Ruth Ben-Ghiat, *Strongmen: Mussolini to the Present* (New York: W. W. Norton, 2021).

34 Zadie Smith, "The Dream of the Raised Arm," *The New York Review* (November 10, 2024), https://www.nybooks.com/articles/2024/12/05/the-dream-of-the-raised-arm-third-reich-of-dreams-beradt-zadie-smith (accessed March 16, 2026).

35 Melvin Goodman, "Trump: the Meanness and Mendacity of Being," *CounterPunch* (February 12, 2025), https://www.counterpunch.org/2025/02/12/trump-the-meanness-and-mendacity-of-being (accessed March 16, 2026).

36 Goodman, "Trump: the Meanness and Mendacity of Being."

37 Étienne Balibar, "The Idea of Revolution: Yesterday, Today and Tomorrow," *Rising Up Seminar Series* 17/18 (August 27, 2027), https://blogs.law.columbia.edu/uprising1313/etienne-balibar-the-idea-of-revolution-yesterday-today-and-tomorrow (accessed March 16, 2026).

38 For a brilliant discussion of this issue see Chandra Talpade Mohanty, *Insurgent Visions: Feminism, Justice, Solidarity* (Durham, NC: Duke University Press, 2025).

39 Etienne Balibar, "Outline of a Topography of Cruelty: Citizenship and Civility in the Era of Global Violence," *We, The People of Europe? Reflections on Transnational Citizenship* (Princeton: Princeton University Press, 2004), 126–7.

40 Balibar, "Outline of a Topography of Cruelty," 119.

41 Bernie Sanders, "We are on the road for democracy and justice," *The Guardian* (February 19, 2025), https://www.theguardian.com/commentisfree/2025/feb/19/trumpism-bernie-sanders (accessed March 16, 2026).

42 Mike Brock, "The Plot Against America," *Notes from the Circus* (February 8, 2025), https://www.notesfromthecircus.com/p/the-plot-against-america (accessed March 16, 2026).

43 Suzanne Schneider, "America's all new economic model," *The New World* (February 5, 2025), https://www.thenewworld.co.uk/suzanne-schneider-americas-all-new-economic-model (accessed March 16, 2026).

44 Jay Salley, "Peter Thiel: The Shadowy Power Behind America's Corporate Control," *Medium* (March 15, 2025), https://jasonsalley.medium.com/peter-thiel-the-shadowy-power-behind-americas-corporate-control-671e8f5a8bbf (accessed March 16, 2026).

45 David Marchese, "The Interview: Curtis Yarvin Says Democracy Is Done. Powerful Conservatives Are Listening," *New York Times* (January 18, 2025), https://www.nytimes.com/2025/01/18/magazine/curtis-yarvin-interview.html (accessed March 16, 2026).

46 David Livingstone, "We Need a Revival of Marxist Class Analysis," *Jacobin* (March 18, 2024), https://jacobin.com/2024/03/marxist-class-analysis-class-consciousness (accessed March 16, 2026).

47 Alain Badiou, *Ethics: An Essay on the Understanding of Evil* (London: Verso, 1998), 9.

Chapter 2

1 Nicole Foy, photography by Sarahbeth Maney, "We Found That More Than 170 U.S. Citizens Have Been Held by Immigration Agents. They've Been Kicked, Dragged and Detained for Days," *ProPublica* (October 16, 2025), https://www.propublica.org/article/immigration-dhs-american-citizens-arrested-detained-against-will (accessed March 17, 2026).

2 Eric Westervelt, Anusha Mathur, and Brent Jones, "Mapping ICE's expanding footprint, and the communities fighting back," NPR (March 23, 2026). https://www.npr.org/2026/03/23/g-s1-114107/ices-growing-detention-footprint-and-the-communities-fighting-back

3 The Associated Press, "Immigration judge rules that Columbia University activist Mahmoud Khalil can be deported," *Politico* (April 11, 2025), https://www.politico.com/news/2025/04/11/immigration-judge-rules-that-columbia-university-activist-mahmoud-khalil-can-be-deported-00287161 (accessed March 17, 2026).

4 Chloe Atkins and Matt Lavietes, "Marco Rubio memo cites Mahmoud Khalil's beliefs in justifying his deportation," *NBC News* (April 10, 2025), https://www.nbcnews.com/news/us-news/mahmoud-khalil-deported-serious-foreign-policy-consequences-rubio-memo-rcna200612 (accessed March 17, 2026).

5 Nawal Arjini, "The Appall," *The New York Review* (November 30, 2024), https://www.nybooks.com/online/2024/11/30/the-appall-jorie-graham (accessed March 17, 2026).

6 Silky Shah, "Khalil Case Shows How Migrant Justice and Palestine Solidarity Are Tied Together," *Truthout* (March 15, 2025), https://truthout.org/articles/khalil-case-shows-how-migrant-justice-and-palestine-solidarity-are-tied-together (accessed March 17, 2026).

7 Niha Masih, Anumita Kaur, Frances Vinall and Julie Yoon, "Tufts student from Turkey detained by masked officers, video shows," *The Washington Post* (March 27, 2025), https://www.washingtonpost.com/immigration/2025/03/27/rumeysa-ozturk-tufts-student-ice-video (accessed March 17, 2026).

8 Nathan Stoltzfus, "Dissent in Nazi Germany," *The Atlantic* (September 1992), https://www.theatlantic.com/magazine/archive/1992/09/dissent-in-nazi-germany/532725 (accessed March 17, 2026).

9 Rumeysa Ozturk, Fatima Rahman, Genesis Perez and Nicholas Ambeliotis, "Op-ed: Try again, President Kumar: Renewing calls for Tufts to adopt March 4 TCU Senate resolutions," *The Tufts Daily* (March 26, 2024), https://www.tuftsdaily.com/article/2024/03/4ftk27sm6jkj (accessed March 17, 2026).

10 Noa Yachot, Anna Betts and Oliver Laughland, "Mahmoud Khalil released from ICE detention after more than three months," *The Guardian* (June 20, 2025), https://www.theguardian.com/us-news/2025/jun/20/mahmoud-khalil-release-federal-judge (accessed March 17, 2026).

11 Jason Stanley, *Erasing History: How Fascists Rewrite the Past to Control the Future* (New York: One Signal Publishers, 2024); Steven Levisky and Daniel Ziblatt, *How Democracies Die* (New York: Broadway Books, 2018).

12 Michelle Butterfield, "Venezuelans deported to El Salvador describe 'horror movie' mega-prison," *Global News* (July 25, 2025), https://globalnews.ca/news/11304222/el-salvador-cecot-conditions-venezuelan-migrants (accessed March 17, 2026).

13 Zak Cheney-Rice, "This Is Fascism. What Trump's affection for El Salvador's Nayib Bukele reveals about the fallen state of American democracy," *New York* (March 21, 2025), https://nymag.com/intelligencer/article/nayib-bukele-donald-trump-deportation-authoritarianism.html (accessed March 17, 2026).

14 Julie Turkewitz, Tibisay Romero, Sheyla Urdaneta, Isayen Herrera and Adriana Loureiro Fernandez, "Inside Trump's Deportation of Venezuelans: Four Months in a Salvadoran Prison," *New York Times* (November 8, 2025), https://www.nytimes.com/2025/11/08/world/americas/el-salvador-prison-migrants.html (accessed March 17, 2026).

15 Hafiz Rashid, "El Salvador's President Makes Sick Argument on Wrongly Deported Man," *The New Republic* (April 14, 2025), https://newrepublic.com/post/193966/el-salvador-bukele-wrongly-deported-man-garcia (accessed March 17, 2026).

16 Al Jazeera Staff, "Who are the students Trump wants to deport?," *Al Jazeera* (March 27, 2025), https://www.aljazeera.com/news/2025/3/27/who-are-the-students-trump-wants-to-deport (accessed March 17, 2026).

17 Chis Geidner, "Judge William Young's ruling against Rubio and Noem is a lesson for all in the Trump era," *Law Dork* (October 1, 2025), https://www.lawdork.com/p/judge-william-youngs-ruling-against (accessed March 17, 2026).

18 Noura Erakat, "The Boomerang Comes Back," *Boston Review* (February 5, 2025), https://www.bostonreview.net/articles/the-boomerang-comes-back (accessed March 17, 2026).

19 Jennifer Mercieca, *Demagogue for President: The Rhetorical Genius of Donald Trump* (College Station: Texas A&M Press, 2020).

20 Chad De Guzman, "President Trump Suggests He's Above the Law in Social Media Post Invoking Napoleon," *Time* (February 18, 2025), https://time.com/7226686/trump-napoleon-post-saves-country-violate-law-reactions-constitutional-crisis (accessed March 17, 2026).

21 Chip Gibbons, "Crushing Dissent Through Immigration Law," *Jacobin* (March 24, 2025), https://jacobin.com/2025/03/khalil-dissent-immigration-law-deportation (accessed March 17, 2026).

22 Ellen Schrecker, *Many Are the Crimes: McCarthyism in America* (Princeton, NJ: Princeton University Press, 1999).

23 Ellen Schrecker, *The Lost Promise: American Universities in the 1960s* (Chicago: University of Chicago Press, 2021).

24 Henry A. Giroux, *Hearts of Darkness: Torturing Children in the War on Terror* (New York: Routledge, 2015).

25 Paul Gilroy, "The 2019 Holberg Lecture, by Laureate Paul Gilroy: Never Again: Refusing Race and Salvaging the Human," *Holbergprisen* (November 11, 2019), https://holbergprisen.no/en/news/holberg-prize/2019-holberg-lecture-laureate-paul-gilroy (accessed March 17, 2026).

26 Primo Levi, *The Black Hole of Auschwitz* (London: Polity, 2005), 34.

27 Martin Wolf, "Fascism has changed, but it is not dead," *Telegrafi* (2025), https://telegrafi.com/en/fashizmi-ka-ndryshuar-por-nuk-ka-vdekur (accessed 14 April 2026).

28 Robert Gellately, *Backing Hitler: Consent and Coercion in Nazi Germany* (New York: Oxford University Press, 2011).

29 Federico Finchelstein, *The Ideological Origins of the Dirty War: Fascism, Populism, and Dictatorship in Twentieth Century Argentina* (New York: Oxford University Press, 2014).

30 G. M. Tamás, "On Post-Fascism: Its central characteristic is hostility to universal citizenship," *Boston Review* (June 1, 2000), https://www.bostonreview.net/articles/g-m-tamas-post-fascism (accessed March 17, 2026).

31 Moira Donegan, "The US government is effectively kidnapping people for opposing genocide," *The Guardian* (February 28, 2025), https://www.theguardian.com/commentisfree/2025/mar/28/rumeysa-ozturk-tufts-trump-immigration-gaza (accessed March 17, 2026).

32 Tamás, "On Post-Fascism."

33 Tamás, "On Post-Fascism."

34 Theodor Adorno, *The Authoritarian Personality* (New York: Verso, 2019).

35 Jason Stanley, *Erasing History: How Fascists Rewrite the Past to Control the Future* (New York: One Signal Publishers, 2024).

36 Jake Offenhatz, "Trump demands admissions overhaul and control of academic department at Columbia University," *PBS News* (May 14, 2025), https://www.pbs.org/newshour/education/trump-demands-admissions-overhaul-and-control-of-academic-department-at-columbia-university (accessed March 17, 2026).

37 Jonathan W. Gray, "Trump Is Cracking Down on the Colleges That Cave to Him," *The New Republic* (March 12, 2025), https://newrepublic.com/article/192543/mahmoud-khalil-detention-warning-higher-education (accessed March 17, 2026).

38 Frank S. Zhou, "Harvard Must Take a Stand for Democracy," *The Harvard Crimson* (March 6, 2025), https://www.thecrimson.com/article/2025/3/6/enos-levitsky-harvard-trump-democracy-fight (accessed March 17, 2026).

39 Umberto Eco, "Ur-Fascism," *The New York Review of Books* (June 22, 1995), http://www.nybooks.com/articles/1995/06/22/ur-fascism (accessed March 17, 2026).

40 Judith Butler, "State Violence, War, Resistance: For a New Politics of the Left," *CCCB* (April 7, 2010), https://www.cccb.org/en/activities/file/judith-butlerstate-violence-war-resistance/217995 (accessed March 17, 2026).

41 Al Jazeera Staff, "Donald Trump threatens opponents with jail in Justice Department speech," *Al Jazeera* (March 14, 2025), https://www.aljazeera.com/news/2025/3/14/in-justice-department-speech-donald-trump-threatens-opponents-with-jail (accessed March 17, 2026).

42 Erakat, "The Boomerang Comes Back."

43 Jonah Valdez and Jessica Washington, "He Sued Trump Over Free Speech. Then ICE Demanded He Turn Himself In," *The Intercept* (March 21, 2025), https://theintercept.com/2025/03/21/trump-free-speech-lawsuit-ice-momodou-taal (accessed March 17, 2026).

44 Amy Goodman with Nader Hashemi, "Georgetown Scholar Badar Khan Suri Remains in Immigration Jail After Masked Agents Snatched Him in D.C.," *Democracy Now* (March 24, 2025), https://www.democracynow.org/2025/3/24/badar_khan_suri_georgetown_nader_hashemi (accessed March 17, 2026).

45 Goodman with Hashemi, "Georgetown Scholar Badar Khan Suri Remains in Immigration Jail."

46 Hafiz Rashid, "Trump Kicks Off Constitutional Crisis with Doctor's Deportation," *The New Republic* (March 17, 2025), https://newrepublic.com/post/192816/trump-constitutional-crisis-doctor-deportation-alawieh (accessed March 17, 2026).

47 Arwa Mahdawi, "The US assault on free speech is not going to end with Mahmoud Khalil," *The Guardian* (March 15, 2025), https://www.theguardian.com/commentisfree/2025/mar/15/mahmoud-khalil-free-speech-civil-liberties (accessed March 17, 2026).

48 Martin Pengelly, "Trump condemned for using 'Palestinian' as slur to attack Schumer," *The Guardian* (March 12, 2025), https://www.theguardian.com/us-news/2025/mar/12/trump-chuck-schumer-palestinian-slur (accessed March 17, 2026).

49 Akela Lacy, "If Protesting Tesla Is Domestic Terrorism, Then What Demonstration Against Musk Isn't," *The Intercept* (March 13, 2015), https://theintercept.com/2025/03/13/trump-musk-tesla-protest-domestic-terrorism (accessed March 17, 2026).

50 Owen Scott, "Trump slams Pope Leo as 'weak' and posts picture of himself as Jesus healing the sick," *The Independent* (April 13, 2026). https://www.independent.co.uk/news/world/americas/us-politics/trump-pope-leo-truth-social-b2956378.html (accessed 14 April 2026).

51 I along with Brad Evans have taken up this issue in great detail. See Henry A. Giroux and Brad Evans, *Disposable Futures: The Seduction of Violence in the Age of Spectacle* (San Francisco: City Lights, 2015).

52 Robert J. Lifton, *The Nazi Doctors* (New York: Basic Books, 2000), 125.

53 Nancy Fraser, "Democracy's Crisis: On the Political Contradictions of Financialized Capitalism," *Weatherhead Center for International Affairs at Harvard University* 33:1 (Fall 2018), https://www.wcfia.harvard.edu/publications/centerpiece/fall2018/transcript_jodidi11-5-2018 (accessed March 17, 2026).

54 Sarah Stillman, "Disappeared to a Foreign Prison," *The New Yorker* (November 24, 2025), https://www.newyorker.com/magazine/2025/12/01/disappeared-to-a-foreign-prison (accessed March 17, 2026).

55 Peter Aitken, "Democrat Lawmaker Blasts 'Alligator Alcatraz' as 'Internment Camp'," *Newsweek* (July 12, 2025), https://www.newsweek.com/debbie-wasserman-schultz-blasts-alligator-alcatraz-internment-camp-2098240 (accessed March 17, 2026).

56 Thom Hartmann, "Alligator Alcatraz Isn't Just a Prison. It's a Mirror. And It's Asking Us: Who Are We, Really?" *The Hartmann Report* (July 2, 2025), https://hartmannreport.com/p/alligator-alcatraz-isnt-just-a-prison (accessed March 17, 2026).

57 Andrew Perez and Asawin Suebsaeng, "Trump Thinks He Can Take Away Citizenship From Anyone He Doesn't Like," *Rolling Stone* (July 12, 2025), https://www.rollingstone.com/politics/politics-news/trump-us-citizenship-rosie-o-donnell-zohran-mamdani-1235384436 (accessed March 17, 2026).

58 Arwa Mahdawi, "The US assault on free speech is not going to end with Mahmoud Khalil," *The Guardian* (March 15, 2025), https://www.theguardian.com/commentisfree/2025/mar/15/mahmoud-khalil-free-speech-civil-liberties (accessed March 17, 2026).

59 Mahdawi, "The US assault on free speech is not going to end with Mahmoud Khalil."

Chapter 3

1 Fred Kaplan, "Hello, Dictators," *Slate* (January 20, 2025), https://slate.com/news-and-politics/2025/01/trump-dictators-putin-xi-kim-jong-un-orban.html (accessed March 17, 2026); Kelly Garrity and Meridith McGraw, "One year of Trump's praise for authoritarians," *Politico* (December 18, 2023), https://www.politico.com/news/2023/12/18/trump-praise-authoritarians-00132350 (accessed March 17, 2026).

2 Amy Goodman, "Mehdi Hasan: Trump Is Weaponizing the Murder of Charlie Kirk to Go After the Left," *Democracy Now!* (September 12, 2025), https://www.democracynow.org/2025/9/12/mehdi_hasan (accessed March 17, 2026).

3 Jeffrey St. Clair, "An Occurrence in Orem: Notes on the Murder of Charlie Kirk," *CounterPunch* (September 15, 2025), https://www.counterpunch.org/2025/09/15/an-occurence-in-orem-on-the-murder-of-charlie-kirk (accessed March 17, 2026).

4 The White House, "Countering Domestic Terrorism and Organized Political Violence," *Presidential Memoranda* (September 25, 2025), https://www.whitehouse.gov/presidential-actions/2025/09/countering-domestic-terrorism-and-organized-political-violence (accessed March 17, 2026).

5 C. J. Polychroniou and Alexandra Boutri, "Trump Is a Fascist, That's Clear. But What Kind Exactly?," *Common Dreams* (September 29, 2025), https://www.commondreams.org/opinion/trump-is-a-fascist-that-s-clear-but-what-kind-exactly (accessed March 17, 2026).

6 Rebecca Falconer, "Trump slams 'radical left' after signing 'organized political violence' memo," *Axios* (September 26, 2025), https://www.axios.com/2025/09/26/trump-organized-political-violence-radical-left (accessed March 17, 2026).

7 Jonathan Chait, "Stephen Miller's Hypocrisy Is Right There in His Speech," *The Atlantic* (September 22, 2025), https://www.theatlantic.com/politics/archive/2025/09/stephen-millers-charlie-kirk-funeral/684301 (accessed March 17, 2026).

8 Hannah Arendt, *The Origins of Totalitarianism* (New York: Harper Collins, 1973).

9 Henry A. Giroux, *Pedagogy of Resistance: Against Manufactured Ignorance* (London: Bloomsbury, 2023).

10 Wendy Brown, "The End of Educated Democracy," *Representations* 116:1(Fall 2011). doi: 10.1525/rep.2011.116.1.19

11 Henry A. Giroux and Anthony R. DiMaggio, *Fascism on Trial: Education and the Possibility of Democracy* (London: Bloomsbury, 2024).

12 Commentary, "Outlawing the Opposition," *Facing History and Ourselves* (August 2, 2016), https://www.facinghistory.org/resource-library/outlawing-opposition (accessed March 17, 2026).

13 PBS, "The Man Behind Hitler," *American Experience* (May 22, 2006), https://www.pbs.org/wgbh/americanexperience/films/goebbels (accessed March 17, 2026).

14 News, "Resurrecting Franco," *Irish Congress of Trade Unions* (January 22, 2016), https://www.ictu.ie/blog/resurrecting-franco (accessed March 17, 2026).

15 Viktor Orbán, "Orbán Viktor's ceremonial speech on the 170th anniversary of the Hungarian Revolution of 1848," *About Hungary* (March 15, 2018), https://abouthungary.hu/speeches-and-remarks/orban-viktors-ceremonial-speech-on-the-170th-anniversary-of-the-hungarian-revolution-of-1848 (accessed March 17, 2026).

16 Julia Conley, "Despite Kirk Shooter's Unknown Identity, Trump Holds Left 'Directly Responsible'," *Truthout (September* 11, 2025), https://truthout.org/articles/despite-kirk-shooters-unknown-identity-trump-holds-left-directly-responsible (accessed March 17, 2026).

17 Chris Stein, "'Despicable': Republicans and Democrats condemn violence after Charlie Kirk killing," *The Guardian* (September 10, 2025), https://www.theguardian.com/us-news/2025/sep/10/charlie-kirk-shooting-reaction (accessed March 17, 2026).

18 Devlin Barrett and Tyler Pager, "Trump Said to Demand Justice Dept. Pay Him $230 Million for Past Cases," *New York Times* (October 21, 2025), https://www.nytimes.com/2025/10/21/us/politics/trump-justice-department-compensation.html (accessed March 17, 2026).

19 Chris Stein, "Charlie Kirk in his own words: 'prowling Blacks' and 'the great replacement strategy'," *The Guardian* (September 11, 2025), https://www.theguardian.com/us-news/2025/sep/11/charlie-kirk-quotes-beliefs (accessed March 17, 2026).

20 Nicholas Bogel-Burroughs and Bernard Mokam, "A Broad Wave of Firings Followed Charlie Kirk's Assassination," *New York Times* (September 26, 2025), https://www.nytimes.com/2025/09/26/us/kirk-critics-fired-free-speech.html (accessed March 17, 2026).

21 Liliana Sequra, "The Absurd Prosecution of a Man Who Posted a Charlie Kirk Meme," *The Intercept* (October 23, 2025), https://theintercept.com/2025/10/23/charlie-kirk-meme-arrest-tennessee-larry-bushart (accessed March 17, 2026).

22 Raphael Satter and A. J. Vicens, "The Charlie Kirk purge: How 600 Americans were punished in a pro-Trump crackdown," *Reuters* (November 19, 2025), https://www.reuters.com/investigations/charlie-kirk-purge-how-600-americans-were-punished-pro-trump-crackdown-2025-11-19 (accessed March 17, 2026).

23 Sam Levin, "UC Berkeley shares 160 names with Trump administration in 'McCarthy era' move," *The Guardian* (September 12, 2025), https://www.theguardian.com/us-news/2025/sep/12/uc-berkeley-trump-administration-antisemitism (accessed March 17, 2026).

24 Ken Klippenstein, "FBI Readies New War on Trans People," *Substack: ken Klippenstein* (September 18, 2025), https://www.kenklippenstein.com/p/fbi-readies-new-war-on-trans-people (accessed March 17, 2026).

25 Amy Goodman, "'Worse Than McCarthyism': Historian Ellen Schrecker on Trump's War Against Universities & Students," *Democracy Now!* (May 30, 2025), https://www.democracynow.org/2025/5/30/mccarthyism_universities (accessed March 17, 2026).

26 Henry A. Giroux, "We can still save education, and that's the key to saving democracy," *Salon* (June 29, 2025), https://www.salon.com/2025/06/29/we-can-still-save-education-and-thats-the-key-to-saving-democracy (accessed March 17, 2026).

27 Joey Esposito, "Fact Check: Fox News host suggested 'involuntary lethal injection' for mentally ill homeless people who refuse help" (September 15, 2025), https://ca.news.yahoo.com/fact-check-fox-news-host-220100337.html (accessed March 17, 2026).

28 Garry Kasparov, "I Saw How Russia Killed Media Freedom," *The Next Move* (September 18, 2025), https://www.thenextmove.org/p/i-saw-how-russia-killed-media-freedom (accessed March 17, 2026).

29 Terry Eagleton, *On Evil* (New Haven: Yale University Press, 2011), 60.

30 John Ganz, "This is it: Obedience and Support are the Same," *Unpopular Front* (September 18, 2025), https://www.unpopularfront.news/p/this-is-it (accessed March 17, 2026).

31 Jeffrey St. Clair, "An Occurrence in Orem: Notes on the Murder of Charlie Kirk," *CounterPunch* (September 15, 2025), https://www.counterpunch.org/2025/09/15/an-occurence-in-orem-on-the-murder-of-charlie-kirk (accessed March 17, 2026).

32 Allan Smith, Michael Kosnar, Kelly O'Donnell, and Ryan J. Reilly, "'No evidence' found yet of ties between Charlie Kirk's shooting and left-wing groups, officials say," *NBC News* (September 20, 2025), https://www.nbcnews.

com/politics/justice-department/no-evidence-charlie-kirk-shooting-left-wing-groups-rcna232513 (accessed March 17, 2026).

33 Art Jipson and Paul J. Becker, "Analysis: What data shows about political extremist violence," *PBS News* (September 22, 2025), https://www.pbs.org/newshour/politics/right-wing-extremist-violence-is-more-frequent-and-deadly-than-left-wing-violence-data-shows (accessed March 17, 2026).

34 Saida Grundy, "Charlie Kirk was a divisive far-right podcaster. Why is he being rebranded as a national hero?," *The Guardian* (September 23, 2025), https://www.theguardian.com/commentisfree/2025/sep/23/charlie-kirk-bigoted-far-right-podcaster (accessed March 17, 2026).

35 Jeffrey St. Clair, "Roaming Charges: United States of Emergency," *CounterPunch* (October 10, 2025), https://www.counterpunch.org/2025/10/10/roaming-charges-121 (accessed March 17, 2026).

36 Toni Morrison, "Nobel Lecture," *Nobel Prize* (December 7, 1993), https://www.nobelprize.org/prizes/literature/1993/morrison/lecture (accessed March 17, 2026).

37 Ashifa Kassam, "Disruption across Italy as tens of thousands protest against Gaza war," *The Guardian* (September 22, 2025), https://www.theguardian.com/world/2025/sep/22/disruption-across-italy-as-tens-of-thousands-protest-against-gaza-war (accessed March 17, 2026).

Chapter 4

1 Laura Meckler, Susan Svrluga, Hannah Natanson, and Danielle Douglas-Gabriel, "With sweeping orders, Trump aims to control race teaching, boost school choice," *The Washington Post* (January 29, 2025), https://www.washingtonpost.com/education/2025/01/29/trump-education-orders-indoctrination-school-choice-antisemitism (accessed March 17, 2026).

2 Presidential Actions, "Ending Radical Indoctrination in K-12 Schooling," *The White House* (January 29, 2025), https://www.whitehouse.gov/presidential-actions/2025/01/ending-radical-indoctrination-in-k-12-schooling (accessed March 17, 2026).

3 Presidential Actions, "Expanding Educational Freedom and Opportunity for Families," *The White House* (January 29, 2025), https://www.whitehouse.gov/presidential-actions/2025/01/expanding-educational-freedom-and-opportunity-for-families (accessed March 17, 2026).

4 Presidential Actions, "Additional Measures to Combat Anti-Semitism," *The White House* (January 29, 2025) https://www.whitehouse.gov/presidential-actions/2025/01/additional-measures-to-combat-anti-semitism (accessed March 17, 2026).

5 Andrea Shalal and Susan Heavey, "Trump administration to cancel student visas of pro-Palestinian protesters," *Reuters* (January 29, 2025), https://www.reuters.com/world/us/trump-administration-cancel-student-visas-all-hamas-sympathizers-white-house-2025-01-29 (accessed March 17, 2026).

6 Henry A. Giroux, *The Violence of Organized Forgetting: Thinking Beyond America's Disimagination Machine* (San Francisco: City Lights, 2014).

7 Dimitrije Curcic, "Global Book Banning Statistics," *WordsRated* (April 14, 2023), https://wordsrated.com/global-book-banning-statistics (accessed March 17, 2026).

8 Maximillian Alvarez, "The End of the End of History," *Boston Review* (Fall 2018), https://www.bostonreview.net/articles/maximillian-alvarez-end-end-history (accessed March 17, 2026).

9 Ezra Klein, "'Now Is the Time of Monsters'," *New York Times* (January 12, 2025), https://www.nytimes.com/2025/01/12/opinion/ai-climate-change-low-birth-rates.html (accessed March 17, 2026).

10 Chauncey DeVega, "The problem with pinning Donald Trump down: Americans' attention spans are too short," *Salon* (September 12, 2025), https://www.salon.com/2024/09/12/the-problem-with-pinning-donald-down-americans-attention-spans-are-too-short (accessed March 17, 2026).

11 Julia Conley, "'He's Not Kidding,' Advocates Warn as Trump Threatens to Defund Schools for Teaching US History," *Common Dreams* (October 18, 2024), https://www.commondreams.org/news/trump-defund-schools (accessed March 17, 2026).

12 Timothy Snyder, "The War on History Is a War on Democracy," *New York Times Magazine* (June 29, 2021), https://www.nytimes.com/2021/06/29/magazine/memory-laws.html (accessed March 17, 2026).

13 Snyder, "The War on History Is a War on Democracy."

14 Kate Petty, "Declining Reading Habits Threaten U.S. Democracy and Social Connection," *Counterpunch* (December 22, 2025), https://www.counterpunch.org/2025/12/22/declining-reading-habits-threaten-u-s-democracy-and-social-connection (accessed April 14, 2026).

Chapter 5

1 William Faulkner, *Requiem for a Nun* (New York: Penguin, 2012), 73.

2 Angela V. Davis, "Black Liberation: The Ghosts of the Past, the Potential of the Future," *Truthout* (March 24, 2016), https://truthout.org/articles/black-liberation-the-ghosts-of-the-past-the-potential-of-the-future (accessed March 17, 2026).

3 Yose Hayim, *Yerushalmi, Zakhor: Jewish History and Jewish Memory* (New York: Schocken Books, 1989), 105.

4 Rita Omokha, "'I See My Work as Talking Back': How Critical Race Theory Mastermind Kimberlé Crenshaw Is Weathering the Culture Wars," *Vanity Fair* (September 2021), https://www.vanityfair.com/news/2021/07/how-critical-race-theory-mastermind-kimberle-crenshaw-is-weathering-the-culture-wars (accessed March 17, 2026).

5 Hannah Proctor, "Psychic Numbing," *Boston Review* (April 18, 2024), https://www.bostonreview.net/articles/psychic-numbing (accessed March 17, 2026).

6 Achille Mbembe, *Necropolitics* (Durham, NC: Duke University Press, 2019).

7 Presidential Actions, "Restoring truth and sanity to American history," *The White House* (March 27, 2025), https://www.whitehouse.gov/presidential-actions/2025/03/restoring-truth-and-sanity-to-american-history (accessed March 17, 2026).

8 Zolan Kanno-Youngs, "Trump Says Smithsonian Focuses Too Much on 'How Bad Slavery Was'," *New York Times* (August 19, 2025), https://www.nytimes.com/2025/08/19/us/politics/trump-smithsonian-slavery.html (accessed March 17, 2026).

9 Dean Blundell, "Trump's War on Black History: Why the Smithsonian (and Black History) Are in His Crosshairs," *Z Network* (August 21, 2025), https://znetwork.org/znetarticle/trumps-war-on-black-history-why-the-smithsonian-and-black-history-are-in-his-crosshairs (accessed March 17, 2026).

10 Amy Goodman, "Historian Rebukes Trump Imposing His Own Views of US History on the Smithsonian," *Truthout* (August 18, 2025), https://truthout.org/video/historian-rebukes-trump-imposing-his-own-views-of-us-history-on-the-smithsonian (accessed March 17, 2026).

11 Henry A. Giroux, "The Nazification of American Education," *Journal of Higher Education Policy and Leadership Studies* (September 2022), https://doaj.org/article/0d4597a3c5e14fb88ac47a3fe9f7ac32 (accessed March 17, 2026).

12 Jake Spring and Hannah Natanson, "National park to remove photo of enslaved man's scars" (September 15, 2025), https://www.washingtonpost.com/climate-environment/2025/09/15/national-parks-slavery-information-removal (accessed March 17, 2026).

13 Primo Levi, *The Drowned and the Saved*, trans. Raymond Rosenthal (London: Abacus, 1989), 158.

14 Antonio Gramsci, *Selections from the Prison Notebooks*, ed. and trans. Quintin Hoare and Geoffrey Nowell Smith (London: Lawrence and Wishart, 1971), 350.

15 Paulo Freire, *Pedagogy of Freedom* (London: Bloomsbury, 2025).

Chapter 6

1 Henry A. Giroux, "The Scorched-Earth Politics of America's Four Fundamentalisms," *Truthout* (March 6, 2012), https://truthout.org/articles/the-scorchedearth-politics-of-americas-four-fundamentalisms (accessed March 18, 2026).

2 Julia Conley, "Trump Adviser Says Those Who Oppose Abrego Garcia Detention May Be 'Aiding and Abetting' Terrorism," *Common Dreams* (April 17, 2025), https://www.commondreams.org/news/donald-trump-free-speech (accessed March 18, 2026).

3 Rob Nixon, *Slow Violence and the Environmentalism of the Poor* (Cambridge, MA: Harvard University Press, 2013).

4 Rebecca Gordon, "It didn't start with Donald Trump," *Salon* (April 22, 2025), https://www.salon.com/2025/04/22/it-didnt-start-with-donald_partner (accessed March 18, 2026).

5 Milton Friedman, "A Friedman doctrine—The Social Responsibility of Business Is to Increase Its Profits," *New York Times* (September 13, 1970), https://www.nytimes.com/1970/09/13/archives/a-friedman-doctrine-the-social-responsibility-of-business-is-to.html (accessed March 18, 2026).

6 Friedman, "A Friedman doctrine."

7 Margaret Thatcher, "Interview for Woman's Own ("no such thing [as society]," *Margaret Thatcher Foundation* (September 1987), https://www.margaretthatcher.org/document/106689 (accessed March 18, 2026).

8 Cited in Nikki McCann Ramirez, "The 'Judicial Black Hole' of El Salvador's Prisons Is a Warning for Americans," *Rolling Stone* (April 3, 2025), https://www.rollingstone.com/politics/politics-features/el-salvador-prisons-warning-americans-trump-1235309721 (accessed March 18, 2026).

9 David Levi Strauss, "Dispatch 62. 'The Homegrowns Are Next'," *Brooklyn Rail* (April 15, 2025), https://brooklynrail.org/2025/04/dispatches/dispatch-62-the-homegrowns-are-next (accessed March 18, 2026).

10 Snyder, "The War on History Is a War on Democracy."

11 Amy Goodman, "Nikole Hannah-Jones on 'The 1619 Project,' Teaching Critical Race Theory & White Supremacy on Trial," *Democracy Now!* (November 21, 2025), https://www.democracynow.org/2021/11/23/nikole_hannah_jones_1619_project (accessed March 18, 2026).

12 Alvarez, "The End of History."

13 Goodman, "Nikole Hannah-Jones on 'The 1619 Project.'"

14 DeNeen L. Brown, "'Lynchings in Mississippi never stopped'," *The Washington Post* (August 8, 2021), https://www.washingtonpost.com/nation/2021/08/08/modern-day-mississippi-lynchings (accessed March 18, 2026).

15 Strauss, "Dispatch 62. 'The Homegrowns Are Next'."

16 Gordon, "It didn't start with Donald Trump."

17 Maria Pia Lara, *Narrating Evil: A Postmetaphysical Theory of Reflective Judgement* (New York: Columbian University Press, 2007), 4–5

18 Zane McNeill, "The State Department Has Revoked the Visas of Over 600 Students at 100+ Schools," *Truthout* (April 10, 2025), https://truthout.org/articles/the-state-department-has-revoked-the-visas-of-over-600-students-at-100-schools (accessed March 18, 2026).

19 McNeill, "The State Department Has Revoked the Visas of Over 600 Students at 100+ Schools."

20 Iveta Silova, "Universities in Nazi Germany and the Soviet Union thought giving in to government demands would save their independence," *The Conversation* (April 9, 2025), https://theconversation.com/universities-in-nazi-germany-and-the-soviet-union-thought-giving-in-to-government-demands-would-save-their-independence-252888 (accessed March 18, 2026).

21 Ian Hodgson, "Florida's DOGE agency asks university faculty to hand over research," *Tampa Bay Times* (April 22, 2025), https://www.tampabay.com/news/education/2025/04/10/floridas-doge-agency-asks-university-faculty-hand-over-research (accessed March 18, 2026).

22 Jeffrey Martin, "Donald Trump Says Critical Race Theory is 'Like a Cancer'," *Newsweek* (September 24, 2020), https://www.newsweek.com/donald-trump-says-critical-race-theory-like-cancer-1534192 (accessed March 18, 2026).

23 Fatima Bhutto, "Want to Experience Fascism First-Hand? Attend Columbia University," *Zeteo* (April 2, 2025), https://zeteo.com/p/want-to-experience-fascism-first (accessed March 18, 2026).

24 Donalyn White and Anthony Ballas, "Settler Colonialism and the Engineering of Historical Amnesia," *CounterPunch* (July 11, 2024), https://www.counterpunch.org/2024/07/11/settler-colonialism-and-the-engineering-of-historical-amnesia (accessed March 18, 2026).

25 Eleanor Clift, "Why Trump Erasing Harriet Tubman Is Worse Than You Think," *Daily Beast* (April 8, 2025), https://www.thedailybeast.com/why-trump-erasing-harriet-tubman-is-worse-than-you-think (accessed March 18, 2026).

26 Hafiz Rashid, "El Salvador's President Makes Sick Argument on Wrongly Deported Man," *The New Republic* (April 14, 2025), https://newrepublic.com/post/193966/el-salvador-bukele-wrongly-deported-man-garcia (accessed March 18, 2026).

27 Eddie Glaude, Jr., "ICE's charge is to 'make America white again': Analyst," *MSNBC* (July 11, 2025), https://www.msnbc.com/the-weeknight/watch/ice-s-charge-is-to-make-america-white-again-analyst-243105861996 (accessed March 18, 2026).

28 Henry A. Giroux and Anthony R. DiMaggio, *Fascism on Trial* (London: Bloomsbury, 2024).

29 Richard D. Wolff, *Understanding Capitalism* (Chicago: Haymarket Books, 2025). On the new billionaire fascist elite, see Heather Gautney, *The New Power Elite* (New York: Oxford University Press, 2023).

Chapter 7

1 Tess Owen, "'The language of authoritarianism': how Trump and allies cast LA as a lawless city needing military intervention," *The Guardian* (June 10, 2025), https://www.theguardian.com/us-news/2025/jun/10/trump-administration-los-angeles-national-guard (accessed March 18, 2026).

2 Anthony L. Fisher, "Kristi Noem says the feds are coming to 'liberate' Los Angeles," *MSNBC* (June 13, 2025), https://www.msnbc.com/opinion/msnbc-opinion/kristi-noem-alex-padilla-detained-los-angeles-ice-rcna212764 (accessed March 18, 2026).

3 Michelle Goldberg, "This Is What Autocracy Looks Like," *New York Times* (June 9, 2025), https://www.nytimes.com/2025/06/09/opinion/autocracy-trump-la-protests.html (accessed March 18, 2026).

4 Ian F. Blair, "The United Police State of America Has Arrived," *The Intercept* (October 4, 2025), https://theintercept.com/2025/10/04/united-police-state-of-america (accessed March 18, 2026).

5 Blair, "The United Police State of America Has Arrived."

6 Rachel Maddow, "U.S. profoundly changed by authoritarian leader; 'We're beyond waiting and seeing now'," *Rachel Maddow Show MSNBC* (August 5, 2025), https://www.youtube.com/watch?v=VQbDgOaOh4c (accessed March 18, 2026).

7 Rebecca Schneid, "'Military-Style' ICE Raid on Chicago Apartment Building Shows Escalation in Trump's Crackdown," *Time* (October 4, 2025), https://time.com/7323334/ice-raid-chicago-pritzker-trump (accessed March 18, 2026).

8 Judd Legum, "How federal agents are terrorizing American citizens," *Popular Information* (October 6, 2025), https://popular.info/p/how-federal-agents-are-terrorizing (accessed March 18, 2026).

9 Legum, "How federal agents are terrorizing American citizens."

10 Greg Sargent, "Inside Stephen Miller's Secret Plan to Normalize Trump's Dictator Rule," *The New Republic* (October 8, 2025), https://newrepublic.com/article/201453/inside-stephen-miller-secret-plan-normalize-trump-dictator-rule (accessed March 18, 2026).

11 Sargent, "Inside Stephen Miller's Secret Plan to Normalize Trump's Dictator Rule."

12 Heather Cox Richardson, "Letters from an American," *Substack* (October 23, 2025), https://heathercoxrichardson.substack.com/p/october-23-2025 (accessed March 18, 2026).

13 Ian F. Blair, "The United Police State of America Has Arrived," *The Intercept* (October 4, 2025), https://theintercept.com/2025/10/04/united-police-state-of-america (accessed March 18, 2026).

14 Solcyré Burga, "White House Anti-Terror Order Targets 'Anti-American' Views," *Time* (October 2025). Online: https://time.com/7322106/trump-nspm-7-domestic-terrorism/

15 Editors, "Expanding the Dragnet: Trump's Threatened Crackdown on 'Antifa,' the Dangerous Mandate of NSPM-7, and the Impending Militarization of Government in the U.S.," *The Lemkin Institute* (October 23, 2025), https://www.lemkininstitute.com/statements-new-page/expanding-the-dragnet%3A-trump%E2%80%99s-threatened-crackdown-on-%E2%80%9Cantifa%2C%E2%80%9D-the-dangerous-mandate-of-nspm-7%2C-and-the-impending-militarization-of-government-in-the-u.s. (accessed March 18, 2026).

16 Aamer Madhani, "Trump directs ICE to expand deportations in Democratic-run cities, undeterred by protests," *Associated Press* (June 15, 2025) https://apnews.com/article/trump-ice-deportations-protests-65fa8d64ea12a78a0ee0ebeea008ee4d (accessed March 18, 2026).

17 Susan Sontag, "Fascinating Fascism," *New York Review of Books* (February 6, 1975), https://www.nybooks.com/articles/1975/02/06/fascinating-fascism (accessed March 18, 2026).

18 Milan Kundera, *The Book of Laughter and Forgetting* (New York: Harper Perennial, 1999), 159.

19 Yuwen Jiang, "The Interview: Ariella Aïsha Azoulay," *Art Review* (April 15, 2025), https://artreview.com/the-interview-ariella-aisha-azoulay (accessed March 18, 2026).

20 Michael Tomasky, "Why Does No One Understand the Real Reason Trump Won?," *The New Republic* (November 8, 2024), https://newrepublic.com/post/188197/trump-media-information-landscape-fox (accessed March 18, 2026).

21 Catherine Caruso, "The Risks of Artificial Intelligence in Weapons Design," *Harvard Medical School* (August 7, 2024), https://hms.harvard.edu/news/risks-artificial-intelligence-weapons-design (accessed March 18, 2026).

22 Brett Wilkins, "OpenAI Cuts 'Military and Warfare' Ban from Permissible Use Policy," *Common Dreams* (January 12, 2024), https://www.commondreams.org/news/openai (accessed March 18, 2026).

23 Brett Wilkins, "Commercial AI Has Become a Key Enabler of Israel's Mass Killing of Palestinians," *Truthout* (February 19, 2025), https://truthout.org/articles/commercial-ai-has-become-a-key-enabler-of-israels-mass-killing-of-palestinians (accessed March 18, 2026).

24 Sibel Duz, "Gaza as a testing ground: Israel's AI warfare," *SETA* (July 3, 2025), https://www.setav.org/en/gaza-as-a-testing-ground-israels-ai-warfare (accessed March 18, 2026).

25 Judith Butler, "Merely Cultural," *Social Text* 52–53, 15:3–4 (Fall\Winter, 1997), 266–77.

26 Theodor W. Adorno, *The Culture Industry: Selected Essays on Mass Culture* (New York: Routledge, 1991).

27 Alex Ross, "The Frankfurt School Knew Trump Was Coming," *The New Yorker* (December 5, 2016), https://www.newyorker.com/culture/cultural-comment/the-frankfurt-school-knew-trump-was-coming (accessed March 18, 2026).

28 C. Wright Mills, "The Cultural Apparatus", *The Politics of Truth: Selected Writings of C. Wright Mills* (Oxford: Oxford University Press, 2008), 203–12.

29 Raymond Williams, *On Culture & Society*, edited by Jim McGuigan (Los Angeles: Sage, 1958), 1–19.

30 Vaclav Havel, "The Power of the Powerless," *The Hannah Arendt Center for Politics and Humanities* (December 23, 2011), https://hac.bard.edu/amor-mundi/the-power-of-the-powerless-vaclav-havel-2011-12-23 (accessed March 18, 2026).

31 Stuart Hall, "Cultural Identity and Diaspora," in *Selected Writings on Race and Difference*, edited by Paul Gilroy and Ruth Wilson Gilman (Durham, NC: Duke University Press, 2021).

32 Bruce Robbins, "A Starting Point for Politics," *The Nation* (October 22, 2016), https://www.thenation.com/article/archive/the-radical-life-of-stuart-hall (accessed March 18, 2026).

33 Stuart Hall, "The Neo-Liberal Revolution," *Cultural Studies* 25:6 (November 2011), 705–28.

34 Thomas Piketty, *Capital and Ideology* (Cambridge, MA: Harvard University Press, 2020).

35 Richard Seymour, *Disaster Nationalism: The Downfall of Liberal Civilization* (New York: Verso, 2025).

36 Daniel Trilling, "Is this Fascism?" *London Review of Books* 47:5 (June 5, 2025), https://www.lrb.co.uk/the-paper/v47/n10/daniel-trilling/is-this-fascism (accessed March 18, 2026).

37 Zoe Williams, "The Saturday Interview: Stuart Hall," *The Guardian* (February 11, 2012), http://www.guardian.co.uk/theguardian/2012/feb/11/saturday-interview-stuart-hall (accessed March 18, 2026).

38 News, "Damning evidence of war crimes as Israeli attacks wipe out entire families in Gaza," *Amnesty International* (October 22, 2024), https://www.amnesty.org/en/latest/news/2023/10/damning-evidence-of-war-crimes-as-israeli-attacks-wipe-out-entire-families-in-gaza (accessed March 18, 2026).

39 Marisa Taylor, Ted Hesson, and Kristina Cooke, "Trump officials launch ICE effort to deport unaccompanied migrant children," *Reuters* (February 23, 2025), https://www.reuters.com/world/us/trump-administration-directs-ice-agents-find-deport-unaccompanied-migrant-2025-02-23 (accessed March 18, 2026).

40 Peter Bake, "As Trumps Monetize Presidency, Profits Outstrip Protests," *New York Times* (May 25, 2025), https://www.nytimes.com/2025/05/25/us/politics/trump-money-plane-crypto.html (accessed March 18, 2026).

41 Dasha Burns, "Trump-aligned club for the ultra-rich launches in Washington," *Politico* (April 26, 2025), https://www.politico.com/news/2025/04/26/donald-trump-washington-club-00311720 (accessed March 18, 2026).

42 Press Release, "U.S. House Passes Trump's Cruel Budget Bill that Ignores Voters' Priorities and Devastates, American Families," *Unidos US* (May 22, 2025), https://unidosus.org/press-releases/us-house-passes-trumps-cruel-budget-bill-that-ignores-voters-priorities-and-devastates-american-families (accessed March 18, 2026).

43 Lisa Mascaro, Kevin Freking, Leah Askarinam, and Joey Cappelleti, "As House GOP grinds ahead, new CBO report says Trump's big tax cuts bill will add to deficit," *PBS News*, https://www.pbs.org/newshour/politics/as-house-gop-grinds-ahead-new-cbo-report-says-trumps-big-tax-cuts-bill-will-add-to-deficit (accessed March 18, 2026).

44 Fintan O'Toole, "A Show of Force," *The New York Review of Books* (July 24, 2025), https://www.nybooks.com/articles/2025/07/24/a-show-of-force-fintan-otoole (accessed March 18, 2026).

45 Henry A. Giroux, *The Burden of Conscience: Educating Beyond the Veil of Silence* (London: Bloomsbury, 2025).

46 Hannah Arendt, *Thinking Without a Banister: Essays in Understanding, 1953–1975*, edited by Jerome Kohn (New York: Shocken, 2018).

47 Jonathan Crary, *Scorched Earth: Beyond The Digital Age to a Post-capitalist World* (London: Verso Books 2022), 16.

48 Henry A. Giroux, "Higher Education Must Champion Democracy, Not Surrender to Fascism," *Truthout* (December 28, 2024), https://truthout.org/articles/higher-education-must-champion-democracy-not-surrender-to-fascism (accessed March 18, 2026).

49 Chris Hedges, "Trump's Useful Idiots," *The Chris Hedges Report* (May 26, 2025), https://chrishedges.substack.com/p/trumps-useful-idiots.

50 Hedges, "Trump's Useful Idiots."

51 Hedges, "Trump's Useful Idiots."

52 Brett Wilkins, "'We'll Own It': Trump Floats US Takeover of Gaza, After Ethnically Cleansing Palestinians," *Common Dreams* (February 4, 2025), https://www.commondreams.org/news/trump-ethnic-cleansing-gaza (accessed March 18, 2026).

53 Judith Butler, "This Is Wrong. Judith Butler on Executive Order 14168," *London Review of Books* (April 3, 2025), https://www.lrb.co.uk/the-paper/v47/n06/judith-butler/this-is-wrong (accessed March 18, 2026).

54 Butler, "This Is Wrong. Judith Butler on Executive Order 14168."

55 Sheldon Wolin, *Politics and Vision: Continuity and Innovation in Western Political Thought* (Princeton: Princeton University Press, 2016), 605–6.

Chapter 8

1 Garrett Graff, "America Tips into Fascism," *Doomsday Scenario* (August 25, 2025), https://www.doomsdayscenario.co/p/america-tips-into-fascism-f51000e08e03254d (accessed March 19, 2026).

2 Norman Solomon, "The Warfare State Paved the Way for a Trumpist Autocracy," *CounterPunch* (February 28, 2025), https://www.counterpunch.org/2025/02/28/the-warfare-state-paved-the-way-for-a-trumpist-autocracy (accessed March 19, 2026).

3 Jackson Lears, "The Righteous Community," *London Review of Books* (July 24, 2025), https://www.lrb.co.uk/the-paper/v47/n13/jackson-lears/the-righteous-community (accessed March 19, 2026).

4 Melissa Gira Grant, "Trump Is Taking Over D.C. Police Because He's a Racist Thug," *The New Republic* (August 12, 2025), https://newrepublic.com/article/199001/trump-dc-takeover-police-racist (accessed March 19, 2026).

5 Paulo Freire, *Pedagogy of the Oppressed* (London: Bloomsbury, 2018).

6 Info, "ICE Leadership," ICE.Gov (2025), https://www.ice.gov/leadership (accessed March 19, 2026).

7 Will Bunch, "Inside Trump's $75B ICE gulag nightmare," *The Philadelphia Inquirer* (July 1, 2025), https://www.inquirer.com/columnists/attytood/ice-dhs-trump-budget-deportations-wnba-20250701.html (accessed March 19, 2026).

8 Tal Kopan, "ICE director: Undocumented immigrants 'should be afraid'," *CNN* (June 16, 2017), https://www.cnn.com/2017/06/16/politics/ice-immigrants-should-be-afraid-homan (accessed March 19, 2026).

9 Bunch, "Inside Trump's $75B ICE gulag nightmare."

10 Timothy Snyder, "Concentration Camp Labor," *Substack* (July 4, 2025), https://snyder.substack.com/p/concentration-camp-labor (accessed March 19, 2026).

11 Kevin Okoth, "The Pessimist's Optimist," *London Review of Books* (July 10, 2025), https://www.lrb.co.uk/the-paper/v47/n12/kevin-okoth/the-pessimist-s-optimist (accessed March 19, 2026).

12 Ryan Bort, "Trump: 'A Lot of People Are Saying Maybe We'd Like a Dictator'," *Rolling Stone* (August 26, 2025), https://www.rollingstone.com/politics/politics-news/trump-says-americans-want-dictator-1235414824 (accessed March 19, 2026).

13 Jodie Ginsberg, "Trump called the press 'the enemy of the people'. Now it's time to defend ourselves," *The Guardian* (February 14, 2025), https://www.theguardian.com/commentisfree/2025/feb/14/trump-press-journalists-enemy (accessed March 19, 2026).

14 Stephen Prager, "New Trump Order Among 'Scariest Things I've Seen in US Politics,' Civil Rights Attorney Says," *Common Dreams* (August 25, 2025), https://www.commondreams.org/news/trump-vigilante-portal (accessed March 19, 2026).

15 Rebecca Shabad, "Trump says he wants to seek the death penalty for murder in Washington, D.C.," *NBC News* (August 26, 2025), https://www.nbcnews.com/politics/justice-department/trump-says-wants-seek-death-penalty-washington-dc-murder-cases-rcna227287 (accessed March 19, 2026).

16 Erical L. Green, "Trump to Sign Order Renaming the Defense Department as the Department of War," *New York Times* (September 4, 2025), https://www.nytimes.com/2025/09/04/us/politics/trump-department-of-war-defense.html (accessed March 19, 2026).

17 Cited in O'Toole; also see, Melissa Chan, "Pete Hegseth's remarks about women in combat are met with disgust and dissent," *NBC News* (November 15, 2024), https://www.nbcnews.com/politics/national-security/pete-hegseths-remarks-women-combat-are-met-disgust-dissent-rcna180136 (accessed March 19, 2026).

18 Julia Carrie Wong, "Pete Hegseth's holy war: the militant Christian theology animating the US attack on Iran," *The Guardian* (April 10, 2026). https://www.theguardian.com/us-news/ng-interactive/2026/apr/10/pete-hegseth-christianity-iran-war-crusade (accessed April 14, 2026).

19 Frank Bruni, "Pete Hegseth's Gospel of Carnage," *New York Times* (April 13, 2026), https://www.nytimes.com/2026/04/13/opinion/pete-hegseths-religious-war.html (accessed April 14, 2026).

20 Dan Mangan, "White House posts video of immigrants in shackles, calls deportation footage 'ASMR'," *CNBC* (February 18, 2025), https://www.cnbc.com/2025/02/18/white-house-x-immigrants-deportation-shackles-asmr-video.html (accessed March 19, 2026).

21 Caleb Kieffer and R. G. Cravens, "Homeland Security deploys white nationalist, anti-immigrant graphics to recruit," *Southern Poverty Law Center* (August 28, 2025), https://www.splcenter.org/resources/hatewatch/dhs-white-nationalist-anti-immigrant-social-media (accessed March 19, 2026).

22 O'Toole, "A Show of Force."

23 Ruth Ben-Ghiat, "Trump's War on America," *Lucid* (August 27, 2025), https://lucid.substack.com/p/trumps-war-on-america (accessed March 19, 2026).

24 Garrett Graff, "America Tips into Fascism," *Doomsday Scenario* (August 25, 2025), https://www.doomsdayscenario.co/p/america-tips-into-fascism-f51000e08e03254d (accessed March 19, 2026).

25 Jonathan Freedland, "Step back and take it in: the US is entering full authoritarian mode," *The Guardian* (August 29, 2025), https://www.theguardian.com/commentisfree/2025/aug/29/us-authoritarian-donald-trump-national-guard (accessed March 19, 2026).

26 Betty Little, "Who Were the Hollywood 10?," *History.com* (August 12, 2025), https://www.history.co.uk/this-day-in-history/20-october/congress-investigates-communism-in-hollywood (accessed April 14, 2026).

27 Greg Sargent, "Transcript: Stephen Miller's Crazed Fascist Rant to Media Is Revealing," *The New Republic* (August 21, 2025), https://newrepublic.com/article/199377/transcript-stephen-miller-crazed-fascist-rant-media-revealing (accessed March 19, 2026).

28 Thom Hartman, "How Fascism Typically Takes Over a Nation by Rhetoric," *The Hartman Report* (March 29, 2024), https://hartmannreport.com/p/how-fascism-typically-takes-over-6db (accessed March 19, 2026).

29 Sargent, "Transcript: Stephen Miller's Crazed Fascist Rant to Media Is Revealing."

30 See Jean Guerrero, *Hatemonger: Stephen Miller, Donald Trump, and the White Nationalist Agenda* (New York: William Morrow, 2021); Jason Wilson, "Leaked emails reveal Trump aide Stephen Miller's white nationalist views," *The Guardian* (November 14, 2019), https://www.theguardian.com/us-news/2019/nov/14/stephen-miller-leaked-emails-white-nationalism-trump (accessed March 19, 2026); Lulu Garcia-Navarro, "Stephen Miller And 'The Camp Of The Saints,' A White Nationalist Reference," *NPR* (November 19, 2019), https://www.npr.org/2019/11/19/780552636/stephen-miller-and-the-camp-of-the-saints-a-white-nationalist-reference (accessed March 19, 2026).

31 Hannah Broughton, "Stephen Miller called 'face of evil' by his own cousin over immigration raids," *The Mirror* (October 6, 2025), https://www.themirror.com/news/politics/stephen-miller-cousin-evil-trump-1430042 (accessed March 19, 2026).

32 Jason Zengerle, "The Ruthless Ambition of Stephen Miller," *New York Times* (July 7, 2025), https://www.nytimes.com/2025/07/07/opinion/stephen-miller.html (accessed March 19, 2026).

33 Robert Tait, "The rise of Stephen Miller, the architect of Trump's hardline immigration policy," *The Guardian* (June 15, 2025), https://www.theguardian.com/us-news/2025/jun/15/trump-immigration-stephen-miller-influence (accessed March 19, 2026).

34 Jason Zengerle, "The Ruthless Ambition of Stephen Miller," *New York Times* (July 7, 2025), https://www.nytimes.com/2025/07/07/opinion/stephen-miller.html (accessed March 19, 2026); Jonathan Chait, "Stephen Miller Is Going for

Broke," *The Atlantic* (October 6, 2025), https://www.theatlantic.com/ideas/archive/2025/10/miller-insurrection/684463 (accessed March 19, 2026).

35 Freedland, "Step back and take it in."

36 Andrew Roth, "Has Trump succeeded in normalizing American autocracy?," *The Guardian* (August 31, 2025), https://www.theguardian.com/us-news/2025/aug/31/trump-american-autocracy-authoritarianism

37 S. Baum, "Stephen Miller Promotes Indoctrination of Children Through the Public School System," *Erin in the Morning* (May 5, 2025), https://www.erininthemorning.com/p/stephen-miller-promotes-indoctrination (accessed March 19, 2026).

38 Thor Benson, "This Right-Wing Culture Warrior Wants Trump to 'Snatch' Activists Off the Streets," *Zeteo* (July 18, 2025), https://zeteo.com/p/this-right-wing-culture-warrior-wants (accessed March 19, 2026).

39 Lauren-Brooke Eisen, "What Trump's Victory Means for the Private Prison Industry," *Brennan Center for Justice* (November 25, 2024), https://www.brennancenter.org/our-work/analysis-opinion/what-trumps-victory-means-private-prison-industry (accessed March 19, 2026).

40 John Ganz, "Death to America," *Unpopular Fron*t (July 1, 2025), https://www.unpopularfront.news/p/death-to-america (accessed March 19, 2026).

41 Ganz, "Death to America."

42 Greg Grandin, "Trump Is Waging War on His Own Citizens," *New York Times* (July 4, 2025), https://www.nytimes.com/2025/07/04/opinion/trump-america-.html

43 Grandin, "Trump Is Waging War on His Own Citizens."

44 Ganz, "Death to America."

45 Rachel Maddow, "Maddow: U.S. profoundly changed by authoritarian leader; 'We're beyond waiting and seeing now'," *MSNBC* (August 11, 2025), https://www.youtube.com/watch?v=VQbDgOaOh4c (accessed March 19, 2026).

46 Mark Peterson, "ICE's Spectacle of Intimidation," *The New Yorker* (August 4, 2025), https://www.newyorker.com/magazine/2025/08/11/ices-spectacle-of-intimidation (accessed March 19, 2026).

47 Chauncey DeVega, "The draw of Trump's spectacle: inhumanity," *Salon* (February 25, 2025), https://www.salon.com/2025/02/25/the-draw-of-spectacle-inhumanity (accessed March 19, 2026).

48 Clarissa-Jan Lim, "Sec. Kristi Noem uses inmates of notorious Salvadoran prison in photo op," *MSNBC* (March 27, 2025), https://www.msnbc.com/top-stories/latest/kristi-noem-el-salvador-prison-cecot-video-rcna198394 (accessed March 19, 2026).

49 Naomi Klein and Astra Taylor, "The rise of end times fascism," *The Guardian* (April 13, 2025), https://www.theguardian.com/us-news/ng-interactive/2025/apr/13/end-times-fascism-far-right-trump-musk (accessed March 19, 2026).

50 Alberto Toscano, "Cathedrals of Erotic Misery," *Ill Will* (October 27, 2025), https://illwill.com/cathedrals-of-erotic-misery (accessed March 19, 2026).

51 Zolan Kanno-Youngs, "In Trump's 2nd Term, More Incarcerations, Less Talk of Reform," *New York Times* (August 27, 2025), https://www.nytimes.com/2025/08/27/us/politics/trump-criminal-justice.html (accessed March 19, 2026). The rise of the carceral state is dealt with brilliantly in Ruth Gilmore, *Golden Gulag: Prisons, Surplus, Crisis, and Opposition in Globalizing California* (Berkeley: University of California Press, 2007).

52 Emma Green, "Inside the Trump Administration's Assault on Higher Education," *The New Yorker* (October 13, 2025), https://www.newyorker.com/magazine/2025/10/20/inside-the-trump-administrations-assault-on-higher-education (accessed March 19, 2026).

53 Anthony L. Fisher, "Kristi Noem says the feds are coming to 'liberate' Los Angeles," *MSNBC* (June 13, 2025), https://www.msnbc.com/opinion/msnbc-opinion/kristi-noem-alex-padilla-detained-los-angeles-ice-rcna212764 (accessed March 19, 2026).

54 Jackson Lears, "The Righteous Community," *London Review of Books* (July 24, 2025), https://www.lrb.co.uk/the-paper/v47/n13/jackson-lears/the-righteous-community (accessed March 19, 2026).

55 Yuwen Jiang, "The Interview: Ariella Aïsha Azoulay," *Art Review* (April 15, 2025), https://artreview.com/the-interview-ariella-aisha-azoulay (accessed March 19, 2026).

56 Ergin Yildizoglu, "Fascism and culture," *Cumhuriyet* (July 7, 2025), https://www.cumhuriyet.com.tr/yazarlar/ergin-yildizoglu/fasizm-ve-kultur-2415735 (accessed March 19, 2026).

57 T. J. Clark, "A Brief Guide to Trump and the Spectacle," *London Review of Books* (January 23, 2025), https://www.lrb.co.uk/the-paper/v47/n01/t.j.-clark/a-brief-guide-to-trump-and-the-spectacle (accessed March 19, 2026).

58 Naomi Klein and Astra Taylor, "The rise of end times fascism," *The Guardian* (April 13, 2025), https://www.theguardian.com/us-news/ng-interactive/2025/apr/13/end-times-fascism-far-right-trump-musk (accessed March 19, 2026).

Chapter 9

1 Toni Morrison, "Nobel Lecture," *Nobel Prize* (December 7, 1993), https://www.nobelprize.org/prizes/literature/1993/morrison/lecture (accessed March 20, 2026).

2 Eric Kin, "The Forbidden Word: How the Suppression of 'Fascism' Obscures the Truth of American Decline," *Medium* (October 1, 2025), https://medium.com/@erickin/the-forbidden-word-how-the-suppression-of-fascism-obscures-the-truth-of-american-decline-e344e1789b9c (accessed March 20, 2026).

3 Morrison, "Nobel Lecture."

4 Morrison, Nobel Lecture."

5 John Ganz, "J.D. Vance's Anti-Declaration," *Unpopular Front* (July 9, 2025), https://www.unpopularfront.news/p/jd-vances-anti-declaration (accessed March 20, 2026).

6 Nathan Taylor Pemberton, "Trolling Democracy," *New York Times* (July 10, 2025), https://www.nytimes.com/2025/07/10/opinion/trolling-democracy.html (accessed March 20, 2026).

7 Lemkin Institute, "Red Flag Alert—Trump's Genocidal Threats Against Iran," *Lemkin Institute* (April 7, 2026), https://lemkininstitute.com/so/acPrfuHkJ (accessed April 14, 2026).

8 Jason Stanley, *How Propaganda Works* (Princeton: Princeton University Press, 2016); Noam Chomsky and Marv Waterstone, *Consequences of Capitalism: Manufacturing Discontent and Resistance* (Chicago: Haymarket, 2021); Noam Chomsky and Nathan J. Robinson, *The Myth of American Idealism: How U.S. Foreign Policy Endangers the World* (New York: Penguin, 2024). The classic work on propaganda is Edward Bernays, *Propaganda* (New York: Ig Publishing, 2004).

9 Leon Wieseltier, "Kulturkampf on the Potomac," *Liberties* 5:4 (Summer 2025), https://libertiesjournal.com/articles/kulturkampf-on-the-potomac (accessed March 20, 2026).

10 Wieseltier, "Kulturkampf on the Potomac."

11 Jared Marcel Pollen, "Unsentimental Education: Peter Weiss's Aesthetics of Resistance," *Liberties* (July 2025), https://libertiesjournal.com/online-articles/unsentimental-education-peter-weisss-aesthetics-of-resistance (accessed March 20, 2026).

12 William Davies, "Repeal the 20th Century," *London Review of Books* (September 25, 2025), 38.

13 Rhoda Feng, "Reclaiming Language: A Conversation With Ngũgĩ wa Thiong'o," *The Nation* (June 2, 2025), https://www.thenation.com/article/culture/ngugi-wa-thiongo-interview (accessed March 20, 2026).

14 Ngũgĩ wa Thiong'o, *Decolonizing Language and Other Revolutionary Ideas* (New York: The New Press, 2025), 30.

15 I take up this issue in great detail in Henry A. Giroux, *Burden of Conscience: Educating Beyond the Veil of Silence* (London: Bloomsbury, 2024).

16 Lawrence Grossberg, *Caught in the Crossfire: Kids, Politics, and America's Future* (Boulder: Paradigm, 2005), 220–1.

17 Henry A. Giroux and Anthony R. DiMaggio, *Fascism on Trial: Education and the Possibility of Democracy* (London: Bloomsbury, 2024); Spencer Ackerman, *Reign of Terror: How the 9/11 Era Destabilized America and Produced Trump* (New York: Penguin Books, 2022).

18 Miami Herald Editorial Board, "Mexican 'rapists' seems so mild compared to what Trump says about immigrants today," *Miami Herald* (September 18, 2024), https://www.miamiherald.com/opinion/editorials/article292632624.html (accessed March 20, 2026).

19 Anne Applebaum, *Twilight of Democracy: The Seductive Lure of Authoritarianism* (New York: Vintage, 2021).

20 Brianna Tucker and Sarah Ellison, "Trump escalates attacks on Mamdani, who says president is attacking democracy," *The Washington Post* (July 2, 2025), https://www.washingtonpost.com/politics/2025/07/01/trump-threatens-deport-zohran-mamdani (accessed March 20, 2026).

21 Federico Finchelstein, *A Brief History of Fascist Lies* (Oakland, Ca: University of California Press, 2020).

22 Finchelstein, *A Brief History of Fascist Lies.*

23 Jamal Kanj, "From Auschwitz to Gaza's 'Humanitarian City'," *CounterPunch* (July 21, 2025), https://www.counterpunch.org/2025/07/21/from-auschwitz-to-gazas-humanitarian-city (accessed March 20, 2026).

24 Amy Goodman and Nermeen Shaikh, "Democrats Abandoned the Working Class: Robin D.G. Kelley on Trump's Win & Need for Class Solidarity," *Democracy Now* (November 7, 2024), https://www.democracynow.org/2024/11/7/robin_dg_kelley (accessed March 20, 2026).

25 David Theo Goldberg, "'Antisemitism' The Making of Our Political Panic" *CounterPunch* (June 4, 2025), https://www.counterpunch.org/2025/06/04/antisemitism-the-making-of-our-political-panic (accessed March 20, 2026).

26 Philip Bump, "What Trump said with his 'very fine people' comments vs. what he meant," *The Washington Post* (June 28, 2024), https://www.washingtonpost.com/politics/2024/06/28/what-trump-said-with-his-very-fine-people-comments-vs-what-he-meant (accessed March 20, 2026).

27 Aaron Blake, "Trump's long history of trafficking in antisemitic tropes," *The Washington Post* (October 17, 2022), https://www.washingtonpost.com/politics/2022/10/17/trump-history-antisemitic-tropes (accessed March 20, 2026).

28 John Ganz, "A Viper in its Bosom," *Unpopular Front* (October 30, 2025), https://www.unpopularfront.news/p/a-viper-in-its-bosom (accessed March 20, 2026).

29 Omer Bartov, "I'm a Genocide Scholar. I Know It When I See It," *New York Times* (July 15, 2025), https://www.nytimes.com/2025/07/15/opinion/israel-gaza-holocaust-genocide-palestinians.html (accessed March 20, 2026).

30 Bartov, "I'm a Genocide Scholar."

31 David Theo Goldberg, "'Antisemitism' The Making of Our Political Panic," *Counter Punch* (June 4, 2025). https://www.counterpunch.org/2025/06/04/antisemitism-the-making-of-our-political-panic (accessed April 14, 2026).

32 Omer Bartov, "I'm a Genocide Scholar. I Know It When I See It," *New York Times* (July 15, 2025).https://www.nytimes.com/2025/07/15/opinion/israel-gaza-holocaust-genocide-palestinians.html (accessed April 14, 2026).

33 David Theo Goldberg, "'Antisemitism' The Making of Our Political Panic," *CounterPunch* (June 5, 2025). https://www.counterpunch.org/2025/06/04/antisemitism-the-making-of-our-political-panic/

34 Omer Bartov "I'm a Genocide Scholar. I Know It When I See It," *New York Times* (July 15, 2025). Online: https://www.nytimes.com/2025/07/15/opinion/israel-gaza-holocaust-genocide-palestinians.html

35 Pankaj Mishra, "The Shoah after Gaza," *London Review of Books* (March 21, 2024), https://www.lrb.co.uk/the-paper/v46/n06/pankaj-mishra/the-shoah-after-gaza (accessed March 20, 2026).

36 Mishra, "The Shoah after Gaza."

37 Amy Goodman, "Genocide Denial in Holocaust Studies: Scholar Raz Segal on Gaza & 80 Years After Auschwitz Liberation," *Democracy Now!* (January 28, 2025), https://www.democracynow.org/2025/1/28/raz_segal (accessed March 20, 2026).

38 See Henry A. Giroux, *Insurrections: Education in the Age of Counter-Revolutionary Politics* (London: Bloomsbury Books, 2023); Henry A. Giroux, *Race, Politics and Pandemic Pedagogy: Education in a Time of Crisis* (London: Bloomsbury Books, 2021); Henry A. Giroux, *The Terror of the Unforeseen* (Los Angeles: Los Angeles Review of Books, 2019).

39 Chris Hedges, *America, The Farewell Tour* (New York: Penguin Random House, 2019).

40 Zachary Sklar and Michael Steven Smith, eds., *From the Flag to the Cross* (London: OR Books, 2025).

41 Ayn Rand, *Atlas Shrugged* (New York: New American Library, 1999).

42 Alia Shoaib, "Church Doubles Down After Preacher Encouraged Prayers for LGBTQ Deaths," *Newsweek* (July 4, 2025), https://www.newsweek.com/church-preacher-lgbtq-deaths-indianapolis-2094734 (accessed March 20, 2026).

43 Sophie Perry, "Indiana church tells LGBTQ+ people to kill themselves or face death penalty under Trump," *The Pink News* (July 7, 2025), https://www.thepinknews.com/2025/07/07/indiana-indianapolis-sure-foundation-baptist-church-lgbtq (accessed March 20, 2026).

44 Zachary B. Wolf, "Elon Musk wants to save Western civilization from empathy," *CNN Politics* (March 5, 2025), https://www.cnn.com/2025/03/05/politics/elon-musk-rogan-interview-empathy-doge (accessed March 20, 2026).

45 Julia Carrie Wong, "Loathe thy neighbor: Elon Musk and the Christian right are waging war on empathy," *The Guardian* (April 8, 2025), https://www.theguardian.com/us-news/ng-interactive/2025/apr/08/empathy-sin-christian-right-musk-trump (accessed March 20, 2026).

46 Wong, "Loathe thy neighbor." See also Christiaan Boonen, "At the Outer Limits of Democratic Division: on Citizenship, Conflict and Violence in the Work of Chantal Mouffe and Étienne Balibar," *International Journal of Politics, Culture, and Society* 33:4 (2020): 529–44.

47 Jed S. Rakoff, "Is Cryptocurrency a Racket?," *Stanford Business* (August 2, 2025), https://casi.stanford.edu/news/cryptocurrency-racket (accessed March 20, 2026).

48 Naomi Klein and Astra Taylor, "The rise of end times fascism," *The Guardian* (April 13, 2025), https://www.theguardian.com/us-news/ng-interactive/2025/apr/13/end-times-fascism-far-right-trump-musk (accessed March 20, 2026).

49 Ruth Ben-Ghiat, "Trump's Brutal & Bellicose Bill; Standing Up for America as a Nation of Immigrants," *Lucid* (July 5, 2025), https://lucid.substack.com/p/trumps-brutal-and-bellicose-bill (accessed March 20, 2026).

50 Henry A. Giroux, *Against the New Authoritarianism: Politics After Abu Ghraib* (Toronto: ARP Books, 2005).

51 Henry A. Giroux and Anthony R. DiMaggio, *Fascism on Trial: Education and the Possibility of Democracy* (London: Bloomsbury, 2024).

52 Ngũgĩ wa Thiong'o, *Decolonizing Language and Other Revolutionary Ideas* (New York: New Press, 2025).

53 Jonah Valdez, "A Pattern of Violence: Documenting ICE Agents' Brutal Use of Force in LA Immigration Raids," *The Intercept* (July 7, 2025), https://theintercept.com/2025/07/07/ice-raids-la-violence-video-bystanders (accessed March 20, 2026).

54 Timothy Snyder, "Concentration Camp Labor," *Substack* (July 4, 2025), https://snyder.substack.com/p/concentration-camp-labor (accessed March 20, 2026).

55 Fintan O'Toole, "A Show of Force," *The New York Review of Books* (July 24, 2025), https://www.nybooks.com/articles/2025/07/24/a-show-of-force-fintan-otoole (accessed March 20, 2026).

56 O'Toole, "A Show of Force."

57 I address this issue in detail in Henry A. Giroux, *The Burden of Conscience: Educating Beyond the Veil of Silence* (London: Bloomsbury Books, 2025).

58 Viktor Klemperer, *The Language of the Third Reich* (London: Bloomsbury, 2006), 167.

59 Melissa Gira Grant, "The Grand Opening of an American Concentration Camp," *The New Republic* (July 2, 2025), https://newrepublic.com/article/197508/alligator-alcatraz-trump-concentration-camp (accessed March 20, 2026).

60 Isabel Keane, "'Alligator lives matter': Trump pal Laura Loomer slammed for saying Florida 'Alcatraz' beasts will get '65 million meals'," *Independent* (July 3, 2025), https://www.independent.co.uk/news/world/americas/us-politics/laura-loomer-alcatraz-alligator-lives-matter-trump-b2782150.html (accessed March 20, 2026).

61 Isabel Keane and Andrea Miller, "Hold Laura Loomer Accountable for Hate Speech Against Hispanics," *Change.Org* (July 6, 2025), https://www.change.org/p/hold-laura-loomer-accountable-for-hate-speech-against-hispanics

62 Primo Levi, *The Black Hole of Auschwitz* (London: Polity, 2005).

63 Judith Butler, *Frames of War: When Is Life Grievable*? (Londo: Verso, 2009).

64 Brian Bennett, "Trump Announces 7 Military Bases Reverting Back to Names Honoring Confederates," *Time* (June 10, 2025), https://time.com/7293047/trump-announces-7-military-bases-reverting-back-to-names-honoring-confederates (accessed March 20, 2026).

65 Chris Cameron, "Trump Administration Will Reinstall Confederate Statue in Washington," *New York Times* (August 4, 2025), https://www.nytimes.com/2025/08/04/us/politics/pike-confederate-statue-trump-dc.html (accessed March 20, 2026).

66 Peter Wade, "Trump Demands Sports Teams Make Their Names Racist Again," *Rolling Stone* (July20, 2025), https://www.rollingstone.com/politics/politics-news/trump-sports-teams-restore-racist-names-1235389673 (accessed March 20, 2026).

67 Henry A. Giroux, *Pedagogy of Resistance: Against Manufactured Ignorance* (London: Bloomsbury, 2022).

68 David Thomas, "Trump imposes US travel ban on seven African countries," *African Business* (June 5, 2025), https://african.business/2025/06/politics/trump-imposes-us-travel-ban-on-seven-african-countries (accessed March 20, 2026).

69 Zolan Kanno-Youngs and Hamed Aleaziz, "'Mission South Africa': How Trump Is Offering White Afrikaners Refugee Status," *New York Times* (March 30, 2025), https://www.nytimes.com/2025/03/30/us/politics/trump-south-africa-white-afrikaners-refugee.html (accessed March 20, 2026).

70 Walter Benjamin, *Reflections: Essays, Aphorisms, Autobiographical Writings* (New York: HarperCollins Publishers, 2019).

71 AK Thompson, "Premonitions: Fragments of a Culture of Revolt," *The Socialist Project* (December 2018), https://socialistproject.ca/2018/12/premonitions-fragments-of-culture-of-revolt (accessed March 20, 2026).

72 Thompson, "Premonitions."

73 Antonio Gramsci, *Selections from the Prison Notebooks*, edited and translated by Quintin Hoare and Geoffrey Nowell Smith (New York: International Publishers, 1971), 276.

Chapter 10

1 Lidice Memorial, "The Children's War Victims Monument," *Pamatnik Lidice* (2015), https://www.lidice-memorial.cz/en/memorial/war-childrens-victims-monument (accessed March 20, 2026).

2 News "Lidice: The Annihilation of a Czech Town," *Holocaust Encyclopedia* (June 1921), https://encyclopedia.ushmm.org/content/en/article/lidice (accessed March 20, 2026).

3 Prem Thakker and Team Zeteo, "Who Says Isreal is Committing a Genocide in Gaza? Everyone on This List," *Zeteo* (July 29, 2025), https://zeteo.com/p/who-says-israel-committing-genocide-gaza-list-politicians-countries (accessed March 20, 2026); Ishaan Tharoor, "Leading genocide scholars see a genocide happening in Gaza," *The Washington Post* (July 30, 2025), https://www.washingtonpost.com/world/2025/07/30/israel-genocide-gaza-scholars-historians (accessed March 20, 2026).

4 Rasha Khatib, Martin McKee, and Salim Yusuf, "Counting the dead in Gaza: difficult but essential," *The Lancet* (July 30, 2024), https://www.thelancet.com/journals/lancet/article/PIIS0140-6736(24)01169-3/fulltext (accessed March 20, 2026).

5 Omer Bartov, "I'm a Genocide Scholar. I Know It When I See It," *New York Times* (July 15, 2025), https://www.nytimes.com/2025/07/15/opinion/israel-gaza-holocaust-genocide-palestinians.html (accessed March 20, 2026).

6 Branko Marcetic, "Israel's Gaza War Is One of History's Worst Crimes Ever," *Jacobin* (August 5, 2025), https://jacobin.com/2025/08/israel-gaza-worst-crimes-ever (accessed March 20, 2026).

7 Amel Guettatfi, "'The Target is Unmistakable': The Shooting of Gaza's Children," *Drop Site* (March 27, 2025), https://www.dropsitenews.com/p/gaza-children-israel-sniper-shoot-jazeera (accessed March 20, 2026).

8 Palestine Chronicle Staff, "Rising Calls for Immediate Ceasefire in Gaza amid Horrific Hunger Crisis," *The Palestine Chronicle* (July 22, 2025), https://www.palestinechronicle.com/rising-calls-for-immediate-ceasefire-in-gaza-amid-horrific-hunger-crisis (accessed March 20, 2026).

9 Mohammad Sio, "Israel dropped 100,000 tons of explosives over Gaza, wiped out 2,200 families: Media office," *Middle East Monitor* (May 8, 2025), https://www.middleeastmonitor.com/20250508-israel-dropped-100000-tons-of-explosives-over-gaza-wiped-out-2200-families-media-office (accessed March 20, 2026).

10 Marc Steiner, "Yes, goddamnit, it's genocide!: A conversation with Norman Solomon," *The Real News Network* (July 23, 2025), https://therealnews.com/yes-goddamnit-its-genocide-a-conversation-with-norman-solomon (accessed March 20, 2026).

11 Arwa Mahdawi, "Seeking bulldozer drivers to demolish Gaza: how a genocide is being outsourced," *The Guardian* (July 9, 2025), https://www.theguardian.com/commentisfree/2025/jul/09/bulldzoer-gaza-genocide-idf-meta (accessed March 20, 2026).

12 Archie Bland, "Thursday briefing: The outlandish plan to turn Gaza into a 'riviera of the Middle East'," *The Guardian* (February 6, 2025), https://www.theguardian.com/world/2025/feb/06/thursday-briefing-first-edition-gaza-riviera-middle-east-donald-trump (accessed March 20, 2026).

13 Joelle M. Abi-Rached, "Gaza and the End of History," *Boston Review* (July 30, 2025), https://www.bostonreview.net/articles/gaza-and-the-end-of-history (accessed March 20, 2026).

14 Joelle M. Abi-Rached notes: "A poll conducted by researchers at Pennsylvania State University and reported in Haaretz earlier this year found that 82 percent of Israeli Jews support expelling Palestinians from Gaza, 56 percent support expelling Israel's own Arab citizens, 47 percent endorse the Israel Defense Forces acting 'as Joshua did in Jericho, kill all its inhabitants,' and, among those who see Palestinians as Amalek, 93 percent believe the biblical injunction to 'wipe out Amalek' still applies."

15 Pankaj Mishra, *The World After Gaza: A History* (New York: Penguin Press, 2025).

16 Ishaan Tharoor, "Leading genocide scholars see a genocide happening in Gaza," *The Washington Post* (July 30, 2025), https://www.washingtonpost.com/world/2025/07/30/israel-genocide-gaza-scholars-historians (accessed March 20, 2026).

17 Alex de Waal, "How to Hide a Famine," *Boston Review* (July 31, 2025), https://www.bostonreview.net/articles/how-to-hide-a-famine (accessed March 20, 2026).

18 Gideon Levy, "Denying Gaza's Starvation Is No Less Vile Than Denying the Holocaust," *Haaretz* (July 27, 2025), https://www.haaretz.com/opinion/2025-07-27/ty-article-opinion/.premium/denying-gazas-starvation-

is-no-less-vile-than-denying-the-holocaust/00000198-47b1-db91-a1df-efff77340000 (accessed March 20, 2026).

19 Heba Almaqadma, "In Gaza, Hunger Has Overtaken Bombs as Israel's Cruelest Weapon," *Drop Site News* (July 30, 2025), https://www.dropsitenews.com/p/gaza-city-famine-israel-starvation-genocide-war (accessed March 20, 2026).

20 Two informative books include: Omar El Akkad, *One Day, Everyone Will Have Always Been Against This* (New York: Knopf, 2025), Rashid Khalidi, *The Hundred Years' War on Palestine* (New York: Metropolitan Books, 2021). Hina Rabbani Khar, "Israel's war on Gaza and the West's credibility crisis," *Al Jazeera* (January 16, 2024), https://www.aljazeera.com/opinions/2024/1/16/israels-war-on-gaza-and-the-wests-credibility-crisis (accessed March 20, 2026).

21 Tharoor, "Leading genocide scholars see a genocide happening in Gaza."

22 William Christou and Quique Kierszenbaum, "Far-right Israeli politicians and settlers discuss luxury 'Gaza riviera' plan," *The Guardian* (July 24, 2025), https://www.theguardian.com/world/2025/jul/24/far-right-israeli-politicians-and-settlers-discuss-luxury-gaza-riviera-plan (accessed March 20, 2026).

23 Christou and Kierszenbaum, "Far-right Israeli politicians and settlers discuss luxury 'Gaza riviera' plan."

24 Christou and Kierszenbaum, "Far-right Israeli politicians and settlers discuss luxury 'Gaza riviera' plan."

25 Jonathan Cook, "Israel's Genocide Is Big Business," *Savage Minds* (July 24, 2025), https://savageminds.substack.com/p/israels-genocide-is-big-business (accessed March 20, 2026).

26 Ben Quinn, "Tony Blair thinktank worked with project developing 'Trump Riviera' Gaza plan," *The Guardian* (July 7, 2025), https://www.theguardian.com/politics/2025/jul/07/tony-blair-thinktank-worked-with-project-developing-trump-riviera-gaza-plan (accessed March 20, 2026).

27 Amy Goodman, "A Ceasefire Deal, But Not a Peace Agreement: What Will Happen in Gaza After Hostages Are Released?," *Democracy Now!* (October 9, 2025), https://www.democracynow.org/2025/10/9/gaza_deal_roundtable (accessed March 20, 2026).

28 Joshu Keating, "Israel Killed More Than 100 Gazans in a Single Day. The IDF Says Just 26 of Them Were Terrorists," *Haaretz* (October 30, 2025), https://www.haaretz.com/israel-news/2025-10-30/ty-article/.premium/israel-killed-more-than-100-gazans-in-a-single-day-just-26-of-them-were-terrorists/0000019a-3231-d36c-a3bf-b675c0c30000 (accessed March 20, 2026); "Netanyahu prolonged the war to save himself. It may have worked," *Vox* (October 7, 2025), https://www.vox.com/politics/463898/netanyahu-political-survival-war (accessed March 20, 2026); Simon Tisdall, "Netanyahu will never accept peace. Where will his perpetual war lead next," *The Guardian* (March 18, 2025), https://www.theguardian.com/commentisfree/2025/mar/18/gaza-benjamin-netanyahu-israel-hamas-palestinian-territories (accessed March 20, 2026).

29 Nir Hasson, UNICEF Report, "Two years of hellish war have devastated Gaza's children," *UNICEF Canada* (October 10, 2025), https://www.unicef.

ca/en/press-release/two-years-hellish-war-have-devastated-gazas-children (accessed March 20, 2026). UNICEF notes that "For more than 700 days, children in Gaza have been killed, maimed, and displaced in a devastating war that is an affront to our shared humanity .... In the last two years, a staggering 64,000 children have reportedly been killed or maimed across the Gaza Strip, including at least 1,000 babies. We don't know how many more have died due to preventable illnesses or are buried under the rubble."

30 Gerry Chidiac, "Gaza war exposes global collapse of conscience," *The Kindersley Clarion* (May 29, 2025), https://theclarion.ca/viewpoint/gaza-war-exposes-global-collapse-of-conscience (accessed March 20, 2026).

31 Arwa Mahdawi, "'Gaza must be eliminated': Israel's airwaves are filled with pro-genocide propaganda," *The Guardian* (June 27, 2025), https://www.theguardian.com/commentisfree/2025/jun/27/israel-gaza-propaganda (accessed March 20, 2026).

32 Achille Mbembe, *Necropolitics* (Durham: Duke University Press, 2019).

33 Abdel Qader Sabbah and Sharif Abdel Kouddous, "Israel Bombs Gaza School With U.S.-Made Missile During Friday Prayers," *Drop Site News* (July 25, 2025), https://www.dropsitenews.com/p/israel-bombs-gaza-school-us-missile-displaced (accessed March 20, 2026).

34 Naomi Klein, Mehdi Hasan, and Team Zeteo, "'How Are You Going to Survive?': Doctor Describes 'Horrific' Humanitarian Situation in Gaza," *Zeto* (July 22, 2025), https://zeteo.com/p/how-are-you-going-to-survive-doctor (accessed March 20, 2026).

35 Heba Almaqadma, "In Gaza, Hunger Has Overtaken Bombs as Israel's Cruelest Weapon," *Drop Site News* (July 30, 2025), https://www.dropsitenews.com/p/gaza-city-famine-israel-starvation-genocide-war (accessed March 20, 2026).

36 Almaqadma, "In Gaza, Hunger Has Overtaken Bombs as Israel's Cruelest Weapon."

37 Howard Zinn, "A Kinder, Gentler Patriotism," *Howard Zinn.Org* (April 13, 2003), https://www.howardzinn.org/collection/kinder-gentler-patriotism (accessed March 20, 2026).

Chapter 11

1 EIU Update, "EIU's 2024 Democracy Index: trend of global democratic decline and strengthening authoritarianism continues through 2024," *Economist Intelligence* (February 17, 2025), https://www.eiu.com/n/democracy-index-2024 (accessed March 21, 2026).

2 Ben Rhodes, "American Descent," *The New York Review* (August 15, 2024), https://www.nybooks.com/articles/2024/08/15/american-descent-wannabe-fascists-america-last (accessed March 21, 2026).

3 Shaun Walker, "Viktor Orbán sparks outrage with attack on 'race mixing' in Europe," *The Guardian* (July 24, 2022), https://www.theguardian.com/

world/2022/jul/24/viktor-orban-against-race-mixing-europe-hungary (accessed March 21, 2026).

4 Steven Levitsky, Lucan Way and Daniel Ziblatt, "How Will We Know When We Have Lost Our Democracy?," *New York Times* (May 8, 2025), https://www.nytimes.com/2025/05/08/opinion/trump-authoritarianism-democracy.html (accessed March 21, 2026).

5 Edward Helmore, "Trump says he doesn't know if he needs to uphold constitutional due process," *The Guardian* (May 4, 2025), https://www.theguardian.com/us-news/2025/may/04/trump-due-process-rights-constitution (accessed March 21, 2026).

6 Peter Thiel, "The Education of a Libertarian," *Cato-Unbound* (April 13, 2009), https://www.cato-unbound.org/2009/04/13/peter-thiel/education-libertarian (accessed March 21, 2026).

7 Editorial, "Steve Bannon joins the 'Nazi salute' controversy after Elon Musk. Has 'Nazism officially taken over the GOP'?," *Economic Times/Panache* (February 21, 2025), https://economictimes.indiatimes.com/magazines/panache/steve-bannon-joins-the-nazi-salute-controversy-after-elon-musk-has-nazism-officially-taken-over-the-gop/articleshow/118456768.cms (accessed March 21, 2026).

8 Judith Butler, "The Compass of Mourning," *London Review of Books* (October 19, 2023), https://www.lrb.co.uk/the-paper/v45/n20/judith-butler/the-compass-of-mourning (accessed March 21, 2026).

9 Butler, "The Compass of Mourning."

10 Maximillian Alvarez, "Trump's Army of Social Vigilantes Are Coming for Payback," *In These Times* (November 12, 2024), https://inthesetimes.com/article/trump-white-supremacy-racism-maga (accessed March 21, 2026).

11 This theme runs through Steven Levitsky and Daniel Ziblatt, *How Democracies Die* (New York: Crown Publishing, 2018).

12 Gerard Dumenil and Dominque Levy, The *Crisis of Neoliberalism* (Cambridge: Harvard University Press, 2011).

13 Ben Rhodes, "American Descent," *The New York Review* (August 15, 2024), https://www.nybooks.com/articles/2024/08/15/american-descent-wannabe-fascists-america-last (accessed March 21, 2026).

14 Daniel Steinmetz-Jenkins, "The Long History of American Cruelty," *The Nation* (August 12, 2021), https://www.thenation.com/article/politics/interview-adam-serwer-cruelty-point (accessed March 21, 2026).

15 Paul Krugman, "Attack of the Sadistic Zombies," *Substack* (May 19, 2025), https://paulkrugman.substack.com/p/attack-of-the-sadistic-zombies (accessed March 21, 2026).

16 Henry A. Giroux, *Zombie Politics and Culture in the Age of Casino Capitalism*, 2nd edition (New York: Peter Lang, 2023).

17 Harriet A. Washington, *Medical Apartheid: The Dark History of Medical Experimentation on Black Americans from Colonial Times to the Present* (New York: Penguin, 2008).

18 Nancy Leys Stepan, *The Hour of Eugenics: Race, Gender, and Nation in Latin America* (Ithaca: Cornell University Press, 1991).

19 Jakob Simmank, "Social Darwinism, Circa 2025, A Chilling German View On RFK Jr.'s Health Agenda," *World Crunch* (May 18, 2025), https://worldcrunch.com/in-the-news/rfk-jr-health-agenda-german-view (accessed March 21, 2026).

20 Simmank, "Social Darwinism."

21 Simmank, "Social Darwinism."

22 Derek Beres, "Maga's era of 'soft eugenics': let the weak get sick, help the clever breed," *The Guardian* (May 4, 2025), https://www.theguardian.com/us-news/ng-interactive/2025/may/04/maga-soft-eugenics (accessed March 21, 2026).

23 Aislinn Shanahan Daly, "Eugenics: From Hitler's Sparta to contemporary legitimacy," *Irish Marxist Review* 9:26 (2020), https://irishmarxistreview.net/index.php/imr/issue/view/26 (accessed March 21, 2026).

24 Rob Eshman, "'America is for Americans and Americans only': How Trump 2.0 evokes the Nazis," *Forward: Jewish Independent* (October 28, 2024), https://forward.com/opinion/668440/miller-trump-madison-square-garden-immigrants (accessed March 21, 2026).

25 Ginger Gibson, "Trump says immigrants are 'poisoning the blood of our country.' Biden campaign likens comments to Hitler," *NBC News* (December 17, 2023), https://www.nbcnews.com/politics/2024-election/trump-says-immigrants-are-poisoning-blood-country-biden-campaign-liken-rcna130141 (accessed March 21, 2026).

26 David Corn, "Donald Trump's War on History," *Mother Jones* (April 2024), https://www.motherjones.com/politics/2025/04/donald-trump-war-on-history-restoring-truth-sanity-propaganda-racism (accessed March 21, 2026).

27 Corn, "Donald Trump's War on History."

28 Yumna Fatima, "The language of genocide: How Israel dehumanizes Palestinians," *Dawn News* (November 7, 2023), https://www.dawn.com/news/1786922 (accessed March 21, 2026).

29 Nesrine Malik, "White South African 'refugees'? The jokes write themselves," *The Guardian* (May 21, 2025), https://www.theguardian.com/news/2025/may/21/white-south-african-refugees-trump-afrikaners-black (accessed March 21, 2026).

30 Eloise Goldsmith, "GOP Cuts to Medicaid 'Will Kill People,' Advocate Warns and New Research Bolsters," *Common Dreams* (May 16, 2025), https://www.commondreams.org/news/medicaid-cuts-nebr-research (accessed March 21, 2026).

31 Sara Murphy, "Head Start avoids Trump's cuts, but advocates are ready to defend it: 'There's too much good in this'," *The Guardian* (May 7, 2025), https://www.theguardian.com/us-news/2025/may/07/head-start-trump-funding-cuts (accessed March 21, 2026).

32 Tyler Kingkad, "Trump administration halts research to help babies with heart defects," *NBC News* (May 10, 2025), https://www.nbcnews.com/news/us-news/

pediaflow-research-babies-heart-defects-trump-administration-rcna197155 (accessed March 21, 2026).

33 Abuko Estrada, "Prescription for Disaster: The Impact of Proposed Medicaid and CHIP Cuts on Children's Health," *First Focus on Children* (March 17, 2025), https://firstfocus.org/update/prescription-for-disaster-the-impact-of-proposed-medicaid-and-chip-cuts-on-childrens-health (accessed March 21, 2026).

34 Henry A. Giroux, *Youth in a Suspect Society* (New York: Palgrave, 2010).

35 Henry A. Giroux, "Scholasticide: Waging War on Education from Gaza to the West," *Journal of Holy Land and Palestine Studies* 24:1 (March 26, 2025), https://euppublishing.com/doi/10.3366/hlps.2025.0348 (accessed March 21, 2026).

36 Quds News Network, "How Many Children Has Israel Killed in Gaza in 700 Days of Genocide?," *Quds News Network* (June 9, 2025), https://qudsnen.co/public/post?id=64342&slug=how-many-children-has-israel-killed-in-gaza-in-700-days-of-genocide (accessed March 21, 2026).

37 Amy B. Wang, "Gates accuses Musk of 'killing the world's poorest children' with DOGE cuts," *The Washington Post* (May 9, 2025), https://www.washingtonpost.com/politics/2025/05/09/gates-musk-killing-poorest-children (accessed March 21, 2026).

38 Wang, "Gates accuses Musk of 'killing the world's poorest children' with DOGE cuts."

39 Wang, "Gates accuses Musk of 'killing the world's poorest children' with DOGE cuts."

Conclusion

1 Henry A. Giroux and Anthony R. DiMaggio, *Fascism on Trial: Education and the Possibility of Democracy* (London: Bloomsbury, 2024).

2 Susan Jacoby, *The Age of American Unreason in a Culture of Lies* (New York: Random House, 2018).

3 Glenn Kessler, Salvador Rizzo, and Meg Kelly, "Trump's false or misleading claims total 30,573 over 4 years," *The Washington Post* (January 24, 2021), https://www.washingtonpost.com/politics/2021/01/24/trumps-false-or-misleading-claims-total-30573-over-four-years (accessed March 21, 2026).

4 Annie Karni and Megan Mineiro, "Mike Lee Draws Outrage for Posts Blaming Assassination on the Far Left," *New York Times* (June 16, 2025), https://www.nytimes.com/2025/06/16/us/politics/mike-lee-minnesota-assassination-democrats.html (accessed March 21, 2026).

5 David Levi Strauss, "Dispatch 73: The Conflict Between Public Opinion and Public Spirit," *Brooklyn Rail* (June 18, 2025), https://brooklynrail.org/2025/06/dispatches/dispatch-73-the-conflict-between-public-opinion-and-public-spirit (accessed March 21, 2026).

6 Chris Hedges, "The Rule of Idiots," *The Chris Hedges Report* (June 6, 2025), https://chrishedges.substack.com/p/the-rule-of-idiots (accessed March 21, 2026).

7 Hedges, "The Rule of Idiots."

8 David Levi Strauss, "Dispatch 88: MAGA Military & Media vs. Enduring Epstein," *Brooklyn Rail* (October 6, 2025), https://brooklynrail.org/2025/10/dispatches/dispatch-88-maga-military-and-media-vs-enduring-epstein (accessed March 21, 2026).

9 Strauss, "Dispatch 88."

10 Strauss, "Dispatch 88."

11 Strauss, "Dispatch 88."

12 Robin D. G. Kelley, "The Responsibility of Intellectuals in the Age of Fascism and Genocide," *Boston Review* (September 2, 2025), https://www.bostonreview.net/forum/the-responsibility-of-intellectuals-in-the-age-of-fascism-and-genocide (accessed March 21, 2026).

13 Kelley, "The Responsibility of Intellectuals in the Age of Fascism and Genocide."

14 Henry A. Giroux, "The neoliberal university faces a crisis: This generation could change everything," *Salon* (June 8, 2024), https://www.salon.com/2024/06/08/the-neoliberal-university-faces-rebellion-this-generation-could-change-everything (accessed March 21, 2026).

15 Jason Stanley, *Erasing History: How Fascists Rewrite the Past to Control the Future* (New York: Atria/One Signal Publisher, 2024).

16 Indigo Olivier, "Trump's War on Higher Education Isn't Just About Crushing Dissent," *The New Republic* (April 29, 2025), https://newrepublic.com/article/194527/trump-war-higher-education-isnt-just-crushing-dissent (accessed March 21, 2026).

17 Ruth Ben-Ghiat, "How Authoritarians Target Universities," *Lucid* (July 11, 2023), https://lucid.substack.com/p/from-fascism-to-hungary-and-the-us (accessed March 21, 2026).

18 Ben-Ghiat, "How Authoritarians Target Universities."

19 Iveta Silova, "Universities in Nazi Germany and the Soviet Union thought giving in to government demands would save their independence," *The Conversation* (April 9, 2025), https://theconversation.com/universities-in-nazi-germany-and-the-soviet-union-thought-giving-in-to-government-demands-would-save-their-independence-252888 (accessed March 21, 2026).

20 David Theo Goldberg, "'Antisemitism' The Making of Our Political Panic" *Counter Punch* (June 4, 2025), https://www.counterpunch.org/2025/06/04/antisemitism-the-making-of-our-political-panic (accessed March 21, 2026).

21 Robert Cohen and Reginald E. Zelnik, *The Free Speech Movement: Reflections on Berkeley in the 1960s* (Berkeley: University of California Press, 2002).

22 Sheila Rowbotham, *Promise of a Dream: Remembering the Sixties* (London: Verso, 2019).

23 Jason Stanley, "Why fascists hate universities," *The Guardian* (September 5, 2024), https://www.theguardian.com/commentisfree/article/2024/sep/05/why-fascists-hate-universities-us-bangladesh-india (accessed March 21, 2026).

24 Ja'han Jones, "Trump's latest attempt to control college campuses hits a snag," *MSNBC* (October 10, 2025), https://www.msnbc.com/top-stories/latest/trump-colleges-universities-compact-academic-excellence-rcna236959 (accessed March 21, 2026).

25 Henry A. Giroux, *Critical Pedagogy*, 2nd edition (London: Bloomsbury, 2020).

26 Perspective, "Trump's Fort Bragg rant: A declaration of war on the American people," *World Socialist Web Site* (June 11, 2025), https://www.wsws.org/en/articles/2025/06/11/zojf-j11.html (accessed March 21, 2026).

27 Foro de Sevilla Collective, "From Auschwitz to Gaza: Education as a Defense Against Hatred and Barbarism," *The Journal of Education* (February 17, 2025), https://eldiariodelaeducacion.com/porotrapoliticaeducativa/2025/02/17/de-auschwitz-a-gaza-la-educacion-como-defensa-contra-el-odio-y-la-barbarie (accessed March 21, 2026).

28 Pierre Bourdieu, *Acts of Resistance: Against the New Myths of Our Time* (London: Polity, 1998).

29 Chris Hedges, "Inside America's Academic Gulags (w/ Rashid Khalidi)," *The Chris Hedges Report* (October 8, 2025), https://chrishedges.substack.com/p/inside-americas-academic-gulags-w (accessed March 21, 2026).

30 Jan-Werner Muller, "US universities must reject Trump's 'compact'. It is full of traps," *The Guardian* (October 7, 2025), https://www.theguardian.com/commentisfree/2025/oct/07/universities-trump-compact (accessed March 21, 2026).

31 Henry A. Giroux, *Burden of Conscience: Educating Beyond the Veil of Silence* (London: Bloomsbury, 2025).

32 Gary Olson and Lynn Worsham, "Staging the Politics of Difference: Homi Bhabha's Critical Literacy," *Journal of Advanced Composition* (1999): 3–35.

33 Cornelius Castoriadis, "Democracy as Procedure and Democracy as Regime," *Constellations* 4:1 (1997): 1–18.

34 Ruth Ben-Ghiat, *Strongmen: Mussolini to the Present* (New York: W. W. Norton, 2020).

35 Alberto Toscano, *Late Fascism* (London: Verso, 2023).

36 Stuart Hall, "Cultural Studies and Its Theoretical Legacies," in *Stuart Hall: Critical Dialogues in Cultural Studies*, edited by David Morley and Kuan-Hsing Chen (London: Routledge, 1996), 442.

37 Angela Y. Davis, "Angela Davis: An Interview on the Futures of Black Radicalism," *Verso* (June 23, 2020), https://www.versobooks.com/en-ca/blogs/news/3421-angela-davis-an-interview-on-the-futures-of-black-radicalism (accessed March 21, 2026).

38 Ernst Bloch, *The Principle of Hope*, Vol. 3, trans. Neville Plaice, Stephen Plaice, and Paul Knight (Cambridge, MA: MIT Press, 1986), 1375–6.

INDEX